From Indians to Chicanos

the dynamics of Mexican American culture

From Indians to Chicanos

the dynamics of Mexican American culture

JAMES DIEGO VIGIL

University of Southern California

WAVELAND
PRESS, INC.

Prospect Heights, Illinois

For information about this book, write or call:

Waveland Press, Inc.
P.O. Box 400
Prospect Heights, Illinois 60070
(708) 634-0081

In memory of my father
Patrick
and mother
Magdalena

Dedicated to my sisters
Viola, Loy, Nany, and Bee

Foreword

To understand the history of the Chicanos is to understand the Chicano movement. It is this complex, multi-layered history that Diego Vigil has chosen to record. Chicano history is still being written, since the movement has not fully matured.

There is, of course, no typical Chicano; they are an amazingly diverse group even though they have certain common interests and associations. This text is of special importance, not merely for its scholarship and research, but because it reflects the intellectual evolution, the maturing point of view, of a representative Chicano, Diego Vigil, who first became interested in the Chicano movement in the middle 1960's. His interest has grown and deepened in the years since then.

The Chicano experience differs in significant respects from that of other ethnic minority groups. It has been affected by many influences that have changed with time and in different geographical and socioeconomic settings. It is an experience that must be patiently unfolded, making allowances for regional and historical differences. Not surprisingly, it has created identity problems for those who have been caught up in it, for it involves racial, class, cultural, and national conflicts in the Southwest, a rapidly developing region of different interests and economies. The Chicano experience has accordingly been marginal and exceptional and has been given a variety of interpretations and definitions. To some extent, it reflects the same syncretic experience that occurred in Mexico but with different causes and results.

The diversity of the experience has spawned the so-called Chicano rebellion, which has altered the consciousness of Mexican-Americans in ways that set them apart from their parents and the older generation of Spanish-speaking people, as well as the dominant Anglo majority. The movement seems to be guided less by ideologies and theories than by the Chicanos' determination to forge their own identity and to reject outside influences and imported schemes and ideas. The legacy of the Chicano movement has not yet been worked out; it changes and is constantly being analyzed and restated. The fact that Diego Vigil reflects this experience, in addition to reciting its history and causes, makes this text an important contribution to Chicano studies.

Carey McWilliams

Preface

This text has a dual purpose. First, it focuses on specific socioeconomic, sociocultural, and sociopsychological issues and problems that affect modern-day Chicanos. These patterns have been forged by their experiences under various dominant groups. Throughout their history they have generally remained in the underclass and have been culturally and racially different members of the social system. By tracing these historical conditions and highlighting several stages of contact, conflict, and change, it is hoped that modern Chicanos will be more clearly understood.

The second purpose of the text is to outline some of the major features (class, culture, and color) integral to sociocultural change. Most of these elements are also instrumental in assessing superordinate-subordinate ethnic relations. In order to clarify the process of sociocultural change and the establishment of ethnic relations boundaries, the text will apply a model of sociocultural change to a Mesoamerican people—the indigenous inhabitants of the present southwestern United States.

The text is divided into four major historical stages. Stage I, "Pre-Columbian Period," deals with the life of Mesoamerican Indians before European contact and ends with the first manifestations of Spanish colonialism. Stage II, "Spanish Colonial Era," a summary of 300 years of rule, is presented to document the beginnings of class inequality and intense cultural and racial discrimination. Stage III, "Mexican Independence and Nationalism," begins with the revolutionary fervor of the Enlightenment and the Latin American wars of independence, outlines the events in early autonomous Mexico, including activities in its northern reaches (now the United States Southwest), and ends with the Mexican-American War of 1846, which began the years of closer Mexican and American ties. Stage IV, "Anglo-American Period," examines the rise of the Mexican-American people and ends with the Chicano movement of the 1960's and its aftermath. The text concludes with some comparative observations that may apply to other minority groups, and a projected synopsis of the Chicano future is provided.

Of course, other people participated in the development and production of the text. Bill and Zele Etchart helped me initiate a summary outline several years ago. I would like to thank all the students in the High Potential Program at the University of California, Los Angeles, in the East Los Angeles community, and at Chaffey College who listened to my lectures. These students offered advice and criticism that aided the conceptualization and refinement of important Chicano issues. I would especially like to thank John Long, who added invaluable editorial suggestions throughout the past several years, and the late Carey McWilliams, who characteristically found the time to write the foreword. Several colleagues read earlier versions of the work and gave encouragement: Sid Silliman, Jim Barreca, and Myron and Estelle Roberts (Chaffey College); Juan Gomez-Quinones, Carlos Velez-I., and Devera Weber (University of California, Los Angeles); Luis Arroyo (University of California, Davis); Steve Arvizu and Raul Isais (California State University, Sacramento); Juan Garcia (Stanford University); Margarita Melville (University of Houston); Henry Torres-Trueba (San Diego State College); and especially Jim Patterson (Eastern Oregon State College). Pete Snyder and Tom Weisner (University of California, Los Angeles) were graduate advisers who helped me in the earlier stages, and Tom Weaver (University of Arizona) gave counsel on the writing. Of the many students offering support and help, these deserve special mention: Carol Edens (for typing also), Leisel Van Balgooy (who read and revised an earlier version), Jessalyn Deputy, Denise Miller, and Miguel Nicasio. Mary Nunez and Jeffrey Huereque produced the fine artwork, Jesus Medina the maps, and John Viencek the photographs. Partial support was provided by a Ford Foundation Grant. And finally, my nieces Monica Hernandez and Jennifer Rubio typed the final manuscript. Without the steady patience of my wife Polly this text would have taken much longer to complete. Although these people are responsible for many of the ideas and advice, I willingly accept the blame for all errors of fact, judgment, and interpretation.

James Diego Vigil

Contents

INTRODUCTION

The Chicano people comprise the second-largest ethnic minority in the United States, numbering anywhere from 8 to 15 million, if one includes undocumented immigrant workers. In several areas of the American Southwest, which some Chicano activists call *Aztlan* after the legendary Aztec name for the region, they are in the majority. Indeed, some of these people's ancestors inhabited the Southwest long before its incorporation into the United States. On the other hand, there are Chicanos who are offspring of recent immigrants from Mexico, often maintaining contacts with close relatives in that country. Although the ethnic label "Mexican-American" is still used by many people who take pride in being American, the recent trend appears to favor the Mexican background and thus the name "Chicano."*

WHY A DYNAMIC HISTORY?

There are several reasons why a historical interpretation of the Chicano is needed. Although many standard histories are available, few works attempt to deal with many of the crucial issues integrally linked to modern Chicano characteristics. Most writers on the Southwest spend more time discussing Indian conditions than those of the Chicano. Not surprisingly, Mexican authors are more concerned with what is happening in Mexico. Chicanos, as the "in-between" people, are either completely ignored or given a quick, cursory treatment. As we shall see, their experience is so

---

* The ethnic label Chicano has many definitions (Nostrand 1975:159-160). A strict colloquial usage is that it is a shortened form of Mexicano. In this text it is used to reflect the multiple-heritage experience of Mexicans in the United States. Although other labels appropriate to the time period or situation are utilized—that is, Indian, Spanish, Mexican, Anglo, or Mexican-American—it is important to note that a Chicano perspective draws from any or all of these cultural orientations to fashion a broader adaptation. The political consciousness-raising events of the 1960's helped develop an appreciation of their multicultural heritage. The term Chicano will be used throughout most of the text because the text is a look backward to trace the historical development of a contemporary people.

1

complex and marked with the stigma of lower socioeconomic status that a more careful interpretative assessment is demanded. In other words, Chicano membership in the class of poor people in this country has tended to blur important features of their sociocultural background.

How have the past four centuries treated the Chicano people? To answer that question we must first state what we know. A series of migrations and settlements, first by the Spanish and then by the Anglo-Americans, have been major influences in molding the contemporary character of Chicanos (Moore 1973). In addition, their early ancestors, the indigenous people, provided them with a rich cultural foundation. (The ethnic label Chicano is a derivative of the Aztec tribal name Mexica, with the "x" pronounced like "ch.") Most of the facts concerning these historical influences are readily available and easily understood.

However, describing the outcome of the merging of Old and New World cultural styles presents a perplexing problem. What was the result of this merging? Were Chicanos forged from that experience? To what degree can one determine the portion of each culture in the mixture? Even more problematic, which Chicano cultural features belong to one group or the other, and which are a synthesis? These questions continue to plague students and researchers alike, as they probe to uncover the complex issues shaping the Chicano people (Trejo 1979; Heisler 1977).

This sociocultural history attempts to resolve some of these issues. In addition, it will introduce new insights into old problems and add a dynamic approach to assessing the Chicano experience (Nisbet 1969). The narrative chronologically highlights important events, people, and the internal dynamics of change. It begins with pre-Columbian Mexico and focuses on over four centuries of problems arising from the struggle for control of land, labor, and consequent wealth between the conquering Europeans and their successors on the one hand, and the indigenous majority population on the other (Frazier 1957:32). Not the least of the problems to be illuminated will be the psychological consequences of the suppression suffered by the Chicano people over these many years. The text will examine how indigenous peoples adapted to new social systems and how social systems also changed.

TWO CONCEPTUAL AIDS—STAGES OF HUMAN MATURATION AND SIX C's MODEL

Two devices are utilized in this text to aid comprehension of such a long, complex epic. One technique is to look at the evolution of the Chicano people by using different stages of human growth to represent each historical period. This illustrative method is not to be interpreted literally, of course, but rather as a basis for comparison. Metaphorically, history can be seen to consist of stages comparable to those that make up the life span of humans. All the stages in an individual life can be found also in the stages in the life of a people. We can distinguish the following stages in humans: embryonic life, infancy, childhood, adolescence, early adulthood, and adulthood. Middle age, old age, and death are excluded here for the obvious reason that Chicanos are still developing, with some people further advanced than others.

The point of comparison is that both historical and human biosocial evolution consist of a progression from one stage to another. Each human growth stage entails a certain type of awareness that allows a person to think and act in special and predictable ways. For example, embryonic life is obviously quite different from any of the other maturational levels, although the difference between early and later adulthood is not so easily appraised. As we proceed, it will be made clear how each human and historical stage interrelates and why a particular type of human awareness is found in one stage and not another. While successive stages often are not qualitatively better, each is more complex than the last, if only from the incorporation of what has been learned in previous developmental levels. Of course, there are instances where stages overlap or one takes priority over another, or when development is blocked or uneven. Nevertheless, the implicit goal here is the establishment of a mechanism to draw parallels and make comparisons. This human growth strategem will facilitate discussion of whether mature, evolutionary progression characterizes various stages of Chicano history or whether the long experience has set Chicanos further back.

For the purpose of this text Chicano history is divided into four major historical periods. Each will be listed first and followed by a comparable human developmental stage in parentheses.

1. Pre-Columbian, pre-1519 (*embryonic life and infancy*). For biological and cultural reasons Chicanos are, in an evolutionary sense, tied to the Indians of Mexico and the Southwest. Aztecs, especially, impressed their culture on surrounding natives and for their time reached the highest level of indigenous civilization. In addition, they became the first large native group to be defeated militarily by the Europeans and to experience a life of subjugation.
2. Spanish colonial, 1521-1821 (*childhood*). This period is one of the most influential in the formation of the Chicano people. Although Chicanos received most of their genetic makeup from Indians, the Spanish were profoundly instrumental in shaping Chicano cultural life, for example, Spanish surnames and language. Their 300-year reign was the longest and perhaps the most significant of all the postcontact stages.

Functionally Intact and Stable Social Order	Breakup and Evolutionary Transformation of Social Order
1. CLASS (land, income, occupation, home, neighborhood, prestige, and esteem; also includes factors from other sectors of the social system)	4. CONTACT (often military force, but also involves the spead of ideas, such as religious or revolutionary principles; often is guided by economic concerns)
2. CULTURE (language, religion, philosophy, values, beliefs, customs, and general world view of the people)	5. CONFLICT (a multiple experience, including military confrontation and resistance and rebellion efforts, as well as a host of religious, sociocultural, and psychological dimensions)
3. COLOR (emphasis, or lack of it, on physiognomic or racial traits in the social system in terms of racist ideology, prejudice, discrimination, segregation)	6. CHANGE (all initial transformations that take place after contact and conflict and before a new class-culture-color system is firmly rooted)

Fig. 1. Six C's model of sociocultural change.

3. Mexican independence and nationalism, 1821-1846 for Mexicans in the United States, but up to 1910 for those in Mexico (*adolescence*). Obviously the experiences of Mexicans on both sides of the border differed markedly on several levels. However, there are still important features that bind them together. On the whole, cultural patterns remained similar, and there was some reciprocal immigration that tended to invigorate and solidify that connection. Often the events in either nation affected affairs in the other. Thus, the awakening of an ethnic and national consciousness must include activities in both regions.

4. Anglo period, 1846-1960's (*early adulthood*). By accident or design, the Anglo "assimilation" policy for foreigners was begun at the time that Chicanos entered the United States. This was the government's predominant cultural adjustment strategy until a massive, concerted effort to change matters began during the 1960's.

In each of these historical stages, the Chicano people were confronted with new realities and problems, but always there was a developing awareness and growth.

The stages of life metaphor aids depiction of a dynamic growth of a people and can be employed flexibly. The model could easily be applied to any one of the stages designated above, thus for example, making a life cycle out of the Aztec and Spanish experience. Every sociocultural beginning is also in some sense an end or a middle, depending on the perspective one takes. Surely the Aztecs and colonial Spanish attained growth pinnacles in their respective eras. The purpose here is not to designate any of the earlier cultural patterns as inferior, but to give emphasis to their role in the blossoming of the Chicano variant: to show how a preindustrial, localized people became integrated into an industrial, multinational entity.

A second method used in the text to clarify Chicano history is a model of sociocultural change, the Six C's: class, culture, color, contact, conflict, and change (Table 1). This model provides a framework for understanding both the structure and the process of a social system (Vogt 1960). Anthro-

Table 1. Historical periods and stages of human growth

	I. Pre-Columbian, pre-1519 *embryonic life and early infancy*	II. Spanish colonial 1521–1821 *childhood*	III. Mexican independence and nationalism 1821–1846 (1910) *adolescence*	IV. Anglo 1846–1960's *early adulthood*
Class	Nobility supported by landholding calpulli (clan) members	Haciendas; native majority debt peons	Criollos take over, some mestizos included	Stripped of land, Chicanos remain low-paid farm and urban workers
Culture	Complex pantheon; rich literary tradition	Hispanicization and rise of mestizaje or blending	Some signs of emerging Mexican style, still mostly imitating Europe	Anglicization; superiority/inferiority connotations; Chicano fusion
Color	Race of minimal importance	Racial barriers create problems for those subjugated	Some mestizos more accepted, Indians not	New dimension to racism, worst for darker "cholos"
Contact	Cortes and conquerors seek riches	Enlightenment; colonial dissolution	Anglo-American land expansionism	Drawn-out human rights struggle peaks again in 1960's
Conflict	Tenochtitlan falls; Spanish introduce new traditions	Independence, New World Spaniards victors	Mexican-American War of 1846	Chicanos confront system at all levels
Change	Early colonial practices, especially land and religion	Era of experimentation and budding nationalism	Anglo occupation of Mexican land, sociocultural struggles	Ethnic consciousness and pride bring advancement

← ———— **Diachronic** ————→

Synchronic ↓

pologists might say that the model aids synchronic and diachronic analysis and interpretation. A synchronic assessment refers to the functional approach to the study of culture in a given time, such as what occurs daily, seasonally, or annually. A diachronic focus emphasizes the historical or developmental approach to the study of culture, such as the interpretation of an evolutionary or macrolevel cumulative change (Vancina 1970).

Each chronological "life stage" in the text is followed by the application of the Six C's model to provide a clearer understanding of the sociocultural change that occurred in that stage. This will provide a framework for a synchronic perspective, or what is functionally operative at any given time (Bloch 1975; Park 1950). Issues and conditions of *class* (sociological or *socioeconomic* conditions and practices), *culture* (anthropological or *sociocultural* change and innovation), and *color* (*sociopsychological* problems caused by racism) are discussed first. Other subjects are not ignored or avoided, but to simplify the presentation they are included under the major headings listed above (Berkhofer 1969:31-32). The sequence in which they are presented is also important. Generally, the class factor is the foundation for developing an examination of the other sectors (Sanjek 1969; Harris

1979). However, there are times when the discussion includes all of the features simultaneously, either because of similar time placement or because they are inextricably interwoven. The categories of class, culture, and color provide a vehicle to highlight the continuous social order and the way in which several major social features intertwine to make a social history (Simpson and Yinger 1972:3; Heisler 1977:2).

The second three categories of contact, conflict, and change aid in explaining the quality and nature of social evolution. *Contact* refers to intrusions that upset an ongoing social system, *conflict* designates the nature of the subsequent struggle, and *change* denotes the reorganization of society in the aftermath (Spicer 1962). A contact-conflict-change analysis enables one to determine how and why a stable social system is disrupted, transformed, and reintegrated. It does this by elucidating how a people evolve from one historical period to another. The result in each stage is the establishment of a new social order, by which Chicanos are progressively shaped and molded according to the dictates of that period.

To summarize, each historical era begins with a relatively intact, stable, *class-culture-color* system, which in time is altered. A *contact-conflict-change* explanatory sequence clarifies the transformations that a fully functional social system undergoes and pinpoints specific aspects of the upheaval.

THEORETICAL IMPLICATIONS FOR THE PRESENT DAY

Application of the Six C's model to each historical period yields a categorical framework within which to describe and discuss similar social system sectors, and more importantly, creates a basis of comparison for all the time periods. Another objective the model fulfills is to document specifically the beginnings of certain modern traits and customs of Chicanos. The model has several dimensions that offer insight into different types of issues in a holistic fashion (Pitt 1972; Hodgen 1974).

With the use of the human stages of growth metaphor and the Six C's model of sociocultural change, this historical study should provide one with an appreciation of the complexity of all these transformations. If it is true that Chicanos have had a diverse contact and change experience, then it follows that there are diverse legacies from which to draw. This diversity underscores the difficulty in comprehending modern Chicano issues and problems. An understanding of the history of these problems will aid in diminishing that difficulty.

As situations of time and place dictate, Chicanos have been affected by many influences (Madrid-Barela 1973). In adapting and adjusting to a multitude of circumstances, they have had to change and rechange customs, values, and beliefs. Their experience is different historically from that of most other national minority groups because they were made to feel culturally and racially inferior by more than one dominant group. Hence, a "layered-on" type of oppression occurred.

Clearly, negative material conditions of land, labor, and wealth are germane to this history (Wolf 1969). Nevertheless, there are also positive inheritances. As one possible reason for their survival, Chicanos epitomize the ability of modern colonized people to fashion multiple-pronged strategies of adaptation. They have learned to integrate and synthesize past racial and cultural mixture experiences. This, in turn, has led to the development of a flexible and comprehensive approach to life, in which first one avenue and then another has assisted their perseverance. Jose Vasconcelos' reference to Mexicans as "La Raza Cosmica" (The Cosmic People) was an early assessment of how cultural diversity makes for strength and vitality. This description also pertains to the even more culturally diverse Chicano people.

REFERENCES

Berkhofer, R. F., Jr.: *Behavioral approach to historical analysis*, New York, 1969, The Free Press.

Bloch, M., editor: *Marxist analyses and social anthropology*, New York, 1975, John Wiley & Sons, Inc.

Frazier, E. F.: *Race and culture contacts in the modern world*, New York, 1957, Alfred A. Knopf, Inc.

Harris, M.: *Cultural materialism*, New York, 1979, Random House, Inc.

Heisler, M., editor: Ethnic conflict in the world today: an introduction, *The Annals of the American Academy of Political and Social Science* **433**:1-5, 1977.

Hodgen, M.T.: *Anthropology, history and cultural change*, Tucson, 1974, The University of Arizona Press.

Madrid-Barela, A.: Towards an understanding of the Chicano experience, *Aztlan: Chicano Journal of the Social Sciences and the Arts* **4**:185-193, 1973.

Moore, J. W.: Colonialism: the case of the Mexican American. In Duran, L. I., and Bernard, H. R., editors: *Introduction to Chicano studies*, New York, 1973, Macmillan, Inc.

Nisbet, R. A.: *Social change and history*, New York, 1969, Oxford University Press.

Nostrand, R. L.: Mexican-American and Chicano. In Hundley, N., editor: *The Chicano,* Santa Barbara, Calif., 1975, ABC-Clio, Inc.

Park, R. E.: *Race and culture*, New York, 1950, The Free Press.

Pitt, H. C.: *Using historical sources in anthropology and sociology*, New York, 1972, Holt, Rinehart, & Winston.

Sanjek, R.: Radical anthropology: values, theory, and content, *Anthropology U.C.L.A.* **1**:21, 1969.

Simpson, G., and Yinger, M.: *Racial and cultural minorities: an analysis of prejudice and discrimination*, New York, 1972, Harper & Row, Publishers.

Spicer, E.: *Cycles of conquest*, Tucson, 1962, The University of Arizona Press.

Trejo, A., editor: *The Chicanos: as we see ourselves*, Tucson, 1979, The University of Arizona Press.

Vancina, J.: Cultures through time. In Naroll, R., and Cohen, E. T., editors: *A handbook of method in cultural anthropology*, New York, 1970, Doubleday & Co., Inc.

Vogt, E.: On the concepts of structure and process in cultural anthropology, *American Anthropologist* **62**:18-33, 1960.

White, L. A.: *The science of culture*, New York, 1949, Farrar, Straus & Giroux, Inc.

Wolf, E.: *Peasant wars of the twentieth-century*, New York, 1969, Harper & Row, Publishers.

STAGE I

PRE-COLUMBIAN PERIOD
30,000 B.C. to A.D. 1519

1

Human evolution in Mesoamerica

Soon after the Spaniards entered Mexico in 1519, they encountered the Aztecs, who had constructed the most advanced civilization on the continent of North America. Before turning our attention to the nature of that civilization, it will be useful to examine the complex process by which it came into being. A look at the thousands of years of American Indian prehistory, the successive achievements of one people after another that culminated in the rise to prominence of the people who called themselves *Mexica*, will provide an understanding of how social institutions began and were refined and perpetuated by the Indian forebears of the Chicano people.

Within the analogy of the stages of human growth, this prehistoric period would compare with the time after initial human fertilization and conception. In the embryonic nine months in the mother's womb, one inherits the results of tens of thousands of years of human adaptation. Stored in that microentity are the germs that soon develop into the marvelous complexity of a human being. Not least, the brain is emerging, an organ that provides the tremendous flexibility of human thought and emotion. In other words, the foundation is being laid for later development.

This is also true for a people who have benefited from the earlier contributions of other peoples. The evolution of more intricate forms of human social and cultural life does not take place unless the groundwork for them is solidly established. Later natives benefited from the adaptations of preceding peoples and thereby fashioned a more complex style of life. This early development, like the womb experience, is remembered only in others' telling of it and in the foundations it has provided. Hence, it is illustrative of how past events, however distant or small, operate to shape the present.

ECOLOGICAL ADAPTATION

The rise of great Mesoamerican civilizations was preceded by many prehistoric events. Beginning in 30,000 B.C. (some experts say it was

earlier), there were great migrations of people from Asia. According to ar-
chaeologists, they wandered across the Bering Straits, which during the last
Ice Age was a land mass connecting Asia and Alaska. These migrations
brought hordes of people whose descendants, over several thousand years,
established themselves throughout North and South America. They were the
original Americans.

These early pioneers were guided down the streams and valleys of
North America by several simple needs: food and water, clothing to keep
them warm and protect them from abrupt weather changes, and shelter for
rest and protection from predators. These basic needs were not entirely satisfied at first. Because of the lack of a ready food supply, the hunters were
forced to follow a nomadic path, restlessly pursuing game wherever it might
lead them. This dependence on large herd animals affected other areas of
life. "Actually, the animals he hunted chose his route for him—doubtless
many routes. Unless he had learned to spear and net fish, the first invader
probably pursued a herd of mammoth or musk ox across the landbridge or
over the frozen ice of later winters" (Macgowan and Hester 1962:23).

Over a period of time, as early humans adapted to their environment, crude flaked stone points gave way to more refined and useful technology. Efforts at self-preservation proved the old adage: "Necessity is the
mother of invention." Tools were invented and perfected to aid in the acquisition of food and the manufacture of clothing. "We know that man controlled fire. . . . He also knew how to make spears, scrapers and knives. He
had the atlatl spear thrower, he knew how to cook meat, he had domesticated the dog, wore skins to protect himself, and he probably knew how to
make baskets" (Peterson 1962:19). Initially, this wandering human found
temporary shelter in natural caves and ledges. Much of what we know about
this time period comes from remains these ancient people left behind in that
part of the United States now most densely populated by Chicanos.

As the years passed, the Ice Age receded and the climate became
warmer and dryer. Groups of natives split off in different directions to find
refuge in a variety of regions and climates. Accordingly, they fashioned a new
relationship to the environment. Some combined the gathering of edible
plants with hunting but in time came to rely mostly on the former: "these
people left behind their querns and mullers, the grinding platforms and the
milling stones, on which they ground their plant food into a palatable
meal. . . . Around 7500 B.C. environmental conditions began to favor their
chances of survival, while lessening the survival opportunities of the big-
game hunters" (Wolf 1959:19).

Other natives, who settled near streams or oceans, learned to
subsist on the surrounding plant and animal life. Those who refused to ex-

periment with new food sources continued the hunting tradition. Nonetheless, because human survival was at stake, in time they too were forced to adopt new subsistence patterns.

Even at this early date one can observe the human propensity to vacillate between conserving the old and creating or adopting the new. Many individuals are reluctant to test new ways of doing things, even if their own existence is threatened. Clinging to age-old traditions is common because familiar patterns are time-tested and thus verify what has been gained. Eventually, however, ecological pressures force them to make the necessary changes for survival. A conservative orientation is not all bad; many old traits and customs persist because they still fulfill important functions. However, certain individuals play a strong role in readapting themselves to changing conditions, and they are at the forefront in selecting the innovative path that hastens human evolution.

During the many centuries when natives confronted the environment, food, clothing, and shelter practices stemmed from the material base. In other words, available natural resources—flora and fauna—determined the time, place, and manner of eating, dress, and sleep. Consequently, a secure environmental relationship developed as human social and cultural institutions evolved.

With the gradual improvement of ecological adaptation that in time brought permanent human settlement, other human traits blossomed. The spiritual concern of humans arose to accompany the material side. While the body finds nourishment in the material world, the soul also strives to participate in life's struggles. Spiritual considerations become involved in the everyday affairs of humans—perhaps to ensure that the environment is not abused, for the human animal is wont to follow purely selfish motives. Often this self-centered tendency needs to be curbed; otherwise, total exploitation of the environment would result.

The early natives were able to reside in permanent cavelike dwellings only where there was an abundance of natural resources. Otherwise they continued the rootless, seasonal, nomadic cycle. Over a period of time, however, there occurred a far-reaching change that shifted natives from the life of nomads to that of a settled people.

AGRICULTURAL REVOLUTION

According to some writers, women were in the forefront of this discovery, for they traditionally gathered fruits, nuts, and seeds near camps while the men were out hunting. One of them may have noticed that a grasslike plant with edible seeds at the tip had grown on the previous year's campsite. She might have further observed that where seeds had been haphazardly strewn in the past, now there were plants that could be eaten right on the spot, and this, surprisingly, could be accomplished without any hunting effort. To test her theory, perhaps she threw some more seeds in a spot that had similar rich-looking soil but no plants. On returning the next year, she found the seeds had grown into plants. Thus began the agricultural revolution (Macgowan and Hester 1962:38-39).

Around 7000 B.C. seed gatherers settled in the Tehuacan Valley, just southeast of present-day Mexico City. Here occurred a concerted program of plant domestication—or what is termed "evolution directed by the interference of man" (Coe 1962:45). The first seeds produced an edible plant the size of a copper penny. After 5500 years of gradual change, the Indians were able to increase its size and yield until they developed the present form of *maize* (modern corn).

Once this discovery was made, others followed. Beans and squash joined maize as the primary staples in the diet known as the American trinity. Other crops and products native to the New World are chile (high in vitamin C and useful in digesting cellulose products), pineapples, tobacco, peanuts, potatoes, avocados, chocolate, tomatoes, cotton, rubber, pumpkins, strawberries, tapioca, quinine, maple syrup, chicle (chewing gum), vanilla, cashew nuts, pepper, and cocaine. These products were the major food source for both natives and later Europeans; in fact, these foods add up to one half of the modern world's aggregate agricultural wealth (Walker 1967:2).

Most modern people are unaware of this early cultivation, and unfortunately Indians have not been given full credit on this account. "Middle America, particularly in the highlands of Mexico and Guatemala, is one of the four or five primary centers of plant domestication in the world. Here . . . an array of other plants were gradually brought under cultivation" (Helms 1975:18). The reliance on these foods, along with small game such as turkeys, decidedly changed the Indians from meat-eating hunters to settled farmers.

One cannot overstate the importance of agriculture. Fertile valleys and water-filled streams were sought out by former hunters and plant gatherers. "Once plants were domesticated . . . they were relayed from one area to another by intervening peoples, thus establishing diffusion as an important contributor to culture growth" (Driver 1969:10).

In this way humankind was brought to an important point in historical development. They had time now to expand on and improve other social and cultural practices. "Once his sedentary life was established, with agriculture taking precedence over earlier activities, man expanded his artifacts. . . . He began to make pottery . . . and began establishing a sedentary, agricultural society with a tribal organization" (Villegas et al. 1974:11-12).

By using technology to improve their ability to adapt environmentally, early natives rose to high levels of civilization. They replaced crude hunting tools with agricultural implements and were spared more time to pursue other activities. Running and chasing were superseded by sitting, thinking, and creating.

REFINEMENT OF SOCIOCULTURAL LIFE

At the outset, social and cultural features remained rudimentary, primarily because farming equipment and tasks were simple. Later, as farming practices became more elaborate and cultivation efforts intensified, sociocultural traits grew in complexity. In effect, advanced technology released human labor for other activities, mainly sociocultural ones. Now, with humans at the threshold of a higher level of civilization, most of their energy was expended in reaching that goal.

By at least 2000 B.C., more intricate institutional changes occurred. Hunter-leaders were joined by shaman-priests, who invoked the blessings of the heavens for the planting, irrigating, growing, and harvesting of maize. Raised earthen platforms were used by the shaman-priests for rituals and ceremonies. Careful observation and scientific study of celestial movements—stars, sun, and moon—became increasingly important. This activity was inspired by their efforts to preserve the agricultural community. The movements of the sun and other stars were keys to the development of calendars, the basis of knowledge of when to sow and when to harvest. Thus the people of the community soon began to seek direction from both hunters and priests.

Crude earthen pit-houses were built as permanent residences (Bushnell 1968:25). "The population grew as the cultivation of corn grew . . . men had time to make life more comfortable. They began to build better shelters, improve their preparations for food, and to accumulate possessions . . . families lived close together near good farming land in order to share in the field work and the protection of the crops, and so the first permanent tiny communities came into existence" (Peterson 1962:31).

Several other factors were involved in the expansion of social and cultural features. They include first, "the appearance of sedentary farming villages; second, the rise of small temples or ceremonial centers; third, the development of civilization with populations clustering around temple centers in true urban zones or living in temple-center-with-outlying-hamlet arrangements; and fourth, the formation of expansionistic civilizations dominating large territorial states" (Willey et al. 1964:488). This ordering corresponds in general to the sequence in which such events occurred. So that the accumulated knowledge could be passed on to future generations, record-keeping devices, including written language, were developed and themselves altered many art forms, such as pottery, jewelry, and murals. The need for specialization arose during this time. Religious leaders, warriors, healers, and potters were only the first in a long line of new occupations.

Religion was undoubtedly the most important profession because of its effect on others. There was a large array of gods, "the most important of which were agricultural in nature, especially the rain gods. To establish a stable relationship between men and his world, these deities had to be constantly propitiated, nourished, and sustained . . . monumental temples were built and much fine craftsmanship devoted to religion" (Sanders and Price 1968:12). As will be noted later, religious customs and duties dominated the life of the Aztecs, especially in their artistic expression.

OLMECS—MOTHER CULTURE

Around 1500 B.C., one group of Indians, the Olmecs, reached a refined and sophisticated level of cultural grandeur. Other groups learned from

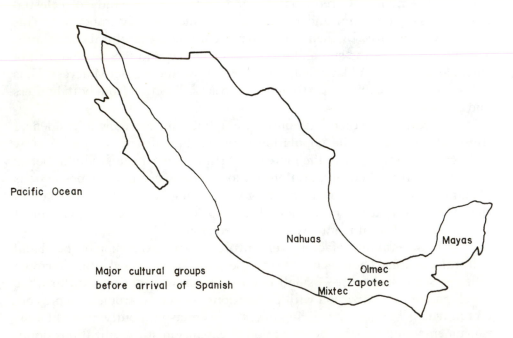

Fig. 1-1. Major cultural groups in Mesoamerica. (Map by Jesus Medina.)

them and prospered. Because of this influence they have been referred to as the *Cultura Madre*, or Mother Culture. They inhabited the lowland region south of Vera Cruz along the eastern coast of Mexico, where the modern states of Tabasco, Campeche, and Yucatan converge. Their cultural glory lasted until 300 B.C. In subsequent centuries other Mesoamerican groups inherited the Olmec tradition and wore the mantle of greatness. In different time periods, the Huastecas flourished in northeastern Mexico; the Mayas in the southeast, going as far as Central America; the Teotihuacanos in the central Mexican plateau; and the Zapotecs in the southwest. These groups "only represent different cultures within a civilization, just as western christianity is but one civilization in spite of differences that exist between Spanish, German, or English cultures" (Bernal 1969:187-188).

The Olmec era is recognized as the time when all the earlier contributions made by unnamed people reached their florescence. In this period the nucleus of cultural achievements took place: the development of the calendar, the invention of the zero concept, and the creation of a system of writing. Other features of Olmec life included stone temples and pyramids, or-

Fig. 1-2. Olmec basalt head. (Drawing by Jeffrey Huereque.)

nate personal dress for the budding elite, commercial networks, defensive fortifications, and sea travel. Hence, this early civilization provided the basis on which the following general cultural foundations were laid.

Some of the features shared by native groups were "hieroglyphic writing . . . books . . . maps . . . a complicated calendar . . . astronomy . . . a team game resembling basketball . . . markets and favoured ports of trade; wars for the purpose of securing sacrificial victims; large-scale human sacrifice; private confession and penance . . . tobacco smoking; and a pantheon of extraordinary complexity" (Coe 1962:17-19). The many basalt stone heads and jaguar art forms found on Olmec sites are a further testimony to the growth of human culture. The gigantic heads "are a psychological record of an early stage of mankind when consciousness was beginning to emerge from the unconscious. No necks, no bodies. Just huge heads emphasizing the new significance of the head-center." The jaguar "served as a cult animal, a spiritual counterpart or guardian" and "each man from birth is associated with such a nagual [spirit], and . . . whatever happens to one happens to the other" (Waters 1975:32-34).

Fig. 1-3. Cache of Olmec jade figures from Gulf Coast plain. (Courtesy Museum of Anthropology and History, Mexico City.)

It is not important whether religious-philosophical beliefs were imported from Asia or conceived in the New World. What is significant is that natives early developed a mythological basis for spiritual endeavors. That spirituality represents a recognition of the contrasting forces all around them. As noted previously, the external, material reality was joined by the internal spiritual world, and this vision of duality permeated other aspects of life. They assigned "the original foundation of the world to a supreme dual principle, Our Mother–Our Father, which was the origin of everything which exists" (Leon-Portilla 1969:30). Thus the rest of the world was viewed in this way. Night-day, life-death, sun-earth, heaven-hell, light-dark, fire-water, male-female, father-mother are but a few of these real and omnipresent contrasting features of life.

Dual existence was the abiding hallmark, the teaching that ordered their life. One side of any duality could not be embraced or thoroughly understood unless its counterpart was acknowledged. Mother-earth took on more meaning when joined by father-sun. Similarly, an appreciation of water-heaven could occur only when fire-hell was introduced. Generally, those who adhered to this spiritual orientation, accepting and integrating these oppositions into their very being, charted a broadened life path.

Thousands upon thousands of Indians participated in the building of Mesoamerica. Like the ocean tide, surging and ebbing, each Indian group took the lead and then lost it to another group through internal decay or foreign encroachment. Of course, during these millenia progressive changes occurred. On the other hand, it is in the nature of human technological and sociocultural evolution to have ups and downs. The periodic moving forward and standing still are universally shared human patterns of evolution. In any event, "from a developmental evolutionary standpoint . . . Mesoamerica remained essentially on a plateau after about 500 A.D., that is, for about a millenium" (Nicholson 1967:58).

CHICHIMECAS—MIGRATION FROM AZTLAN

Beginning in A.D. 900, midway through that thousand-year cultural plateau, a wave of migrations lasting several centuries swept the valley of Mexico and upset the stability of the area. The Chichimecas (meaning "descendants of dogs") came from the far, dry desert northwestern region. These "wild nomads, driven to desperation by drought and starvation, pushed south into regions that were formerly occupied by tillers of the soil, raiding the outposts of civilization. . . . It is thus that we can account for the great Chichimec invasions which took place" (Coe 1962:134). The Chichimecas either forced their way into the region or simply filled the vacuum left by others or both. According to legend, they had migrated from Aztlan, their homeland, which is now the southwestern United States.

In time the Chichimecas absorbed the cultural traits of previous residents of the area, but "warfare and military expansion on the one hand, intensive agriculture and the appropriation of surpluses through tribute payments on the other, are the hallmarks of this new period" (Wolf 1959:117).

The Toltecas were the first of several subgroups within the generic Chichimeca population to establish hegemony in Central Mexico. Borrowing from earlier people, especially the Teotihuacanos and Mayas, they settled at Tula in A.D. 968. Here blossomed a cultural showpiece of excellence from which their rulers could dominate others in the valley. "They soon acquired much of the civilization of these groups and of the settled inhabitants of the valley of Mexico, so much so that the later Aztecs looked back on their time as a golden age" (Bushnell 1969:72).

Many other Chichimeca subgroups eventually found a niche in the area. Most of them spoke the Nahua language and generally followed a militaristic way of life. Before incorporating the cultural habits of the valley, they filled active roles as mercenaries in the power struggles that were under way.

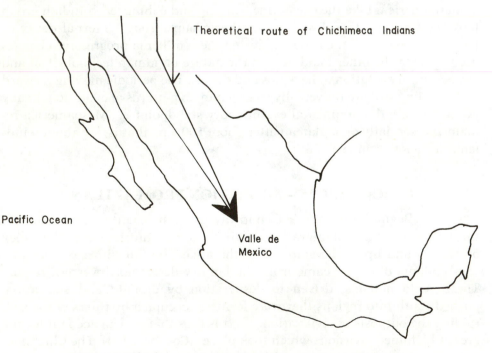

Theoretical route of Chichimeca Indians

Pacific Ocean

Valle de Mexico

Fig. 1-4. Chichemeca migrations. (Map by Jesus Medina.)

After Toltecan rule ended in A.D. 1156, another wave of migration brought a group later to gain power and fame: the Aztecs. With most of the tillable farmland already occupied, the Aztecs at first wandered about, hiring themselves out as mercenaries. Later they found a temporary refuge in Michoacan in western Mexico. Still not satisfied with that location, they finally moved to a most undesirable spot in A.D. 1325.

According to myth, the Aztec warrior-god leader Mexitli followed explicit instructions from heaven to find a spot suitable for his people. This location would be visibly apparent. They were to look for an eagle with a serpent in its mouth, stationed on a lone cactus in the middle of a large lake. And so it happened as foretold. "The place was called Tenochtitlan, in token of its miraculous origin, though only known to Europeans by its other name of Mexico City, derived from their war-god, Mexitli" (Prescott 1843:16). This event notwithstanding, it was not until A.D. 1430, after much intrigue and warfare, that the Aztecs were able to secure a stable foothold in the area. With this beginning, they established themselves as the last Indian group to reign over the central plateau.

2

Intact and stable social order

Most of the basic attributes of civilization were firmly established during the Aztec period. It was an age metaphorically similar to infancy, when the human animal internalizes the first mechanisms to handle external reality. After the embryonic period (those thousands of years during which Indians evolved to the threshold of a more intricate form of life) humans began to seek other outlets to fulfill themselves. Of course, just as infancy is not the same for everybody, a society's cultural customs do not offer the same value for every member of the society. In spite of this fact, it is still fair to state that Aztec society had surely made a more refined style of life available to its citizens.

It is clear that Aztec society aided the direction of human drives such as hunger and thirst, established the willpower to fulfill needs, and demonstrated the social purposefulness to preserve these patterns. With the social and cultural institutions they had developed, the possibilities of further innovation and growth bloomed. This period parallels the infancy stage of human development, then, in three ways: (1) biological drives were certainly better met; (2) learning was becoming increasingly important to societal maintenance; and (3) in spite of these accomplishments, a sense of uncertainty still pervaded the scene. The comparison of Aztec cultural attainment with the stage of human infancy is generally valid for pre-Columbian life.

CLASS *(Nobility supported by commoners)*

Much controversy surrounds the exact nature of the Aztec social stratification system. One school maintains that it was a nonegalitarian aristocracy (Coe 1962:165), while another interpretation seems to support a very democratic situation indeed (Morgan 1963:217). Because of the transitional nature of the relatively new social system, it appears certain that both views are correct for different times. "The Aztec nobility ... began to

Fig. 2-1. Life of Indian nobility. (Drawing by Jeffrey Huereque.)

grow. . . . The continual expansion of the aristocracy undoubtedly diminished the importance of the tribal organizations—the calpullis [groups of houses]—which comprised the common people" (Villegas et al. 1974:39). The system was initially egalitarian and had, over a century, gradually become less so. And yet there were moments when older practices prevailed in the midst of the new ones. "If not a precisely democratic scheme, it did provide for a measure of equity" (Padden 1967:15).

Recognizing that role-class assignments were necessary, the Aztecs sought to prevent social conflict and disintegration with a community-oriented ideological framework. This was undertaken at the expense of the individual, who now was taught to integrate his interests and direct his duties to those of the total group. In a very strict sense, "it was the Aztecs who were to undertake the creation of a political unit matching the area of cultural and economic unity" (Soustelle 1967:253). Thus, as a state-level society, they took on the responsibility of developing a collective ideology and destiny.

Land system

The basis of Aztec society was a land system that evolved around the most important natural resource: the people. In general, land belonged to the people in common; their labor produced basic necessities, and consequently a large share of the wealth was returned to them. However, as noted earlier, this arrangement had undergone important transformations with the rise of a ruling elite, and with the gradual eroding away of a people-oriented land system there arose a new practice, perhaps an incipient form of *latifundia* (large landed estates).

The backbone of the earlier arrangement was the *calpulli*, a socioeconomic unit based on kinship (blood and social relations) and territoriality (ownership of the land required for subsistence). Although some observers question the importance of "blood" in the kinship network (Wolf 1959:135), it nevertheless is clear that the emphasis on "social" kin relations operated to make the calpulli a cohesive unit. Each calpulli possessed a set amount of territory for its own use. Rights of land tenure and ownership were carefully outlined, as were water and irrigation rights, timberland rights, hunting privileges, and farming for household consumption and market bartering. Each calpulli set boundaries with maguey plants, stonewalls, and worn footpaths. Those citizens from another calpulli who trespassed were subject to prosecution and punishment (Whetten 1969:76-81).

Social classes and life

The members within each calpulli were known as *macequales* (commoners, or citizens of the confederacy). Most macequale household heads, working on about a ten-acre plot, had enough food to support themselves and their families. If more was desired by those ambitious ones who labored harder and longer each day, they were granted the right to farm untilled calpulli land. This added incentive and investment allowed them to use the extra amount for bartering at the marketplace. The macequales numbered about eighty-five percent of the population.

Family life was well ordered, with each member learning about and carrying out his responsibilities. Children were taught to respect their parents, grandparents, and aunts and uncles. Living arrangements followed

Continued.

Fig. 2-2. **A,** Stela in Copan, Honduras. **B,** Center of Palenque, Chiapas, Mexico.

Fig. 2-2, cont'd. C, Uxmal, Yucatan, Mexico. **D**, Chac-Mool statue in Chichen Itza, Yucatan, Mexico. **E**, Temple ruins in Tulum, Quintana Roo, Mexico.

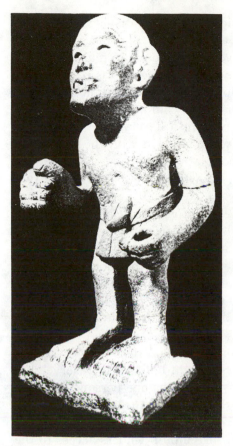

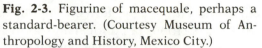

Fig. 2-3. Figurine of macequale, perhaps a standard-bearer. (Courtesy Museum of Anthropology and History, Mexico City.)

a pattern: "each house was surrounded by a little garden. . . . These more modest homes had foundations made of stone; their adobe walls supported a flat roof of beams. . . . One rectangular room sufficed to lodge an entire family; for the kitchen, granary, and bathhouse were separately installed in the garden" (Villegas et al. 1974:37). "They lived chiefly on maize, which they planted in hillocks with pointed sticks; when the maize was ripe, the women ground it into flour and moulded the flour dough into tamales [a type of turnover with meat, vegetables, and chile] or beat it into flat tortillas [round toasted pancakes] which were cooked over charcoal fires. They also cultivated frijoles [beans] and certain other fruits and vegetables, and seasoned their food with chile" (Parkes 1969:6). Most of the food and cooking techniques were native creations and were named with Nahuatl words: *metate* (grinding stone), *mano* (stone hand grinder), and so on.

In addition to the macequales in social class status there were two other groups: the *mayeques* and the *tlalmaites*. The mayeques, never more than two or three percent of the population, were like "displaced persons" without citizenship rights. They worked the fields for the rulers on a permanent basis. Similar to serfs, they received only enough to maintain their households. Another slave-type status, the tlalmaite class, was reserved for those who sold themselves to the rulers for a set amount of time and lived on their land as permanent laborers. Their tenure could last a few years or a lifetime, but their offspring could not be born into slavery. They comprised three or four percent of the people, and when coupled with the tlalmaites never rose above ten percent of the total population.

It is important to note that the growth in numbers of these two groups increased in direct proportion to the steady expansion of a ruling elite—the latter being former calpulli members who had left agricultural work for positions of political and cultural leadership.

Each calpulli was composed of a group of families related by kin. Often the members of one calpulli would number into the thousands. "Tenochtitlan itself was divided into four great quarters, and every quarter into its constituent calpulli, every calpulli into tlazilacalli, or streets . . . this was an ideal system for administrative control of a large population. The individual calpulli had its own temple and some of the more high-ranking of them had schools for . . . military education" (Coe 1962:164).

Several local *tlatoques* (speakers) would be elected to serve as a "natural" calpulli high council, and from their ranks one person would be designated the calpulli "speaker" (Padden 1967:15). All the supreme calpulli leaders met as a council to advise the head of government (Valiant 1956:115). However, this egalitarian practice of allowing calpulli leaders access to the higher echelons of government was rapidly phased out.

Rise of the state

Since the Aztecs profited from earlier technologies and thus were able to support a larger population, it similarly followed that social relations would also change. In early Aztec society, tlatoques were selected from the ranks of the people. These natural leaders knew the people well, for they were of the people and made decisions with their consent. The gradual replacement of a grassroots democracy with an aristocracy was one of the major social changes. "But it must not be forgotten that plebians could reach the highest honours: although this aristocracy was jealous of its prerogatives it was not ossified; it could still renew and strengthen itself by recruiting new men of value" (Soustelle 1961:93).

It can be hypothesized that a particular calpulli eventually became entrenched as the leading group. Perhaps they became all-powerful because of their military prowess. At first their actions benefited the total community, but before long they had become a hereditary ruling body and no longer took the interests of the community to heart. Coe states that "a society evolved from a primitive organization in which all lands were originally held by the clans . . . there was no higher authority than clan chiefs, into a fully fledged state with the appearance of a privileged class. . . . Given time, the clans would have certainly declined to total insignificance" (Coe 1962:165). "The city was not merely the tribe enlarged; it had become something else, a state launched upon a career of aggrandizement, a society in which differentiation was continually growing and in which enmity between the classes was beginning to appear" (Soustelle 1961:93).

The members of this ruling group became known as the *pipiltin* (nobles). Never more than two to ten percent of the populace, they directed religious and political concerns from the center of the city. Although power was concentrated in their hands, they still were burdened with the responsibilities of administration, government, and religion. Because these obligations were handled fairly and efficiently, the people generally supported their rule. As a matter of fact, the rule of Texcoco, one of the neighboring city allies, was very democratic. "In Tezcuco [Texcoco] the . . . arrangements were of a more refined character; and a gradation of tribunals finally terminated in a general meeting or parliament . . . held every eighty days in the capital" (Prescott 1842:23).

The primary support for the pipiltin came from the tribute of the macequales. This was paid in two ways: contribution of a set amount of produce and labor service for a certain number of days on pipiltin land. As a result of this relationship, the pipiltin would still keep an open ear to macequale demands, for it was the macequales' extra efforts that released the pipiltin from working the land, allowing them to focus their energy on civic and religious duties.

Priestly duties were closely linked to the pipiltin rule. For example, the emperor Montezuma, who will be discussed later, was "the head of an immensely complicated social, political, and economic system, . . . an emperor embodying all the temporal power of an autocratic despot. As the nominal head of a state religion, he was in addition a high priest to whom was ascribed the attribute of divinity" (Waters 1975:72). The early chronicler Fray Bernardino de Sahagun describes the great array of deities and the priests who served them, but especially noteworthy in his account was how priests were selected. "These two pontiffs were equal in standing and honor, even if they should be of very low birth and of very lowly and poor parents; the only reason why they were elected to be the high pontiffs was their having faithfully complied with and followed all the customs, rules, exercises and teachings" (Sahagun 1932:202).

Occupations other than those based on agrarian life were held by the macequales. They were "divided into social classes with residence in either town or rural settlements, based primarily on occupation. In the town were the professional warriors or tectecuhtin, the pochteca or merchants, and such full-time professional craftsmen as the goldsmiths, lapidaries, and featherworkers. The merchants and craftsmen were organized into hereditary guilds occupying residential wards within the town" (Sanders and Price 1968:152). In short, the pipiltin held the leadership positions in the city and the macequales filled the agrarian roles in the country and skilled occupations in the city.

As trade with other Indian groups throughout Mesoamerica developed, there came into being a class of merchants known as *pochteca*. They provided a dual service when away on trading expeditions: they gathered foreign information as spies, and they represented Aztec commercial interests. However, because Aztec leaders feared the potential power of the pochtecas, they were watched very closely. Some pochtecas harbored entrepreneurial ambitions and desired to build a separate business dynasty, but if detected in this activity, they were put to death and their wealth was redistributed. As a result, they "made a special effort to appear humble and poor" (Wolf 1959:140).

Caution should be taken here to avoid perceiving the pochteca and pipiltin as bourgeois and aristocratic classes comparable to those of Europe. They were very different, and according to Prescott: "It cannot be denied that we recognize, in all this, several features of the feudal system, which, no doubt, lose nothing of their effect, under the hands of the Spanish writers, who are fond of tracing analogies to European institutions. But such analogies lead sometimes to very erroneous conclusions" (Prescott 1842:22). Thus, these two classes should be viewed in the context of their own historical development.

Every civilization that has grouped over one-half million citizens in one location, as the Aztecs did, has had to establish and maintain a system of law and order. The people of Tenochtitlan were instructed in a code of laws ordering behavior, and if they deviated or were remiss, well-defined methods of enforcement were taken. One supreme judge, chosen for life with veto powers over the king, interpreted the law and meted out decisions for all the people. Lesser judicial officials were appointed for each calpulli district and for the remaining outlying provinces of the confederacy, or league of states. A network of higher and lower courts ensured that every citizen, no matter where he resided in the central region, would receive a swift and fair legal decision when a law was broken. Social stability was also maintained by a police force.

Confederacy and trade

To further the interests of the people, it was necessary for the Aztecs to establish diplomatic alliances and commercial relations with other groups. In 1430 they created an alliance that was later to expand into a confederacy. Two other Nahuatl-speaking groups, the cities of Texcoco and Tlacopan, joined the Aztecs to share obligations and increase their security. During the later expansionist wars, both cities aided in the Aztec military campaigns: Tlacopan provided supply carriers and Texcoco sent warriors. This triple alliance was able to gain and maintain control over the whole central plateau of Mexico.

In the process of expansion and conquering other tribes the prevailing type of rule was "[a] confederation of autonomous cities rather than a centralized state . . . which contained Nahuatl-speaking peoples along with others who spoke Otomi, Mazahua, Matlaltzinca, Huaxtec, Totonac, Mixtec, Zapotec, Maya and other languages" (Soustelle 1967:253). This ruling system benefited the Aztecs, for they could not afford to station a permanent military force in the outlying provinces. Nevertheless, in comparison to most imperial sistems it was rather egalitarian. One sixteenth-century observer states that "it should be noted that the Mexican kings . . . left the natural lords of their provinces in command of all the land they conquered and acquired. . . . They also allowed all the commoners to keep their land and property, and permitted them to retain their customs and practices and mode of government" (Zorita 1963:112).

On the whole, in spite of some rivalry among the main allies, the confederacy was able to function fairly smoothly. Under this political unit, far-reaching trade activities were undertaken with other regions—north to the modern state of Durango, east and west to the Atlantic and Pacific Oceans, and as far south as Nicaragua (Loya 1958:21). Tenochtitlan, as the leading city of the triple alliance, provided these conquered regions with military protection from other warring tribes and in exchange received a "wide variety of goods . . . from the 38 tributary provinces which composed the Mexica domain. Annual payments of basic subsistence items including maize, beans, amaranth, dried chile peppers, and maguey honey, along with items of clothing, pottery bowls, native paper, and the like" (Helms 1975:104). Groups that were unable to contribute agricultural products gave tribute in the form of labor.

Tenochtitlan reigned supreme over the entire valley. Tlaltelolco, its twin marketplace city, served up to 60,000 people daily. There the shoppers would purchase the innumerable items and services available and pay for them by bartering or with money, the latter being either cacao beans or quetzal bird quills filled with gold.

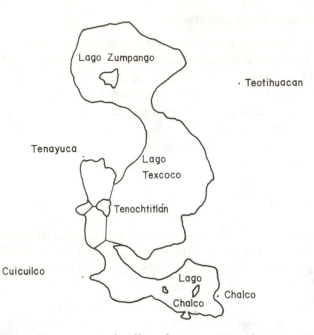

Fig. 2-4. Main cities in central valley of Mexico. (Map by Jesus Medina.)

Generally, then, the socioeconomic and political practices of the Aztecs were shaped to benefit the total community. Interestingly, although the pipiltin were the elite group, macequales who showed talent and intelligence were given the opportunity to attend their schools. Thus, some egalitarianism yet remained.

CULTURE *(Pantheon of gods, moral order, and literary tradition)*

"If the Aztecs were bloodthirsty barbarians with an itch for power, they were also a sensitive people with high moral ethics. They were, in short, a people like most people, expressing both sides of their dual nature. Only on their own terms can we understand them" (Waters 1975:72). This cultural theme embodies all that the Aztecs represent. Learning from the world around them and from the teachings of earlier Indians, they embraced the dual nature of reality. They were similar to the Greeks who combined the body (materialism) and soul (spirituality) in their paideia: A man should become a speaker of words (soul), and a doer of deeds (body). Here is how the Aztecs phrased their ideal (Leon-Portilla 1963:135):

The mature man
is a heart solid as a rock,
is a wise face,
possessor of a face,
possessor of a heart,
he is able and understanding

To this end, all people from youth onward were taught by their parents and teachers to develop their "hearts" (soul) and "faces" (body). Always uppermost in their minds as they pursued this goal was how best to serve the community.

Religious principles encompassed this view of mankind and guided the people to be as one with nature. Hence, "religion, with its scrupulous and exacting ritual and profusion of its myths, penetrated, in all its aspects, deeply into the everyday life of men. Continuously and totally, it moulded the existence of the Mexican nation. Everything was under its domination: public life and private life; each stage of each person's progress from birth to death; the rhythm of time; the arts and even games—nothing escaped" (Soustelle 1961:119).

Education

The educational system was structured to fulfill that lofty goal. Accordingly, regardless of socioeconomic background, all male citizens were entitled to participate in a universal system of education. As noted previously, many intelligent children of humble origins were placed in the higher schools, where all the spiritual and intellectual knowledge was found in great books. "The priests were in charge of educating the young people; they were custodians of esoteric knowledge, wisdom, and tradition, of the two calendars, and of the art of writing in painted books and inscriptions" (Leon-Portilla 1969:4). All instruction was conducted in the Nahuatl language.

This constant, daily struggle to balance the dual human drives of environmental adaptation and spiritual betterment was not always successful. There were numerous instances when either material or spiritual practices, or both together, failed completely. And yet, in spite of the many failures, there were more successes, and this undoubtedly stemmed from the almost obsessive religious devotion of the Aztecs. It appeared that the guidance they sought from the heavens enabled them to change and readapt on a continuous basis.

School life was built around two types of learning environment. The *calmecac* (higher college) was devoted to the intellect and spirit, and

Fig. 2-5. A and **B,** Natives of Chiapas, Mexico.

there the leaders and priests received training. In the *telpochcalli* (arsenal) the crafts of the military warrior were taught. Because military prowess was a highly valued skill, most young men attended the telpochcalli. Of course, the fact that Aztecs maintained authority over the valley through military might had something to do with that. Many liberties were granted those trained at this institution, but a rigorous upbringing that instilled physical and mental discipline ensured the development of hardy warriors. In brief, one might say that the calmecac was an intellectual and spiritual school (perhaps analogous to the best of Harvard and Notre Dame), while the telpochcalli was strictly military (like West Point) (Peterson 1962: 109).

Official state instruction began at about six years old, when parents would take their sons to school. However, education was initiated much earlier in the home, the father ministering to the sons and the mother to the daughters. "Education began after weaning in the third year. Its purpose was to induct the child into the techniques and obligations of adult life as promptly as possible" (Valiant 1956:90). Females learned skills and duties to complement their future roles as wives and mothers. Some became priestesses and were active in certain religious sects, but most were excluded from such positions.

Religious practices and moral code

As noted previously, religion was more than a segment of Aztec life. Accordingly, every day was a holy day and every member of the community was a part of the collective worship. "It was by religion that the city and tribe were one, and by religion that variety was unified" (Soustelle 1961:93).

Aztecs believed that beyond mortal life were heaven, hell, and purgatory (these differed in many particulars from the Christian counterparts, however). Warriors who died in battle were rewarded with heaven, a serene place of flowers, birds, clouds, and sunshine. Those who died in sin fell to a dark forbidding hell. A neutral, intermediate purgatory awaited those who had not given service to the community. Forgiveness for one's sins was possible through confession, in which both spiritual and temporal absolution were granted. As Aztec law allowed only one confession for each individual lifetime, not surprisingly most waited until old age to confess their sins.

There were many other rituals and ceremonies in which citizens actively participated, including baptism with holy water to ward off the evil spirits, and dozens of supplicatory prayers—incantations, poems, or songs—directed to one of the many deities, a commemorative holy day, or for a cure for a particular ailment (Prescott 1842:41-42; Leon-Portilla 1963:124-128).

The people's faith in these practices equalled the height of fervor and devotion reached by other world religions.

Worshipping the gods by prayer was not enough, for the community also undertook large-scale projects in building pyramids (and, for lesser deities, smaller buildings). A whole pantheon of deities was honored in this way, each with his own temple of a size to reflect the patron god's importance or insignificance. Among the most important of the pantheon figures was Huitzilopochtli, the sun god. According to tribal myth, the Aztecs were now in the fifth world of creation—the previous four had been destroyed by wind, water, fire, and the earth. This fifth world was named *El Quinto Sol* (The Fifth Sun). Because of the failure of past worlds through one catastrophe or another, the natives feared the destruction of this one. Thus, they took it upon themselves to conduct ceremonies to keep the sun alive.

Every day, with the rising of the sun, the priests would sacrifice human beings, tearing out their hearts. Offerings of hearts made at the top of the temple dedicated to Huitzilopochtli guaranteed his daily return. This important act of creation, the rising of the sun, kept the people from total darkness and had to be propitiated. Thousands of people were sacrificed in this manner for their precious blood, *chalchihuatl*, was the only suitable

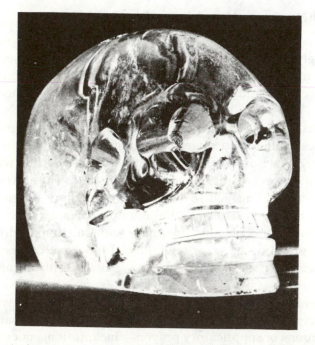

Fig. 2-6. Symbol of Aztec god of death. (Courtesy Museum of Anthropology and History, Mexico City.)

nourishment for the sun (Padden 1967:73). Interestingly, many of the intended sacrificial victims faced the affair in a solemn manner, and often they received special treatment. Leon-Portilla depicts the austere ceremony in this way: "There were dialogues between different choirs, solemnly recalling myths and religious beliefs. . . . They were all trained to act just once in the cosmic drama of the Aztec perpetual theater. They were messengers from the people, collaborators with the Sun, carefully chosen to begin their journey to the beyond" (Leon-Portilla 1969:98-99). Many of those chosen for sacrifice received royal attention and were granted special privileges for weeks prior to the event. On the whole, like most people who die for a cause, the sacrificial victims bravely served their community.

Other victims were not so blessed. This was especially true of the many prisoners captured in actual or acted-out "flower wars" (Waters 1975:71). Mock battles were organized with neighboring tribes, and the captured prisoners were later sacrificed to each tribe's respective gods. Like contemporary wars, this practice was brutal and savage but was also adaptive. According to one writer: "It was essential to remain in a state of war, and from this arose the strange institution of the war of the flowers, Xochiyaoyotl, which seems to have come into being after the terrible famines which ravaged central Mexico in 1450" (Soustelle 1961:101). Aztec warriors captured by other tribes were subjected to a similar fate.

This overview of cultural life highlights the most salient customs. Other activities worthy of mention are the arts and music, architecture and stone carving, and the many fine crafts, such as sculpture and gold and silver jewelry-making. One can observe that here was a people in infancy, barely beginning to develop their form of civilization. According to the evidence, and despite certain paradoxes, Aztec life was both culturally sophisticated and generally contoured to the requirements of the total population.

COLOR *(Intragroup racism)*

The emphasis on racial features, or racism, as we know it today, did not exist in Aztec society. Of course, there were physiognomic differences between Indian tribes: some were taller than others, higher cheekbones characterized Mayas, broad noses appeared to be an Olmec trait, and so on. These intraracial differences are similar to the heterogeneity found among Caucasian Europeans. Presumably, Frenchmen fit the Alpine mold, Swedes are typical Nordics, and Italians are Mediterranean, at least in a general way. In the main, this is also true of pre-Columbian Indians. Certainly, the Aztecs oppressed and exploited other groups in Mesoamerica. In some respects their rule was as severe as that found elsewhere in the world, then and now. Nevertheless, it was not purely *racial criteria* that determined who was to be subjugated and kept that way.

Culture as a basis for oppression

Indeed, racial appearance was not enough to prevent a capable person from rising to the highest position. Cultural cues—dress, gestures, language, and so on—motivated the Aztecs to act. Whether the cultural sign brought positive or negative Aztec behavior depended on whether or not the person or group was an ally. Enemies, of course, caught all the abuse humans are capable of heaping on one another—including death.

So, in brief, the whole notion of racial superiority and inferiority and the attendant psychological ramifications were not present in the social system, at least not on a large scale. This was a system in which the conquering peoples maintained control for as long as possible, dominating the hinterland from an urban center. When they finally experienced a downfall, a new group would absorb their culture and become the new culture carriers. According to Wolf, myth was then used to legitimize the successors' claims to dominance. "Some Toltec were undoubtedly real; but others were Toltec through myth-making, . . . all conceptions of Tollan and Toltec soon passed into the realm of myth. Those who came after [including the Aztecs] regarded these mythical original Toltec as a race of supermen, taller than ordinary men and able to run faster than decadent later breeds. They were the master artificers, the first scientists, the first astronomers" (Wolf 1959:120). Ruler designation and legitimacy, then, were inconsistent and usually had a cultural basis.

Breakup and transformation of the social order

CONTACT *(Conquerors seek riches)*

After years of reconnoitering various parts of the Caribbean region, the Spanish accidentally discovered Mexico. Early expeditions to that land, directed by Governor Diego Velasquez of Cuba, failed, but they returned with rumors of fabulous wealth and set the stage for an enterprise that succeeded, the expedition of Hernando Cortes. In February 1519, Cortes set out with 11 ships, over 600 Spaniards, 16 horses, 10 brass guns, several large dogs, and over 200 Indian and African slaves of both sexes (Loya 1958:38; Diaz del Castillo 1956:40-41).

European exploration of the Caribbean region had begun with Columbus' voyage in 1492, of which one historian has aptly noted: "Columbus did not discover a New World; he established contact between two worlds, both already old" (Parry 1971:65). By 1519, the Spanish had subdued many natives in the Caribbean islands and established a strong colony in Cuba. From there they moved north, west, and south, seeking other territories to conquer and settle. Aiding them in this exploration and discovery were recently vanquished natives and many imported African slaves.

Background to exploration and discovery

The background to these events begins in Europe. The European desire for goods from the Orient ignited an age of expansionism. The defeat of the Moors, who controlled Mediterranean sea commerce, opened the door for further commercial relations. With this success, significantly, Spain and the other European states concerned themselves with building empires. However, "Spain started overseas discovery later than Portugal. Not until the marriage of Ferdinand and Isabella in 1469 were the two main Spanish kingdoms of Aragon and Castille finally united, and not until the capture of Granada in 1492 was the last Moslem stronghold in the peninsula destroyed" (Nowell 1954:47). In the aftermath nationalist consolidation was speeded up.

Navigational science developed because of the search for riches and commercial ties with the East and made possible the age of discovery and exploration. Adventurous expansionism became fashionable, and many Spaniards were swept away with get-rich-quick schemes.

Spanish success can be attributed to several factors:

1. The tension brought about by the establishment of a centralized government under Ferdinand and Isabella, which encouraged Spanish nationalism and expansionism
2. The control of the strategically located continental gateway between the Mediterranean and the Atlantic
3. The evangelical Catholic zeal and nomadic adventurous ambitions born during *Reconquista* (expulsion of the Moors)
4. The obsession to become rich, particularly on the part of dispossessed *segundones* (second sons not entitled to a full share of the family estate because of inheritance laws favoring senior sons), who sought to become *hijos de algo* or *hidalgos* (noblemen, "son of something or someone") through military achievements (Vives 1969:315-316)

The last two influences were particularly crucial. Many segundones were eager for adventure and enterprise. Joined by other, nonaristocratic, soldiers of fortune, they set out for the New World. One writer says that the messianic missions were a carryover from earlier times: "these Spaniards were all imbued with the sense of common fellowship fostered in Spain as in all the Latin world by the twofold tradition of Rome—the Imperial and the Christian" (Madariaga 1947:6).

The motivation provided by fellowship and adventure was strongly augmented by personal ambitions. Spanish soldiers of fortune also sought to become landed aristocrats, along the lines of the old Roman principle of *occupatio*, or occupancy: "Occupancy, one of the time-honored 'natural' means of acquisition, was broadly inclusive," for it allowed the newcomers to take total possession of all lands. "This was the legal engine of the Spanish Reconquista and was firmly rooted in the conqueror's mind when he invaded the western hemisphere" (Padden 1967:135). Thus, *conquistadores* (conquerors) had reason to expect a prestigious title and landed estate in the Americas. "The original impelling motive of discovery and colonization was economic, and the exploitation of the resources of the colonies for the benefit of the crown and of the colonists who supported the imperial system always remained the paramount factor in determining the character of administration" (Scholes 1946:530).

Cortes begins conquest

Upon setting foot in Mexico, the Spaniards under Cortes immediately established themselves as conquerors. In the first encounter over 1500

Yucatan Mayas died, while the victors lost only 37 men. Moving toward the center of Mexico, the Spaniards repeated this bloody pattern. To maintain military superiority, they often wiped out whole Indian groups. Numerous tribes were met and dealt with summarily. Some small disorganized tribes were quickly subjugated. Others, larger and socially united, required more time and effort. Cortes directed this process with skillful (although unfeeling) military genius.

Cortes and his men were initially ignorant of Indian languages. As a result, most of their early contacts with natives lacked any exchange of information. However, luck was on the Spaniards' side. Early in the expedition the army met Aguilar, a shipwrecked Spaniard who had learned the Maya dialect (Diaz del Castillo 1956:43; Prescott 1842:162-163). This chance meeting enabled Cortes to use Aguilar as an interpreter, or interrogator, of Indians in the area. Later, as Cortes marched closer to the heart of Mexico, he encountered more good fortune. It was an Indian custom to present gifts to any conqueror, and the offerings often included young maidens. One such woman, Malinche, known to the Spaniards as Doña Marina, played a crucial role in the conquest (Diaz del Castillo 1956:66). Malinche was originally bilingual, speaking the Nahuatl Aztec language and the Maya dialect Aguilar had learned, but she soon learned Spanish. Consequently, although Cortes understood only Spanish at the outset, he quickly utilized the two translators to become totally apprised of Indian designs. He used this tactical tool to speed up the march and to guard against attack.

Other tactics benefited the Spanish military juggernaut. For example, some dissident Indians welcomed Cortes as a liberator and assisted in the conquest. "It is pretty clear that Cortes was able to carry out his awe-inspiring feat only because most of the Mexican people welcomed him as their deliverer from the unbearable exactions of the Aztecs" (Simpson 1967:25). Tlaxcala was one of these groups; more than 20,000 Tlaxcalans aided campaigns against other Mexican Valley Indians. In some instances Cortes resorted to psychological ploys to prove the power of his Christian God. Once he had cannon sharpshooters blow up an Indian statue of a god set on a temple top. Thus, by exhibiting a technological advantage, in one stroke he demonstrated the superiority of the Spanish deity and the impotence of Indian gods (Loya 1958:41).

When all else failed, Cortes turned to the simple and time-proven practice of rhetorical bravado, inspiring his men to extraordinary acts of military prowess. "The utterances of Cortes . . . are replete with references to Caesar, Pompey, and Hannibal. Cortes plays not only at being himself, he is also the amadis of Gaul celebrated in the medieval books of chivalry . . . he . . . translated each act into a symbolic statement, an evocation of a superhuman purpose" (Wolf 1959:154).

Montezuma and the legend of Quetzalcoatl

It appeared that the Indian gods had forsaken the defenders. At every turn Cortes undermined native plots and intrigues. Paradoxically, a most curious legend furthered the Spanish cause and explained to a degree why many Indians openly received the Spaniards. The legend concerned a tall, bearded, white god, Quetzalcoatl (The Feathered Serpent, or Kukulcan to Mayas). This legendary character had gained prominence several centuries earlier, during Toltec rule. According to the legend, the beneficent Quetzalcoatl left the valley because of troubled times—mainly the downfall of the Toltec empire—with the promise that he would return. The Indians inferred that Cortes was Quetzalcoatl incarnate, returning from the east intent on bringing back the good, moral, and just life (Padden 1967:103; Leon-Portilla 1962:13; Prescott 1931:191).

Cortes exploited this legend when he discovered that the Indians connected him with the returning Quetzalcoatl. Like many other Indian groups, the Aztecs had already incorporated this god into their pantheon. As a result, the Aztec ruler Montezuma believed that Cortes was a god-man. This fateful decision made him waver and vacillate, delaying action.

Fig. 3-1. Temple of Quetzalcoatl at Teotihuacan, near Mexico City.

Montezuma "had been mistaken about Cortes' identity and mission from the very beginning" (Padden 1967:190), and he ignored the advice of the royal family. Such men as Cacama and Cuitlahuac early advocated the extermination of foreign interlopers. The legend of Quetzalcoatl notwithstanding, they felt that Cortes' intent was evil. And yet, Montezuma "could not run away, could not go into hiding. He had lost his strength and his spirit, and could do nothing . . . now he was weak and listless and too uncertain to make a decision. Therefore he did nothing but wait" (Leon-Portilla 1962:36). Meanwhile the conquerors moved ahead, tribe by tribe, province by province.

At first gifts of gold and other rare objects were offered to placate the Spanish. These were to no avail, however, and only stimulated conquistador appetites. As Cortes himself said, the Spanish suffered from "an affliction of the heart, and gold was its only remedy" (Diaz del Castillo 1956). The more offerings to the Spaniards in return for their retreat, the more they pushed forward. Finally an Aztec retinue escorted them into the great city of Mexico-Tenochtitlan.

Mexico-Tenochtitlan

Cortes' men viewed the central urban area of Mexico-Tenochtitlan with awe, for they had never seen such a splendid place. "Spaniards . . . had seen nothing better during the twenty-five years of exploration of America than the houses of poles and thatch of Indian tribes, none of whom had risen above a state of barbarism" (Diaz del Castillo 1956:202).

Although Europeans were skeptical of creations made by "barbarians," they agreed the city was beautiful. In all their previous contacts with regions and cities of the Old World, nothing had impressed them more. All the buildings of the central plaza were plastered a brilliant white, and the streets were lined with trees and flowering shrubs at regular intervals. At night, well-tended braziers in wall brackets illuminated the streets. Canals were filled with canoes carrying passengers to and fro, and after dark the light from crude lighthouses guided them (Zorita 1963:157).

The city was dominated by the main ceremonial precincts, and a huge marketplace was located in the neighboring community of Tlatelolco (Adams 1977:31). The temple enclosure itself held twenty-five pyramids, several palaces, two ball courts, and many civil buildings. Activities abounded throughout the city: policemen made the rounds, anxious crowds gathered near medical and dental facilities, teams played on the ball courts, and schools bustled with children. Tlatelolco, the greatest Indian trading center of the Americas, offered a variety of services and foods: tattooers, barbers, leather tanners, jewelers, healers, basket and pottery makers, tailors, storytellers, magicians, wood carvers, cotton, turkeys, bells, slaves, edible dogs, sweets of all kinds, fish, tomatoes, tortillas, rubber, lentils, peanuts, pineapples, iguanas, firewood, perfume, toys, pumpkins, maté, tobacco, vanilla, parrots, pepper, sweet potatoes, strawberries, meal, jade, turtles, and many more.

CONFLICT *(Destruction of Tenochtitlan)*

There were many sources of conflict. Some caused more friction than others, yet in one way or another all reflect the results of Spanish-Indian contact. The conquistadores sought wealth, in whatever form, and this ambition generally brought problems. Their motives were "their restless greed for gold, for land and slaves; their traditional ambition to strike down the heathen and to win souls for Christ, and, more subtle but no less compelling, their love of great deeds for their own sake" (Parry 1971:84). After the available supply of mineral wealth dwindled, the Spaniards turned to other sources of support. This caused the escalating conflict between Spaniards and Indians to reach its apex.

Cortes entered Tenochtitlan and was welcomed by many of the inhabitants. Fearing reprisals from the antagonistic Aztecs, and to secure his

Fig. 3-2. A, Main temple complex of Mexico-Tenochtitlan. **B,** Scale model of temple complex. **C,** Ruins of Tenochtitlan in Mexico City. (**A** and **B** courtesy Museum of Anthropology and History, Mexico City.)

Fig. 3-2, cont'd. For legend see opposite page.

own tenuous position, he made Montezuma a prisoner in his own land. Cortes believed the Spaniards needed a hostage to prevent their annihilation. What better one than the main leader who was respected and obeyed by all the people—and who, of course, played willingly into their hands? At the outset, relations between the two groups remained steady. Only after Cortes left for the east coast of Vera Cruz did warfare break out in the city. His departure was prompted by an invasion of other Spaniards, sent from Cuba by Governor Velasquez to reassert control over Cortes and to appropriate his gains. Although many Indians were uncomfortable with the Spanish presence, it was the Spanish who initiated the fighting. One of the captains, Alvarado, was charged with maintaining order while Cortes was away. Instead, fearing a plot, he viciously attacked the Aztecs during a dance ceremony. Of course the Indians fought back, if only to protect themselves from being massacred (Leon-Portilla 1962:76). On Cortes' return everything turned to chaos. There was nothing for the Spanish to do but flee, and so they did, driven from the city by angry warriors. In the words of Bernal Diaz del Castillo, who was there: "Had it been in the day-time, it would have been far worse, and we who escaped did so only by the Grace of God. To one who saw the hosts of warriors who fell on us that night and the canoes full of them coming along to carry off our soldiers, it was terrifying" (Diaz del Castillo 1956:315).

While the Aztecs celebrated that night, it was *La Noche Triste* (The Sad Night) for the defeated Spaniards. Many of the conquerors tried to escape with gold but succeeded in saving only their skins. Others, not so fortunate, drowned because of the heavy weight of gold they carried. Seeking sanctuary and aid from friendly Indians, the Spanish nursed their wounds and regrouped. Afterwards, they returned, laid seige to the city, and eventually subdued the defenders.

Causes of Aztec defeat

The Aztec defeat stemmed from a combination of factors: the technological superiority (weapons) of the Spaniards, their psychologically astute diplomatic strategy, and their temporary alliances with dissident Indians. Many Aztec customs weakened the Indian cause and added to the Spanish strength. For instance, Cortes was captured by Aztec warriors on several occasions but was not slain. This occurred because the Indian goal in warfare was to capture, not kill, so that the prisoners could later be ceremonially sacrificed to the gods. Spaniards were able to recapture their leader in the heat of a battle. In addition, fighting against mounted men was new to the natives. Since the Aztecs had never seen horses before, the animals naturally terrified them.

Most important of all were the eager Indians who helped Cortes, reasoning (incorrectly, as it developed) that they would benefit in the aftermath. When the Aztecs realized that certain defeat was ahead, it was already too late to build alliances with other similarly besieged Indians. Hence, the conquistadores conquered the tribes piecemeal, without facing coordinated resistance. Perhaps, like so many other humans who are convinced their way is right, the Indians felt that the gods would not abandon them.

This modern comment describes the Aztec view of the fall of the city (Leon-Portilla 1962:149):

Nothing but flowers and songs of sorrow are left in Mexico and Tlatelolco, where once we saw warriors and wise men. . . .

We know it is true that we must perish, for we are mortal men. You, the Giver of Life, you have ordained it.

We wander here and there in our desolate poverty. We are mortal men. We have seen bloodshed and pain where once we saw beauty and valor.

We are crushed to the ground; we lie in ruins. There is nothing but grief and suffering in Mexico and Tlatelolco, where once we saw beauty and valor.

Following the downfall of Tenochtitlan in 1521, over twenty years passed before most major Mesoamerican tribes were conquered. "Bands of Spaniards were dispatched by Cortes to gain the subordination of major native cities and to seek the sources of Mexica gold. In this way various Spanish communities, new centers for expansion, were also established" (Helms 1975:143) (Wagley and Harris 1958:50). Despite their earlier defeats in numerous skirmishes, the Mayas in 1846 were the last important group to be conquered. Some groups such as the Yaquis of the northwest resisted much longer and never accepted subordination (Spicer 1962:46). The Spaniards usually sought out groups living in heavily populated settlements. The Aztecs fit this criterion in two ways: dense groupings and strategic location. This settlement pattern made it possible to bring the area under immediate subjugation with a few heavy battles. Those who fled to the hinterland and mountains were more fortunate, for they escaped the worst excesses of contact and conflict (Loya 1958:108-109).

Friction over land and religious practices

Land and religious practices were serious conflict issues, often affecting other areas of life. With the defeat of the Aztec confederacy, the Spaniards replaced the old elite and became the new collectors of tribute, which directly involved the land system. However, the most serious and intense confrontation occurred in the area of religion. The Spanish earnestly focused attention on the Indians' minds and hearts. They reasoned that control over the natives' laboring bodies would be assured after a new ideology was implanted. Their program of implementation, reminiscent of the heated European holy wars and inquisitions, was vicious and effectively merciless. "It is easy to see why the phobia about heresy that raged in Spain was exaggerated in America among the religious who were perpetually in contact with a pagan civilization" (Ricard 1966:35).

A well-organized campaign led to the destruction of many of the temples, which were quickly replaced by Christian structures on the same sites. Native religious roles and activities of all types were banned. All resisters secretly upholding the old "pagan" way were punished or exterminated.

Missionaries, beginning with the Franciscans in 1524, followed by the Dominicans and Augustinians, were charged with the Indian Christianization policy. Many ascetic, humanistically inspired clerics undertook the Christian salvation of Indian souls and worked against great odds to convert them. The missionaries' protective intervention softened the cruel impact of military contact. No matter how lofty their goals, though, the church fathers actually further aided the Spanish crown by more completely oppressing the Indians—soul as well as body. They also placed a wedge between generations, causing intratribal conflict. Church schools taught Aztec children the catechism to combat Indian religious beliefs. Children were instructed to spy on their elders and report parents who continued in the old ways (Madsen 1967:374).

The missionaries initiated a campaign of indoctrination to make Christianity and "paganism" incompatible to the neophytes. Some of the frictional contrasts were these: Aztecs believed in multiple creations, and Christians in one beginning and one God. Christians spoke of the pains of hell for sinners, whereas afterworld torture was unimportant to the Aztecs. (One young catechist, when told he would go to heaven, answered, "I haven't seen anyone go there.") In addition, clerical sects competed for Indian souls, each with its own conversion program and all with the intention of rescuing them from damnation.

On the whole, Indians underwent a traumatic period because of these conflicting religious philosophies. Missionaries constantly preached that individual salvation of the soul resulted from practicing Christianity. If one hesitated, then eternal hell awaited him. Significantly, one early observer was already laying the groundwork for both their conversion and subjugation: "These Indians are free of almost all the impediments to salvation that hinder the Spaniards, for they are content with very little. . . . They are incredibly patient and long suffering, and meek as sheep. I do not once remember having seen one of them nurse a grudge. They, the humble and scorned, live only to serve and work" (Zorita 1963:164).

As a result, many Indians attempted a balancing act, worshipping both the old and the new religions and symbols simultaneously. Hence, "friars detected a shifting of position and posture that they interpreted as backsliding and even outright apostasy. . . . At the same time the friars were horrified at the plethora of old religious ideas the Indians were carrying over" (Padden 1967:241).

Religious conversion programs brought superficial native acceptance, especially following atrocities against natives in the name of God. One such example of a conversion method is "the water torture in which the mouth was fastened open with a stick and water was poured in until the abdomen swelled up, after which the investigator stood on top of the victim until water mixed with blood came out of the mouth, nose, and ears" (Madsen 1967:385). This method was common for that time, as various European religious sects performed such acts on each other.

"The military conquest and political consolidation of Mexico were accompanied and reinforced by a spiritual conquest which was considered the chief justification for the Spanish presence in the New World" (Quirk 1971:29).

CHANGE *(Colonial practices begin)*

Sixteenth-century Mexico, and for that matter the New World, was probably among the fastest moving transitional societies ever, "and initiated the most dramatic and far-reaching cross-fertilization of cultures in the history of the world" (Driver 1969:1). Contact, conflict, and change between the peoples of the Old and New World caused havoc in all sectors of life. Centuries passed before any semblance of stability was established. During that time an empire grew. Owing to the Spanish initiatives the period bore the earmarks of their culture, even though Indians also participated in the events (Wolf 1959:154-155).

Adoption of Christianity

At first Christianity was accepted reluctantly; therefore the Spanish resorted to other means of teaching religion. These techniques proved more successful, although Spanish leaders no doubt considered such innovations a retreat from the original goal. "From the moment it was established that they were not seeking to Hispanicize the Indians and that the task of civilizing them was to be done completely and solely in the native languages, books had to be put into the hands of all the religious" (Ricard 1966:48). Despite such efforts, conversion went slowly.

In part, this was due to the conquistadores who had become *encomenderos* (landowners and tribute collectors), for they held responsibility for Catholic conversion of the natives even though clerics actually administered the program (Whetten 1969:810). The crown sought to mediate here, but government officials, far from Spain, often competed for the same resources. These recently arrived gentry often took much more interest in the Indians' labor than in their souls.

A unique and far-reaching incident became the turning point of this era. In 1531, Juan Diego, a recent Indian convert, had a vision affecting all of Indian Mexico's future. According to legend, his miraculous experience occurred on a former Indian holy site dedicated to the Aztec mother goddess Tonantzin (Madsen 1967:377-378). Juan Diego reported that he had seen the embodiment of the Virgin Mary in a saintly, brown-skinned apparition. At first skeptics dismissed the report as the superstitious preachings of an Indian, but to prove his point, Juan Diego returned to the same place and the vision reappeared. This time he allegedly brought back evidence: roses and the facial imprint of the Virgin on a shawl. Bishop Zumarraga, who at this time played a vital role in the Christianization program, was finally convinced and, recognizing the significance of the event, sanctioned Juan Diego's vision. Thus began the "Virgin de Guadalupe cult" (Ricard 1966:188).

This miraculous affair built on native pride and hastened their acceptance of Christianity. They found it easier to embrace the Catholic faith, if for no other reason than that one of their own kind was accorded a saintly status. In time the effect of the Virgen de Guadalupe incident spread throughout Mexico. "Increasingly popular during the sixteenth century, the Guadalupe cult gathered emotional impetus during the seventeenth" (Wolf 1973:248).

During this time the same bishop, Zumarraga, participated in wiping out other vestiges of Indian religion (Prescott 1931:59). "Zumarraga, in his famous letter of June 12, 1531, wrote that he had destroyed more than five hundred temples and twenty thousand idols" (Ricard 1966:37) (Padden 1967:244).

Altogether, clerics burned over 400,000 manuscripts. The Spaniards considered written words too powerful in supporting the religiophilosophic beliefs of the Aztecs. They reasoned that destroying books would somehow rub out the spiritual ideology in Indian minds and hearts. (Again, book burning also took place among Europeans who were vying for their particular brand of Christianity, mostly Catholics against Protestants.) Most unfortunately, almost all the knowledge the Indians had accumulated was lost. Moreover, human lives were destroyed—several million died in the decade after the conquest (Loya 1958:58, 126).

Many clerics taught the liturgy and cathechism in the native languages in order to contribute to a better understanding of the doctrine. "The friars of Mexico, from the moment of their arrival, recognized that the knowledge of Indian languages was the essential prerequisite of serious evangelization" (Ricard 1966:46). Patterning themselves after Jesus Christ, many also gave an excellent example in their daily lives. This further influenced native adoption of Christianity. Some outstanding, humane priests felt that the Indians should learn all that European education could offer. Because this goal did not coincide with Spanish interests, it was unfortunately eliminated (Padden 1967:274; Ricard 1966:52). Other reasons, to be discussed in Stage II, will clarify the reversal of Spanish policy.

Religious syncretism

An apparently unexpected outcome of the conversion program was the merging of Indian and Spanish religious features—words, symbols, and so on. For instance, certain Indian ceremonial dates were retained with Christian symbols being commemorated. In some respects this adapation eased native adjustment, gaining their cooperation by showing respect for their culture. Naturally, it also aided the dissemination of Catholicism: "the Indians are not truly Catholic; they have not really accepted the dogma and moral system of Roman Christianity, but have contented themselves with taking over a certain number of foreign ceremonies and practices, and have mixed this entirely formal and superficial Catholicism with their ancient superstitions and traditional rites" (Ricard 1966:276).

This kind of religion was known as "syncretic." Syncretism is a process whereby different cultural elements are combined into an entirely new system. This occurred in Mexico because: "The total possible range of Indian reaction at this time was relatively extensive . . . [since] two complicated societies were intermeshing, opportunities for new combinations continually arose" (Gibson 1964:404). By blending the Indian and Spanish views of the world, the Spaniards clearly enhanced the colonization program. This beginning sparked overall cultural changes: "a new culture was arising from the fusion of both, an interaction made the more effective by blending of the indigenous people with the Spaniards" (Alba 1967:22).

This cultural and biological cross-pollinization is sometimes referred to as *mestizaje* (mixing). Mexican culture is especially known for this, although few can pinpoint with accuracy what portion of the culture was Spanish or Indian. Furthermore, the process was dynamic and unfolded differently for different people. Some were able to avoid total immersion into

Spanish culture by introducing their own traditions. However, others were assimilated almost overnight, becoming Hispanicized Indians.

Initial changes in land, labor, and wealth

The people's relationship to the land remained essentially the same. What did change was land ownership: who controlled the land, why, and how and for whom resources were extracted. The introduction of large-scale mining enterprises required the relocation of many Indians. Calpulli members once tied to the land were forced to change residences and work in the bowels of the earth (Vives 1969:320; Alba 1967:26-27).

"In their new status as a minority (or better, as a series of minorities) in the Spanish colony, the Indians were exploited as a source of cheap labor" (Wagley and Harris 1958:52). Thus, the early decades of the colonial period begin with a series of changes in the labor and landholding system, each change having a new name—*encomienda, repartimiento,* or *hacienda.* The name might change and so might the social relations, but the result was always the same: the natives remained oppressed. In short, "a number of Indians were 'entrusted' or 'distributed' to Spanish settlers to be educated in the Christian life in exchange for their services" (Madariaga 1947:17).

A new socioeconomic system was introduced and gradually transformed Indian society. "If Aztec society is . . . a graduated complex of progressively more inclusive units, from the family and Calpulli at one end to the total empire at the other, it becomes evident that conquest eliminated all the more comprehensive structures while it permitted the local and less comprehensive ones to survive" (Gibson 1964:403). The calpulli kin- and territory-based system was no longer the primary land ownership unit. Colonial authorities ignored kin networks, broke up and separated families, calpullis, and even whole villages, and sent their members to various regions to labor for the ever-expanding colonial empire. However, Spaniards preserved many calpulli land boundary lines, creating encomiendas or haciendas (landed estates) from them. The Spaniards reasoned that the calpulli kin system was in the way; it made for a united Indian group. Therefore they broke it up to better exploit workers. The motto of the new overseers was, "Just give us some hands and backs." The important fact is that Indians no longer controlled or owned their land. The Spaniards had appropriated it, making the natives subjects in their own land (Frank 1979).

Missionary program

To offset these abuses, the missionaries entreated the crown to establish separate Indian and Spanish towns. By this program some Indians were shielded from ambitious colonists who aggressively pursued lucrative careers on landed estates, and Indian land rights and cultural traditions were protected and preserved. This plan was not altogether successful, for later colonists were still able to partition Indian lands. Furthermore, during this period the colonists' struggle over the control of Indian subjects reached tremendous proportions. First the encomenderos gained the upper hand, followed by the clerics, then the crown, and the cycle was repeated in a continual battle. This rivalry over natives consumed the energies of each competing group in New Spain: Should Indian souls be Christianized (church)? Should their labor be exploited (encomenderos)? Should they be made into good Spanish subjects (crown)? The three factions agreed, however, that it was all for the natives' benefit to become Christianized laboring subjects (Villegas et al. 1974:45-46; Parkes 1969:88; Gibson 1966:49).

To achieve this objective, many Indian leaders (former pipiltin and local caciques, or chieftains) who collaborated with the Spanish were absorbed as minor colonial administrators. They "were able, through their traditional powers over the common people, to maintain control over the local communities and to exact tribute for themselves and for their Spanish masters. But, as Spanish power was stabilized throughout the colony, and particularly as Spanish numbers were increased by immigration and by their mixed off-spring, this indigenous aristocracy was gradually deprived of power" (Wagley and Harris 1958:51) (Alba 1967:24). By assisting in the subjugation of their fellow Indians they became *endonado* (Hispanicized, entitled to use the gentlemanly "Don" before their names), but this conciliatory treatment was short-lived.

Beginnings of instability

. Clearly the postconquest period was chaotic, especially when contrasted with the relatively more stable indigenous system that had existed previously. As will be noted, the colonial period introduced a host of phenomena that radically altered society. These include: (1) Spanish, Indian, and African racial intermixture (known as miscegenation, or *mestizo* in Spanish); (2) incipient racist practices, a peculiarly Mesoamerican type affecting both social class and mobility; (3) a program of Spanish racial and cultural superiority, which made the native and darker-hued people feel inferior; and (4) racial and cultural marginality, in which the masses found themselves torn between Old and New World cultural patterns and racial appearance (the Aztecs called this mental state *nepantilism*). These conditions brought economic and sociocultural problems and generally a native pattern of thought and action best termed a "psychology of colonization."

"Their culture, so suddenly destroyed, is one of those that humanity can be proud of having created . . . and our common inheritance is made up of all the values that our species has conceived, it must take its place among our previous treasures—precious because they are so rare" (Soustelle 1961:244).

Thus ended the embryonic and infancy years in Mesoamerica. Although human imperfections pertained to Indians, as to all groups, they had established a great tradition, one in which they took pride. To them it was a time when a closer rapport with nature prevailed, when their decisions, right or wrong, determined their common destiny. Now that came to an end.

The original humans in Mexico no longer had control of society. Their infancy years were interrupted by the arrival of the Spaniards and the subsequent contact, conflict, and change. Now a stern childhood of rigidly enforced conformity to new Spanish-based social rules awaited them. Although even without the Spanish the Indians would still have had to undergo a childhood period, the usurpation of this stage of development by the Spanish made the process and outcome quite different from what would have occurred otherwise.

REFERENCES

Adams, R. E. W.: *Prehistoric Mesoamerica*, Boston, 1977, Little, Brown & Co.

Alba, V.: *The Mexicans: the making of a nation*, New York, 1967, Praeger Publishers.

Bernal, I.: *The Olmec world*, Berkeley, 1969, University of California Press.

Bushnell, G. H. S.: *The first Americans*, New York, 1968, McGraw-Hill Inc.

Coe, M.: *Mexico*, New York, 1962, Praeger Publishers.

Diaz del Castillo, B.: *The discovery and conquest of Mexico: 1517-1521*, New York, 1956, Farrar, Straus & Giroux, Inc.

Driver, H. E.: *Indians of North America*, Chicago, 1969, University of Chicago Press.

Frank, A. G.: *Mexican agriculture, 1521-1630: transformation of the mode of production*, New York, 1979, Cambridge University Press.

Gibson, C.: *Aztecs Under Spanish rule*, Stanford, 1964, Stanford University Press.

Gibson, C.: *Spain in America*, New York, 1966, Harper & Row, Publishers.

Helms, M. W.: *Middle America: a culture history of heartland and frontiers*, Englewood Cliffs, N.J., 1975, Prentice-Hall, Inc.

Leon-Portilla, M.: *Broken spears: the Aztec account of the conquest of Mexico*, Boston, 1962, Beacon Press.

Leon-Portilla, M.: *Aztec thought and culture*, Norman, 1963, University of Oklahoma Press.

Leon-Portilla, M.: *Pre-Columbian literatures of Mexico*, Norman, 1969, University of Oklahoma Press.

Loya, D. G.: *Mosaic of Mexican history*, Mexico, D. F.: Editorial CVLTVRA, T.G. S.A., 1958.

Macgowan, K., and Hester, J. A., Jr.: *Early man in the New World*, New York, 1962, Doubleday & Co., Inc.

Madariaga, S.: *The rise of the Spanish American empire*, New York, 1947, Macmillan Inc.

Madsen, W.: Religious syncretism. In Wauchope, R., editor: *Handbook of Middle American Indians*, vol. 6, Austin, 1967, University of Texas Press.

Morgan, L. H.: *Ancient society*, New York, 1963, Meridian Books.

Nicholson, H. B.: The efflorescence of Mesoamerican civilization: a resume. In Bell, B., editor: *Indian Mexico: past and present*, Los Angeles, 1967, University of California, Latin American Center.

Nowell, C. E.: *The great discoveries and the first colonial empires*, New York, 1954, Cornell University Press.

Padden, R. C.: *The hummingbird and the hawk: conquest and sovereignty in the Valley of Mexico; 1503-1541*, Columbus, 1967, Ohio State University Press.

Parkes, H. B.: *A history of Mexico*, Boston, 1969, Houghton Mifflin Co.

Parry, J. H.: *The Spanish seaborne empire*, New York, 1971, Alfred A. Knopf, Inc.

Peterson, F. A.: *Ancient Mexico*, New York, 1962, G. P. Putnam's Sons.

Prescott, W. H.: *History of the conquest of Mexico*, New York, 1931, Random House, Inc. (originally published in 1842).

Quirk, R. E.: *Mexico*, Englewood Cliffs, N.J., 1971, Prentice-Hall, Inc.

Ricard, R.: *The spiritual conquest of Mexico*, Berkeley, 1966, University of California Press.

Sahagun, B.: *A history of ancient Mexico*, Glorieta, N.M. 1932, The Rio Grande Press, Inc.

Sanders, W. T., and Price, B. J.: *Mesoamerica: the evolution of a civilization*, New York, 1968, Random House, Inc.

Scholes, F. V.: Spanish policy and the Yucatan. In Locke, A., and Stern, B. J., editors: *When peoples meet: a study in race and culture contacts*, New York, 1946, Hinds, Hayden and Eldredge.

Simpson, L. B.: *Many Mexicos*, Berkeley, 1967, University of California Press.

Soustelle, J.: *Daily life of the Aztecs*, Stanford, Calif., 1961, Stanford University Press.

Soustelle, J.: *The four suns*, New York, 1967, Grassman Publishers.

Spicer, E.: *Cycles of conquest*, Tucson, 1962, The University of Arizona Press.

Valiant, G. C.: *The Aztecs of Mexico*, New York, 1956, The Viking Press.

Villegas, D. C., et al.: *A compact history of Mexico*, Los Angeles, 1974, University of California, Latin American Center.

Vives, J. V.: *An economic history of Spain*, Princeton, N.J., 1969, Princeton University Press.

Wagley, C., and Harris, M.: *Minorities in the New World: six case studies*, New York, 1958, Columbia University Press.

Walker, E. F.: *World crops derived from Indians*, Highland Park, Calif., 1967, The Southwest Museum.

Waters, F.: *Mexico mystique: the coming sixth world of consciousness*, Chicago, 1975, The Swallow Press, Inc.

Whetten, N. L.: *Rural Mexico*, Chicago, 1969, University of Chicago Press.

Willey, G. R., et al.: The patterns of farming: life and civilization. In West, R. C., editor: *Natural environment and early cultures. Handbook of Middle American Indians*, vol. 1, Austin, 1964, University of Texas Press.

Wolf, E.: *Sons of the shaking earth*, Chicago, 1959, University of Chicago Press.

Wolf, E.: The Virgin of Guadalupe: a Mexican national symbol. In Duran, L. I., and Bernard, H. R., editors: *Introduction to Chicano studies*, New York, 1973, Macmillan Inc.

Zorita, A.: *Life and labor in ancient Mexico*, New Brunswick, N.J., 1963, Rutgers University Press.

STAGE II

SPANISH COLONIAL ERA
1521 to 1821

Childhood is not always an enjoyable or fulfilling experience. The Indians of Mexico, like many in childhood, were unprepared for what they had to undergo. The Spaniards dictated what roles Indians would fill and doggedly supervised them to ensure compliance. As a result, many who resisted were shaped into a distinctive culture of their own, rather than incorporating a culture that had grown out of the transition from infancy (Aztec) to childhood (Spanish).

Not all the experiences of the colonial period were negative. What was taught during the colonial era was not uniformly learned by everyone, nor were the consequences the same for each individual. Many of the natives benefited from the experience. Nevertheless, colonial instruction was forceful enough to restrict the range of behavior; the majority of Indians were subjected to a harsh pattern. "The colonial relationship . . . chained the colonizer and the colonized into an implacable dependence, molded their respective characters and dictated their conduct" (Stein and Stein 1970:vii). In the end, Indian society broke down because of an experience that was largely damaging and unrewarding. It was not a time when supportive parental backing helps the child to proceed from one step to another, gaining in confidence with the assurance of mastering future tasks. Instead, it was a childhood largely controlled by cruel, selfish step-parents who concerned themselves only with duties and accomplishments and not with personal development.

Since the Spaniards were masters of the environment, they largely determined the extent of autonomy and coercion—who would do what, when, where, and why. This arrangement decisively affected the character and health of each person in the social system. The Spanish in large measure controlled learning experiences and therefore all lives.

Of course, there were many instances in which the native peoples sought to liberate themselves from the Spanish and seek a more rewarding path, if only temporarily. Also, the group of Spanish customs ordering human practices was not entirely absorbed by the Indians. Still, the Indians were taught how to respond to events (beliefs), to know the difference between good and bad events (values), to integrate the details of proper or improper performance (rules), and, finally, to understand that their behavior would be rewarded by positive or negative treatment (sanctions). These instructions were unevenly impressed upon the Indian population, causing many maladaptions, similar to those made by a poorly instructed or rebellious child. With all its vicissitudes, the colonial period is of major importance because (as in one's childhood) the experiences of that period became so ingrained in the people's minds that many traits lingered in later years.

4

Intact and stable social order

CLASS *(Haciendas and debt peons)*

The Spanish totally revamped the socioeconomic system—in their favor. While different in certain major respects, modern problems involving the relationship between developed and underdeveloped societies often parallel those generated by the Spanish colonial system in Mexico. One country develops by exploiting another country, leaving it underdeveloped; thus, development and underdevelopment can often be viewed as two sides of the same coin. Political and social actions support this system. This is the story of Spain's colonization policies—mercantilism and imperialism—and of how Indian society became underdeveloped (Frank 1969:123-142).

Spanish motives

First, let us briefly review the motives behind this socioeconomic class structure. Conditions in Spain, even before contact with the New World, had led to the establishment of a centralized, crown-controlled economy. Ferdinand and Isabella sought to establish a monopoly on gold and silver resources. This led to consolidation by maintenance of a favorable trade balance and control of the colonial economy, in order for the crown to retain strict control of American metal imports. These monopolistic ventures follow the principles of mercantilism (Haring 1963:293-294).

At the outset of the occupation of the New World, the Spanish seized and sent to Spain the most readily available sources of wealth. Indian jewelry, often consisting of fine specimens of art, was smelted into bullion. After the available supply of Indian gold and silver was exhausted, the Spaniards forced the natives to work the mines. "Finding only a few mines previously worked by the Indians, the Spaniards endeavored to discover new ones. A part of every step of the Conquest, and a concomitant of the occupation of territory, was the search for mines" (Diffie 1945:112).

Many mining techniques were used to extract the minerals, but the crucial resource was always indigenous labor. During the period from

1503 to 1660 and including New World areas other than Mexico, more than 185,000 kilograms of gold and 16,886,000 kilograms of silver were shipped to the Old World. The value of the gold alone was in billions of dollars, calculated at twentieth-century prices. Silver would bring the total worth close to five billion dollars in mineral resources (Diffie 1945:107-109; Vives 1969:322-324). This economic activity was an important feature of mercantilism.

One would assume that Spain's future was secure with all these riches. However, the Spaniards were concerned with establishing a nonlaboring, genteel, aristocratic life; they "inherited a tradition of prodigality and extravagance that may be said to have come down to them from the feudal society of medieval times" (Haring 1963:178). To maintain this lifestyle, they generally used their liquid wealth to purchase manufactured products from others. Spain actually aided the rise of manufacturing in other European nation-states while unevenly developing their own industries (Elliott 1963:119-120; Stein and Stein 1970:26). Nevertheless, since Spain still had an abundance of colonial land and labor to exploit, their decline was gradual.

Encomienda

As one observer has noted, "The real treasure was the Indian. So Cortes distributed Indians" (Sierra 1969:97). Furthermore, the European concepts of private property and large feudal landholding units were important factors shaping colonial social organization. When depleted mineral resources slowed mining activity, a return to the land was indicated. Since mere land ownership does not produce a commodity, there had to be a means whereby Indians could work the land to benefit those who controlled it. Thus, land and laboring natives were immediately brought under Spanish control: "Until the middle of the sixteenth century the labor system in New Spain rested upon slaves, who were employed mainly in the mines and at other hard tasks, and upon the personal service rendered on the encomiendas by way of tribute" (Zavala 1943:93). The encomienda established a relationship in which the conquistador was given tribute by the Indian. At this time a conquistador who served the crown traditionally earned a parcel of land as reward. This trusteeship of land, together with the granting of Indian subjects to military leaders (known as encomenderos), was the basis of the encomienda system. Since the encomenderos only replaced Indian overlords, accepting tribute from native labor, at first the transition was relatively easy (Diffie 1945:66; Simpson 1966:59-63). However, the encomenderos and other Spaniards, who settled late but were eager to exploit, intensified the oppression, and difficulties later surfaced. The encomenderos abused Indians by forcing them to work harder and longer. In addition, many were uprooted and sent to northern mining and lowland plantation regions.

Many humanitarian clerics influenced the crown in limiting the worst excesses of encomienda: "the duty of the church . . . was to save the race in order to save souls" (Sierra 1969:98). Royal authorities were also motivated by self-interest. So that they would share in the profitable exploitation themselves, their representatives undermined growing encomendero power, which was increasingly dominating Indian land and labor, and thus wealth. Many encomenderos were challenged for this reason. For example, Cortes, the Marquis de Oaxaca, was the biggest landowner in Mexico, controlling an Indian population of over 20,000. "His tremendous riches—it is likely that he was at one time the wealthiest person in the entire Spanish world—depended chiefly on encomienda, which furnished him a large annual tribute income and labor for his various enterprises" (Gibson 1966:55). He was recalled to Spain to answer charges of treason, for the crown feared his growing power (Chevalier 1966:128).

Repartimiento

To prevent decimation of the native population, which had occurred in the Caribbean, the crown initiated a twofold policy: save the natives from total exploitation, and restructure the colony to provide a broader Spanish ruling elite in place of a few enterprising individuals. This new program was called *repartimiento* (distribution or allotment of workers). It was intended to provide wages for Indian labor—but it did not (Gibson 1966:143).

Under this policy laborers were to work for wages a limited number of days per year and thus have time for their own needs. Not surprisingly, the results were otherwise. Self-interest motives guided the adoption of repartimiento, for exploitation of Mexico's resources would stop if native labor disappeared. Consequently, the crown's acceptance of pagan Indians as worthy of Christian salvation (as urged by the missionaries) was something of a subterfuge for preserving labor services. However, it was unsuccessful in this: The indigenous population fell from twenty-five million in 1519 to a little over a million by 1650 (Borah and Cook 1960:88; Stein and Stein 1970:37; Gibson 1966:63).

From the beginning, repartimiento was almost totally ignored by the colonists. The conquistadores were joined by lawyers, merchants, doctors, government officials, and some enterprising missionaries in a continuing program of native exploitation (Chevalier 1966:23-35). As a general practice, colonists either casually avoided the repartimiento policy or tactfully manipulated it to their advantage. By controlling large parcels of good fertile land, land required for the necessities of life, the landowners held the

Indians at their mercy. The latter, in turn, accepted any wages the Spaniards deemed fair. Usually the wages were low, for the Spaniards were interested in high profits. The adage of buying cheap and selling high took precedence over human need.

Most natives were unable to work only the exact number of days required by repartimiento. These specified days were a safeguard to allow them time to work their own land, but generally they had little land and were rapidly losing even that. Instead laborers sought more work on Spanish-held land for subsistence. Because of this need and the landowner's demand for low-paid laborers, the owner-worker relationship became asymmetrical. The landowners enthusiastically participated, for their empire would quickly crumble if labor demands went unmet. "They solidified their hold on the workers by depriving them of freedom to leave the farm at will. The legal means of accomplishing this purpose was found in advances of money and goods, which bound the workers to the land by placing him in debt. This method, . . . constitutes the true precursor of the Mexican hacienda" (Zavala 1943:99).

Hacienda system and debt peonage

Undoubtedly, the mechanism that established a bonded landowner-laborer network leading to the hacienda system was the practice of advancing Indians money or credit for future work (Chevalier 1966:285; Diffie 1945:467-471). Offering advancements, landowners or their emissaries scoured the countryside for prospective workers, even infringing on mission domains and free Indian communities. Since money was desperately needed for basic necessities, the temptation was too great for Indians to ignore. If the contract was accepted, the worker fulfilled his part by working for a set period. Indians who defaulted were sought by the authorities and punished. In this way they were bonded to the land as debt peons, and the landowners became their overseers and creditors.

With the available labor pool thus drawn to the land, the hacienda system began. Its evolution and the gradual consolidation of the native work force became the socioeconomic features that marked the colonial epoch. Peonage, and specifically debt peonage, was the trademark of the hacienda system. At first Indians were given money or credit to work a specified time, but later, with meager wages and *hacendado* (landowner) demands for a permanent work force, the relationship changed. For example, workers frequently extended their stay on a job by accepting more credit or money. A vicious circle resulted in which they seldom completed the contract without asking for more credit ahead of time. They found themselves as poor at the end of the contract as at the beginning and signed on again for more credit.

Whenever a family need or crisis required extra money, they might mortgage away a year or two of the future. If the household head died before fulfilling the contract, the sons would inherit the debt. In effect, the sons were weighed down even before starting their own families.

Besides being held to the soil by debt peonage, Indians were affected by other hacienda practices. For instance, they were required to use credit in the *tiendas de raya* (hacienda stores), which additionally benefited the Spaniards. Dwellings provided by landowners were poor in quality, since good homes cost money and might lower the hacendado's profits (Chevalier 1966:289; Whetten 1969:99).

As has been noted, the hacienda itself was an offshoot of the medieval feudal system. Many Dark Age customs flourished in the New World. "The process of estate formation and labor recruitment on hacienda and plantation in the New World between 1500 and 1700 should not be examined solely in microcosm . . . a macrocosmic view . . . is required to put the process in the perspective of the colonial heritage [In other words, the phenomenon should be viewed in relation to regional transformations in other parts of the world.] In central and eastern Europe it became the 'second serfdom.' In America it took various forms: encomienda, repartimiento, mita, and ultimately debt peonage and chattel slavery" (Stein and Stein 1970:43).

In contrast, there were many instances when natives escaped the worst effects of a hacienda-type system. This was especially true in mission or communal towns in southern Mexico (Chance 1978), where natives were either in complete control or assisted the church fathers; in both cases they avoided debt peonage. Despite these exceptions, the native majority, especially the growing mestizo population, came under the hacienda system in the other regions.

Social role of hacendados

The quasi–medieval manor complex of the hacienda became the cornerstone of colonial society, although with significant variations from region to region (Brading 1979). In an almost knightly fashion, the hacendado patron protected and cared for the natives, workers who obediently served the interests of the empire.

"Individualism or personalism is the key to the genius of Spain" (Schurz 1964:92). Each of the strong-willed hacendados—be he a conquistador, late-arrival civilian, lawyer, or merchant—established a miniempire. A patronage system of social relations prevailed, in which the hacendado opted for the parent role and forced the peons to play children (Hewes 1954:214). If they misbehaved, he sternly upbraided them; if they were hard

working and respectful, he solemnly patted their heads in a gesture of assurance. The patron hacendado was a god-figure on the landed estate, regardless of how well or badly Indians conducted themselves (Paz 1961:102).

Much of this paternal quality stemmed from the strong assertive
manner of the conquistadores. From the start they "tended to depress the
spirit of the new race. The conquerors were not workmen, but soldiers, who
had to utilize the vanquished race in order to take advantage of their new
possessions. . . . Wealth was not acquired by work but by the unjust privilege
which permitted exploitation of the poor" (Ramos 1962:33).

Colonists who followed adhered to this type of manly behavior.
Spanish tradition supported this strong, lordly male image that was readapted to New World conditions. *Caudillismo* (charismatic leadership) was
the result of this tendency. Beginning on a small scale on haciendas or in
minor military engagements, many caudillos rose to high positions of national leadership. Caudillismo is associated with the drive to acquire an economic empire and, later, political leverage. The Indian population served as
the backdrop for this scenario.

The Spaniards continued to use Indian labor for farming, now
turning to cash crop commerce. Sugar, coffee, maize, rice, bananas, wheat,
tobacco, chocolate, and other crops were the mainstays of a growing economic empire. Much of the harvest was processed for export to the Old
World (Diffie 1945:95-98; Stein and Stein 1970:43).

Specializing in sugar and pulque in the central region and cattle
hides in the north, the haciendas supported the colony. Moreover, as self-
sufficient estates, the haciendas provided the landowner and peons with all
the necessities of life. On some of these estates, particularly the *mestas* (cattle
or livestock ranches), the hacendados ruled on horseback. "The introduction
of domestic animals into Spain's overseas possessions was an important concomitant of the conquest, occupation, and settlement of the new lands. Stock
raising was essential to Spain's experiment in imperialism and acculturation" (Dusenberry 1963:205).

Hacendados who controlled the largest parcels of land sought
higher rewards, such as prestige and esteem from their fellow citizens. Consequently, social life revolved around the *gentil* (genteel) population, who
maintained city residences along with their landed estates—the city for living and the country estate for supporting that life-style. Many enjoyed leisure and recreation in both urban and rural settings. Colonial society was
based on hacendado-peon relationships, which included an array of thought
and activity denoting superordinate/subordinate and superior/inferior conditions. Today, even though the hacienda system has presumably ended, this
climate of feeling persists in a large part of Latin America (Wagley and Harris 1958:52).

Fig. 4-1. A, Maize field in Michoacan, Mexico. **B,** Boy hauling wood in Guatemalan highlands. **C,** Muleteers loading maize in Guanajuato, Mexico.

Fig. 4-2. Modern Mayas in Santa Clara La Laguna, Guatemala. **A,** Family in native dress. **B,** Man weeding maize field. **C,** Girls carrying water. **D,** Men playing native flute and drum.

Life of the debt peons: Mechicanos

As previously noted, the ethnic label "Chicano" was probably derived from the word "Mechicano," a sixteenth-century pronunciation of Mex(ch)icano. After the conquest and subjugation of central Mexican natives, the Spaniards generally referred to them as Mechicanos and later used the term for other similarly vanquished Indians. The word finally became synonymous with the dispossessed lower-class peons. It is interesting and somehow symbolic that the Aztec tribal name, Mexica, became fixed in this way. Because of the social class relationships of the colonial period, an ethnic label for the lower class became instituted to remind people of their station so that they would presumably remain there.

All of the pre-Columbian Indian classes—pipiltin, macequales, and so on—were compressed into one: peons. Limited exceptions were members of the Indian nobility (such as Malinche, or Doña Marina) who cooperated during the early sixteenth century. Although some remained in leadership positions, most eventually found themselves in the lowest class. According to the thinking of that time, the "doctrine of natural slavery was entirely applicable to the Indians on the grounds of their inferiority" (Elliott 1963:71-72). Noble collaborators either were assimilated with the Spanish, racially or culturally or both, or were eased out of their higher status.

One important incentive was held before the peon masses throughout this period: If they wanted to improve their standard of living, they had to adopt the dominant culture. This often meant learning to supervise people of a lower status. Thus, in attaining social mobility for themselves, many Indians became oppressive instruments of the Spanish (Simpson 1966:83, 87).

Rationale of social classes

Spanish colonial authorities defined socioeconomic class rankings simply. Usually, "colour-class became . . . to a certain extent entangled with labour-class" (de Madariaga 1947:240). In addition to race, place of birth and occupation determined social status. Spaniards born in Spain were at the top. Known as *gachupines* ("those who wear spurs"), they occupied the highest positions of religious, political, economic, and social life. Gachupines were primarily responsible for curbing overexploitation of Indians by *criollos* (Spaniards born in the New World) and maintaining control of the colony for Spain.

Below gachupines in the social order were criollos, some of whom carried a slight amount of Indian or African blood, a fact they preferred to conceal (Loya 1958:135). The criollos adopted the attitudes and behavior of gachupines, but most were artisans, mineowners, parish priests, merchants, and landowners. "Their businesses were always the poorest, they could never prosper, and their lives were full of resentment against the Spaniards" (Loya 1958:136). By the end of the eighteenth century close to one million criollos held these secondary positions. It was not until foreign encroachments, primarily by the expansionist British, threatened the colonial empire that new opportunities opened for them in the military. Before this military calling (which also offered social advancement for many mestizos and Hispanicized Indians) criollos were barred from the highest church and state offices.

An interesting group of this period, almost as unfortunate as the Indians, were the *mestizos*, individuals defined as racially mixed (Loya 1958:136). Many racial and social class subdivisions, based on various combinations of Spanish, Indian, and African descent, existed within this category. Their rise was woefully slow; in this period they were mineworkers, *vaqueros* (cowboys), craftsmen, soldiers, hacienda peons, and small-store owners. A few could be found in the lower clerical ranks.

At the bottom of the socioeconomic ladder of colonial Mexico, and also today, were Indians and Africans. According to colonial law, Indians were given a high legal status, but social practice placed them below almost everybody else (Morner 1967:60). In some respects their treatment was similar to that of Africans, who were without legal rights and remained peons/slaves throughout this time. To escape the grasp of land-hungry Spaniards, and aided by protective clerics, a sizable minority of Indians established communal villages (Zavala 1943:104-106). However, the majority worked on

Fig. 4-3. Regal life of gachupines. (Drawing by Jeffrey Huereque.)

estates or in enterprises owned by others. High positions in any realm of society were outside their command.

An additional explanation may clarify this social class system. The population of urban areas (mostly gachupines, criollos, and some mestizo workers) were the beneficiaries of the socioeconomic network. The Indians, mestizos, and Africans making up the population of the satellite rural enterprises (agrarian or livestock haciendas, mines, small Indian communal farms, or towns specializing in particular crafts) increasingly fell behind economically because they functioned primarily to provide urban areas with the products of their labor. This arrangement deprived them of a fair share of production and forced them to live a hand-to-mouth existence. Esteem, prestige, and power were retained by the Spaniards. This invidious social structure, which developed one group by underdeveloping another, lasted for 300 years. Even to this day, "the 'problem' of the Indian and his community, from his point of view, is one of constant struggle for bare survival in a system in which he, like the vast majority of other people, is the victim of uneven capitalist development. . . . It is a losing battle the Indian has fought for over four centuries" (Frank 1969:141).

Wolf's words are reminders of colonization and imperialism: "The conquering Spaniard became a mining entrepreneur, a producer of commercial crops, a rancher, a merchant . . . he wanted to organize and press the human resources under his command, to enlarge his estate, to take his place among the other men grown rich and powerful in the new utopia" (Wolf 1959:176).

CULTURE *(Hispanicization and mestizaje)*

Cultural life during this period was complex. Many natives quickly absorbed the dominant culture; however, even to this day others remain Indian. Escape from Spanish jurisdiction usually meant moving to the hinterland or hidden mountain valleys. A few refused to leave and somehow retained strong elements of Indian culture. Spanish instruction was occasionally ambiguous and incomplete, probably because of the different cultural goals each Spanish group had for the indigenous population; various interests were working at cross-purposes. This variance also stems from the diverse roots of Spanish culture, expecially the Iberian regional differences (Hewes 1954:215).

Shift in cultural orientation

Although a complete description of cultural life in the colonial period is not possible here, certain phenomena should be mentioned. The prevailing cultural confusion caused Indians, and later mestizos, to shift cul-

tural orientations often, sometimes daily. This lack of a stable cultural adaptation ensured their permanent placement in the lower classes. In addition, many cultural maladaptions—drinking, fighting, envy, and so forth—
eventually became norms for thought and action, further guaranteeing low-
class status. A discussion of Spanish colonial culture necessarily involves the
process by which the dominant group made the learning of their culture the
gateway to success, and conversely, the way in which the subordinate majority was moved to cultural disorientation, instability, and confusion.

Ironically, early in the colonial period, Indians and mestizos became the carriers of either Spanish culture or a hybrid version. For example,
Spanish conquistadores moved north after the pacification of most Mesoamerican people. Many Hispanicized Indian and mestizo settlers accompanied them to the legendary Aztlan, home of the Chichimeca tribes (this
area, known as the Spanish borderlands by writers focusing on the colonial
period, is now the United States Southwest). There, as early as 1539, the
Spaniards searched for gold and silver. Continuing the pattern set in Mexico,
they later initiated other enterprises. In 1598 the "silver king" Juan D'Onate
moved north from the mines of Zacatecas and founded the first permanent
colony in New Mexico. Thus Indians and mestizos came to play a cultural
role in the further expansion of the colonial empire. Many of them oppressed
and exploited the Indians in the new territories. Others became settlers. The
pueblo of Los Angeles, known then as the Indian community of Yang-na, was
settled in 1776 by two Spaniards, one mestizo, two Africans, eight mulattoes,
and nine Indians from Mexico (McWilliams 1969:36).

During the territorial expansion, both Spanish and native culture
changed. Many new patterns emerged, but three basic types stand out: (1) a
culture taken directly from Spain, with some New World alterations; (2) a
culture primarily native to the New World; and (3) a wide, variable cultural
spectrum derived from the merging of Old and New World traits.

Introduction of Catholicism

Religion provides an example of cultural merging. "Under the
cloak of Christian rites they (Indians) retained their old religious concepts—
the cult of nature and its forces—and even worshipped their ancient gods in
secret. The Church had to be content with conformity with externals" (Haring 1963:187-188). "The degree of culture they absorbed depended on the
character and docility of the tribes reduced" (Haring 1963:184-185).

Religion and Spanish language instruction influenced the shaping
of a new Indian view of life. Clerics admonished neophytes who failed to
serve their hacendados faithfully. While teaching the Indians religion, the
missionaries taught respect for authority (Simpson 1966:170; Haring 1963:182-
183). Natives were continually reminded that, no matter how bad the con-

ditions or difficult the times, they would surely go to heaven if they remained obedient and dutiful; however, hell was the certain destination if they disobeyed and rebelled. Furthermore, they were told that the Christian God favored especially those who suffered and remained strong in the faith. According to the teaching, earthly experience was merely a testing ground to determine where one would go after death. "Backed by the influence, prestige, and force of the conquistadores, the missionaries gathered the children into doctrinal schools where they learned the rudiments of Catholic practice" (Diffie 1945:248).

Because the Indians were deeply religious anyway, they followed many Christian teachings perfectly (Diffie 1945:250). Of all realms of colonial life, religious worship was the most open to Indians and so they devoted their available leisure time to church-related activities. In addition, many Indians built and maintained missions and churches and established permanent residence there. They were very devout subjects indeed.

Fig. 4-4. Interior of church near Zocalo, Mexico City.

Only one God was placed before them, but the many Christian saints, and especially the Virgin de Guadalupe, found ready acceptance by a people accustomed to a pantheon. Baptism, rituals, ceremonies, prayers, fasting, confessions, heaven, hell, and purgatory were not new concepts to the Indians and were thus easily adopted (Madsen 1967:370). Oddly, the symbolic sacrifice of the Catholic mass, with bread and wine representing the body and blood of Jesus Christ, was also reminiscent of Indian rituals. According to some writers, the sacrifice in the Catholic mass is a legacy of pre-Christian ceremonies when a lamb was slain and offered to the gods. Such similarities simplified the enforced transition to a new spiritual reality. When possible, missionaries incorporated Indian practices to teach Catholic dogma (Gibson 1966:72). For example, in pre-Columbian times towns honored a patron deity with a processional. The clerics staged the affair on the already established day but replaced Indian idols with Christian saints; thus, a mixed Indian-Spanish ceremony evolved (Ricard 1966: 277). This syncretism, the combination of two distinct cultural styles into a wide-ranging new one, also occurred in other areas of life.

Mestizaje: cultural blending

"And here a new culture is coming into being, a mixed culture derived not only from the Spain of colonial times, but also from the aboriginal cultures of America. . . . Not only do the mode of life and point of view appear to be emerging as a fusion of diverse elements from other cultures, but, in the process of synthesis, local adaptations and innovations have been added, so that the total configuration of the culture seems to be developing aspects of uniqueness" (Gillin 1957:158-160).

Neither totally Indian nor Spanish, Mexican culture is the result of this merging. "It is the period in which the clash of civilizations (which ethnographers love to talk about) occurred in the sharpest form, a period in which native American elements and imported Spanish traits are sometimes fused and sometimes juxtaposed, together giving Mexico its present personality" (Ricard 1966:3). "It is precisely this success [of cultural blending] which sets Mexico apart . . . in Latin America" (Madsen 1967:370) (Vasconcelos and Gamio 1926:118).

Even the Spanish language underwent a syncretic change. Indian words aided the transmission of European concepts. Some words were integrated into the Spanish language because they represented a feature of Indian reality that was totally alien to the Spaniards. Language borrowing, creating, and synthesizing developed a linguistic spectrum of native and Spanish patterns. "Some 5,000 Nahuatl words—like metate (from Nahuatl metlatl, 'quern'), chiquihuite (from Nahuatl chiquihuitl, 'basket'), tepescuin-

gle (from Nahuatl escuintli, 'little dog', in Mexican Spanish, 'little boy')—
came into everyday use among speakers of Mexican Spanish" (Wolf 1959:46).
Moreover, many Indians who learned Spanish fashioned a new sound and
style. This resulted in the many regional patterns and intonations found today. Some Indians became well versed in Spanish and shed their Indian idi-
oms. Others even today speak mostly the Indian dialect: "certain native
groups, protected by their isolation, have not yet given it up" (Ricard
1966:276) (Hewes 1954:216). Unfortunately, this linguistic diversity has led
to critical adjustment problems for many people.

A syncretic style also pertained to art and architecture, although
perhaps these were more dominated by Spanish traits. "Hispanic American
arts and crafts, while owing much to Indian developments, reveal profound
and far-reaching European influences" (Foster 1960:4). The European culture of that time, including Moorish elements (which go back to the early
Middle East), was reflected in official buildings, churches, and domestic
dwellings. Indians made their biggest contribution in their labor and construction materials. "The adobe walls of houses may reflect both Spanish
and native techniques, but the common red tile roof is but one of a number
of Moorish elements that found their way to the New World" (Foster 1960:4).
Furthermore, "contact with the New World began to put a distinctive stamp
on traditional forms of Spanish poetry: ballads, Christmas carols, and med-
leys in honor of some saint [and] poetry helped to spread the Catholic faith
by supplying symbols comprehensible to the people, and also contributed to
the new linguistic sensitivity of the Spanish language . . . religious festivals
were the clearest and most colorful symbol of the interrelation of the Spaniard and the native" (Picon-Salas 1965:54, 63). This mixing process also occurred in other creative activities: philosophy, jewelry, pottery, and music.

Several social customs and cultural perspectives evolved through
syncretism. Equally important, though, is that many of these traits were
adaptive reactions, fashioned for survival reasons. For instance, the Indian
emphasis on kinship, family and neighbor relationships, persisted for several
reasons. For one, kin ties became a valuable social resource in time of need.
Furthermore, Catholic tradition maintained that a baptized person must
have godparents, who would assume child-rearing duties if anything happened to the parents. Indians used *compadrazgo* (co-parenthood) to establish
social ties with nonfamily members, replacing in part the traditional calpulli networks that the Spaniards were breaking up. Consequently, the Indians quickly readapted to social conditions.

Close ties between brothers and sisters continued long after they
married and established separate households. They actively participated as
uncles and aunts in raising each other's children. Grandparents represented

the top level of the authority hierarchy in extended families. Children were taught to respect and honor their elders at all times. Whenever an adult was absent, supervision fell on the shoulders of the eldest child. (With adulthood, however, the male members, even those who were younger than female siblings, usually assumed a higher status.)

Cultural resistance and marginality

As pressure for Indian assimilation to Spanish ways intensified, forcing Indians into a mold, many rejected Spanish culture entirely at the same time their own was being destroyed. As a result, they were without solid roots in any culture. In contrast to those who had undergone a cultural syncretism—that is, adopted Mexican or mestizo culture—there were many who remained culturally indecisive. This led to widespread anomie—cultural normlessness, or the equivalent of the Aztec nepantilism. Such a person lives in a cultural limbo, searching for firm moorings, and is generally perceived as culturally marginal.

The marginal person is caught between two cultural worlds. "This fusing, however, is not a smooth blending. Even in the individual it is a violent and unconscious conflict between opposite polarities which wrings from the heart that ironic laugh known as vacilada, derived from the verb to vacillate" (Waters 1975:vii). Racial intermixture contributed to this difficulty (Ramos 1962:31), because "the mixed breeds were torn between the parent cultures" (Schurz 1964:90). Significantly, "what the colonial society feared was not the creation of mixed offspring but the growth of a large mass of unattached, disinherited, rootless people in its centers and along its margins" (Wolf 1959:237).

For people in this quandary, certain problems arise when selecting one cultural world or another. One kind of problem comes when members of the dominant culture reject members of the subordinate culture who seek to join them. Another occurs when subordinate members remain in their original cultural milieu but are totally dissatisfied with its offerings. Thus the group to which they aspire rejects them, and they despise the group to which they belong. Furthermore, "they were generally marginal, socially, culturally, or politically, in their relations with other groups, notably the dominants in the seats of power and also with other people in the same society who represented different racial or cultural strains" (Gist and Dworkin 1972:7).

After experiencing unrewarding cultural shifts, many marginal individuals have become revolutionaries or social activists who struggle to change the cause of their marginal condition. Many Indians reacted to Spanish contact, conflict, and change in this fashion.

Problems of adaptation

The colonial period reflected a number of sociocultural problems. One that seriously affected demographic conditions stemmed from the diseases brought to Mexico by Europeans. Smallpox, typhus, measles, typhoid fever, and diphtheria epidemics wiped out whole towns. Because they were "isolated from the rest of the world . . . Amerindians had developed no resistance at all against these diseases" (Morner 1967:32). As noted previously, the native population suffered radical losses (Gibson 1966:63). And this was only the immediately observable part of the destruction—the aftermath had similarly dire effects.

For example, certain calpullis lost eighty percent of their people through disease, but those who remained still were held to the same tribute quota. "Of more importance is the fact that the recounts and reassessments consistently lagged behind the rapid shrinkage in the number of tribute payers, with the result that the survivors had to bear the tribute burdens of those who had died or fled" (Zorita 1963:12). How were these tribute quotas met? Simply by having survivors work harder and longer, with little time for anything else, to fulfill the tribute goal (Gibson 1964:138-144).

The colonial social structure was established to benefit the Spanish materially. It is important to stress, though, how the inclusion of new cultural habits complemented new social relations. Programs for Indian cultural awareness were designed to help them take their place in the new social order: ideas about life fitted in with one's position in the social structure.

Thus, "although Indians continued to speak their native languages and retained much of their aboriginal belief and custom, by the end of the colonial period they were Catholics, had a Spanish community organization, and had acquired many Spanish customs and beliefs" (Wagley and Harris 1958:57). Indian acceptance of Spanish authority also meant alteration of their attitudes and behavior toward leaders. To help natives in acting the "right way," their value system was revised to include highly formal rules of etiquette—all, of course, denoting a superordinate/subordinate relationship. Since Indians were already instilled with a respectful demeanor, they learned the new terms and actions quickly. The preexisting Indian humility was part of their philosophical view, which stressed the immensity of the world and deemphasized egoism or self-importance. Humans were only a small part of the vast universe; they must coexist with other elements in it.

While Indians fulfilled their part of the bargain, remaining honorable and dutiful, the Spanish skirted theirs. In the words of an early colonial Indian: "You have deprived us of our good order and way of government. . . . Now all is confusion and without order and harmony. The Indians have given themselves to fighting because you have brought it upon them . . . those who are not in contact with you do not fight; they live in peace" (Leon-Portilla 1963:151). The native people are still patiently waiting for the successors of the Spanish to lead in a way beneficial to all.

Political structure

The Spaniards controlled the political institutions, which were linked to economic practices. Political power was concentrated in the hands of the Spanish king. Beginning with the introduction of the encomienda system, twenty percent of all production extracted by a colonist was paid to the king. Thus, the king was at the top of the political hierarchy. Stationed in Spain, and directly under the king in authority, was the Council of Indies. They approved subordinate leaders and groups, made general policy decisions, and curbed the power and influence of ambitious colonists (Gibson 1966:90-111, Elliott 1963:161-178).

The various *audiencias* (advisory and judicial bodies) in the New World were next in importance. Each of these was composed of *oidores* (justices), whose number varied depending on audiencia land size. Each audien-

Fig. 4-5. A, Aqueduct. **B,** Building from colonial period, Queretaro, Mexico.

cia controlled its separate domain, serving as the supreme court, council, and executive and legislative bodies. Depending on the time period and individual personalities, the audiencias were often more powerful than the Council of Indies. Since an ocean separated the council from the colony, it was easy for the audiencia to control affairs. The viceroy was the only barrier to audiencia dominance; he was appointed by the king to protect royal interests in the New World. Since the audiencia legally had the final word in checking the viceroy's actions, but the viceroy had the imprimatur of the king, political power often was determined by the personal strength or weakness of the viceroy.

Corregidores (governors) and *alcaldes mayores* (mayors) were in charge of smaller administrative units. By collecting tribute, they also could assign Indians to public works (Diffie 1945:297-302).

Local town government followed a Spanish pattern that was a legacy of Roman times. New World natives filled positions in this framework, however. The town leader, usually a criollo, was the municipal secretary. His authority was paramount. Indians served under the secretary as a council of elders (*principales*), or one was selected by the elders as the alcalde mayor. Others filled lower positions as *aguaciles* (constables). The Indians provided administrative and judicial services under the secretary's continual supervision. The secretary dictated policy and could veto native political decisions (Cancian 1967:283-297; Foster 1960:163-164).

The Spaniards used Indian cultural tradition to govern town members. This pattern was based on the Indian practice in which leaders carried out duties in both the political and religious sectors (Carrasco 1965:73). For example, if a man became an aguacile, later rising to the higher rank of principale, he would have a dual role; he would perform civic duties and also lead group participation in religious ceremonies. Different roles made up the civil-religious hierarchy, almost like a stepladder. This tradition was continued because colonial administrators realized that it would serve their purposes. Real political power remained in Spanish hands, and natives were given more the form of authority than the substance. This format strengthened the double-pronged strategy the Spanish favored: The crown (civil) and the church (religious) would guide natives, the latter actively.

Education: a double standard

The education and training required for important colonial occupations relegated Indians and mestizos to menial, manual labor. "It should be added that they considered their Indians to be a little like children, to be kept in tutelage and led by the hand. Knowledge of Castilian [language] would have been the first step toward dangerous freedom" (Ricard 1966:52).

At first, concerned missionaries provided a sound education, especially in mission schools. Frequently some bright Indian students were given special attention. For these Indians, education meant becoming priests to instruct others in the new faith and doctrine (Haring 1963:201). However, this approach soon ran counter to the overall Spanish policy, which demanded an unlimited number of illiterate manual workers. Once educated, the Hispanicized Indians, especially teachers or priests, did not support Spanish subjugation policies but instead led fellow natives against domination (Padden 1967:274).

In the late sixteenth century the Indian education experiment was abandoned. It appears that the clerics, in this case anyway, had undermined the colonists' designs, precipitating a clash between the church and civil authority. Consequently, in around 1570 Jesuit priests and secular clergy more responsive to the crown were brought in to reverse the practice of favoring Indians. The new clerics developed programs that catered to Spaniards born in the New World.

"The emphasis on religious orthodoxy led to the belief that learning was dangerous for the masses and should be confined to a select few" (Diffie 1945:492). Thus, the educational about-face had two purposes: to deemphasize native intellectual development, focusing instead on craft training, and to improve and expand criollo instruction in order to enhance their leadership skills. Basic understanding of the Spanish language and reading and writing were kept from most Indians. "In the . . . villages only the chiefs or principales understood Castilian or could read and write, and the same may be said of many Indian communities in the Spanish American republics of today" (Haring 1963:209). Except for a few humanist missionaries, the Spaniards made no effort to teach and preserve the many Indian languages. Consequently, Indian education was eliminated, and Spanish policy kept them from European education. However, this action had some benefits. Isolated communal Indian villages and dozens of Indian mission towns were left alone and thus were able to preserve aspects of native culture—in many cases even to the present day.

As noted before, missionaries often tried to help Indians, even though their goal was native integration into a Christian society. Many socioeconomic benefits resulted from clerical intervention, such as preservation of village land holdings. Ostensibly the clerics intended to shield Indians from exploitative and oppressive encomenderos. However, as mentioned previously, these benefits were nullified before the end of the sixteenth century.

Instead of higher education—poetry, rhetoric, history, science, mathematics, and the many calendars—Indians were instructed in elemen-

Fig. 4-6. Colonial society was supported by native labor. (Drawing by Jeffrey Huereque.)

tary, vocational subjects. Already mentioned were the many occupational roles Indians filled and the blending of styles into what was increasingly becoming a Mexican culture (Foster 1960:101-102). In addition, missionaries taught the Indians masonry, carpentry, blacksmithing, horticulture, pastoralism, and the domestic chores necessary to operate colonial society fully (Haring 1963:210). Thus, Indian cultural life was limited because their occupations were basic.

Native reactions and resultant problems

The Indians and mestizos reacted in a variety of ways to the patterns by which Spaniards selfishly shaped conditions to their own benefit (Gibson 1964:404-405). One generalized type of reaction that arose intermittently was nativist resistance, which stressed self-determination and the survival of Indian culture. "Probably the easiest generalization to make which would apply to all the Indians of the region is that all offered resistance and at some time fought to maintain their independence of white domination"

(Spicer 1962:16). Some refused to risk failure, inasmuch as the Spaniards maintained military superiority, and instead retreated into wild, unsettled regions (Edmonson 1960).

On numerous occasions sporadic, unorganized resistance escalated into large-scale rebellions. One example was the Pueblo Revolt of 1680, which occurred in the northern outposts of the Spanish empire (now the United States Southwest) (Bolton 1921:179). In this case thirteen years passed before the Spaniards returned, and then only after the Indian coalition had dissolved. Likewise, tribes such as the Apaches and Comanches, and many others, successfully resisted for the duration of the Spanish presence.

Nativist resistance became a cultural characteristic of many Indians and later mestizos; one might say that they had a permanent chip on their shoulders. Although resistance was seen by the Spaniards as deviant because it undermined their social order, it could also be interpreted as a highly adaptive human mechanism to correct injustices and deprivations. In other words, deviant behavior may become a norm when it fulfills some socially useful function (Ricard 1966:264-282).

The Spaniards, of course, attempted to suppress native resistance: "the colonists developed new techniques anticipating . . . similar methods to be employed two and a half centuries later on the expanding United States frontier [such as the] covered wagon . . . ; soldiery . . . organized itself into flying detachments for purposes of patrols and escort. The fort or presidio made its appearance alongside the mission . . . and Spaniards established colonies of armed Indian peasants from the urban area as strategic outposts in the hostile countryside" (Wolf 1959:193).

An emphasis on male physical strength and prowess was closely associated with native reaction. With roots in Spain and the Mediterranean area, Mexican male dominance evolved into an institutionalized behavior. A *macho* (masculine, virile person) equates physical with social power (Hewes 1954:218; Ramos 1962:59-60); he is a fighter and a hard-working protector of home and family. Because of the misfortunes that befell the natives at this time, there was a need for this male attitude and behavior, especially to defend the honor of females, many of whom were victims of Spaniards. On the other hand, the macho syndrome includes some negative traits, such as masculine tyranny in the home and locality. Both aspects were shaped by political and social oppression.

Another legacy linked to machismo was an increase in drinking and fighting. Before Spanish contact, "the use of *pulque* [liquor from the maguey cactus] had ordinarily been confined to the sick and aged . . . for public ceremonies and religious celebrations. Consistent popular drunkenness had been unknown. But following the conquest the native population rapidly took to drink" (Gibson 1964:150). The Spaniards encouraged drinking by expanding maguey plantations and opening more *pulquerias* (bars and stores). While the Spaniards benefited from this enterprise, the Indians used drinking as an escape from the reality of oppression and a safety valve to allow for violent and aggressive behavior.

As a result, along with the drinking habit, intragroup fighting became the norm. The Indian "chip on the shoulder" became a cumbersome burden that dared any man, usually the closest one and preferably one without the power to retaliate, to knock it off on any pretext. Fearlessness in the face of death, a positive Indian trait accepting the inevitable end of life, made matters worse, for now they accelerated a confrontation with death by being overly sensitive to imagined insults and indulging in fighting. Indians released pent-up frustrations on fellow Indians or mestizos who experienced similar conditions of oppression (Wolf 1959:238-239).

Social mobility was adversely affected by jealousy. Many foremen of haciendas and owners of small Indian stores, who had become part of the colonial social order, were considered traitors by their people. This early atmosphere of competition for the few relatively higher-class positions open to Indians (even though low by Spanish standards) gave rise to an attitude of *envidia* (hate and envy) rather than support and elation for those who were successful (Foster 1965:310; Wolf 1959:228). It kept Indians competing against each other for the few available positions, instead of cooperating to create more opportunities. Another consequence, closely related to envidia, is the way in which peons censured those who attempted to become assimilated into the Spanish mainstream.

The days of calmecac (higher education) were gone; no longer were Indians intellectually and spiritually in control under the new social order. Their advanced military training, received in the telpochcalli, gave way to lower positions as supply-carriers and unskilled foot soldiers. Although Indians and mestizos were the backbone of the military, they did not receive the credit for victories or the hero worship. Except for the tribes that allied themselves with the Spaniards, it was a long time before natives were allowed to participate actively in military affairs.

COLOR *(Roots of racism and racial barriers)*

"Contact of Europe with new territories . . . created new social and cultural problems. One of these problems . . . has been the creation of mixed blood populations who are both biologically and culturally marginal.

Wherever Europe had penetrated, these mixed blood populations have developed into race problems. The patterns of the relations have tended to follow the economic pressures inherent in the nature of the contact" (Johnson 1946:220). Indians also experienced these problems, and social relations were structured to keep natives and mestizos socially immobile. For this purpose Spaniards made race, and a host of conditions associated with it, a crucial feature of the social system (Morner 1967:54). Much of the thinking behind these developments revolves around ethnocentrism, the orientation in which each sociocultural group emphasizes the superiority of their world view while downgrading that of another group. Practically all human groups succumb to an ethnocentric attitude, including Indians (Wagley and Harris 1958:259). In this case, however, the Spaniards were responsible for its introduction and execution.

Ethnocentrism and development

The Spaniards used racial criteria to consolidate their ethnocentric program. Racial prejudice and discrimination cemented the economic relationships underway—this was the introduction of an early type of racism (Cox 1970:322). As noted previously, in order for one ethnic group to advance and develop, another group is often kept in a state of underdevelopment. Barriers placed between the groups help the operation and longevity of such a system. Since the age of exploration and discovery, racial prejudice has often been an integral aspect of the formation of a class system based on inequality (Link 1947:18). Individual differences based on innate intelligence could not make this system work, for the Indians had at least an equal percentage of potentially intelligent members as the Spanish. Therefore, a simple device was introduced to act as a barrier to upward mobility: One group was credited with superior qualities to become and remain dominant, while the other was assigned inferior traits to keep them subordinate (Wolf 1959:236; Wagley 1965:531-545).

"Among Spaniards, Indians had a reputation for sullenness, laziness, and meekness, qualities that Spaniards did not admire. With very rare exceptions white society looked down on Indian society" (Gibson 1966:114). Cultural habits and customs are often the criteria for a superior/inferior relationship, and the Spanish cultural imperialism program, as noted previously, made natives feel culturally inadequate (Parkes 1969:85). But what happens when the subordinate group assimilates the dominant culture? This possibility was foiled by introducing racial barriers. Changing one's culture is far easier than changing one's race or face. "By an irony as strange, the more capable the so-called inferior races prove themselves of attaining emancipation, the more emphatic grows the assertion of racial dogma, stiffened by the coloured races' acquisition of a minimum of political rights or by their emergence as competitors" (Leiris 1958:8).

The Indians found themselves in this predicament and suffered accordingly, particularly in view of the changes in the Spanish educational program. In establishing the colonial class system, the Spaniards viewed dark-complexioned natives as biologically and physically inferior (Zavala 1943:106-107). Of course there is no basis for such a perspective, but people's beliefs about race had significant social consequences. Thus, one's physical appearance determined how high he would climb on the social class scale. The paternalistic attitude the conquerors held toward natives was also a contributing factor (Zavala 1943:109).

Mestizaje: racial mixture

The first Spaniards, the conquistadores, came to the New World without European wives or female companions (van den Berghe 1967:46; Morner 1967:22). When Indian nobles presented young women to the conquerors, the Spanish soon recognized another benefit of this event besides satisfaction of their sexual appetites. By accepting this overture they gained legitimate entrance into Indian society. In future years their sons could claim dual leadership status: by right of conquest and through the line of native aristocratic descent (Gibson 1964:160-162).

More often Spanish males consummated sexual unions by force. Many of the first mestizo offspring resulted from incidents of forcible rape (van den Berghe 1967:48-49; Padden 1967:231-232). "Because formal marriages between Indians and non-Indians were rare, it is safe to say that the great majority of first generation mestizos were the bastard offspring of Spanish men and Indian women" (Gibson 1964:144). Rare indeed was a mestizo who could claim an Indian father and Spanish mother, regardless of the nature of the union.

Years later this continued to be true. Bands of mestizo children, fifty or more in number, wandered the countryside seeking sustenance and security but were rejected by both Spaniards and Indians. Mestizos were shunned by their Spanish fathers because of their native features and non-Christian, illegitimate birth. Similarly, because they represented a living physical memory of the rape of Indian women and Indian civilization, they were turned out from indigenous communities (Wolf 1959:233). "Relegated to the byways and back alleys of society, all these varieties of . . . people encountered one another in common destitution along the trail, in mining camps, in hostelries, in city taverns. Recognizing their common fate, they produced common offspring, resulting in an ever increasing number of mixed physical types" (Wolf 1959:235).

Mestizo mentality

"The growing mestizo element in the population suffered even more than the legally protected Indian communities, and was further stigmatized with being the product of casual liaisons of Spanish men and Indian women" (Hewes 1954:217). Not surprisingly, the mestizo learned to see himself as alone in the world. The unjust rejection by the original (parental) participants in the New World accounts for a state of mind in which the mestizo felt abandoned and unaccepted by nearly everyone. This gave rise to the mestizo mentality, an approach to life that was new, unconventional, and sometimes deviant. "His chances of survival lay . . . in an ability to change, to adapt, to improvise. The ever shifting nature of his social condition forced him to move with guile and speed through the hidden passageways of society, not to commit himself to any one position or to any one spot. Always he would be called upon to seem both more or less than what he was, to be both more or less than what he seemed" (Wolf 1959:238). "Undoubtedly, much of the aggressive, boisterous, and untrusting nature of the early mestizo mentality grew from this experience" (Ramos 1962:57-63). In the mestizo philosophical framework fearlessness and apprehension alternated as important forces according to the situation. "Where the Indian saw power as an attribute of office and redistributed it with care lest it attach itself to persons, the mestizo would value power as an attribute of the self, as the personal energy that could subjugate and subject people" (Wolf 1959:239).

An interesting corollary to the mental state of mestizos was the racial variety found among them. Coming from Spanish-Indian or Indian-African racial backgrounds, they were a hybrid race representing a color spectrum from white to black. Mestizos were referred to as *Ladinos*, a term that originally meant Hispanicized Indian. Later, Ladino became synonymous with those (usually mestizos, but often Indians) who had acculturated and risen above the Indian masses (de la Fuente 1967:432-448).

Mestizos played a significant role in the operation of the socioeconomic class system. Although mestizos were legally ranked below Indians, many appeared European and moved up in the social scale simply because of their white appearance. Furthermore, hybrid bloods, a new breed neither totally Spanish nor Indian, also in time found themselves a niche above the peon Indians. Many mestizos resembled natives or Africans and therefore probably remained peons throughout their lives.

Race and social class

Detailed baptismal records listed racial heritage: pure blood, mixed once, mixed twice, and so on. Here is an example of how they were recorded:

1. Spaniard and Indian beget mestizo
2. Mestizo and Spanish woman beget *castizo* (pure blood)
3. Castizo woman and Spaniard beget Spaniard (Some liken this to cleaning one's blood!)
4. Spanish woman and African slave beget mulatto
5. Spaniard and mulatto woman beget *morisco* (Moorish)
6. Morisco woman and Spaniard beget *albino* (brownish color)
7. Spaniard and albino woman beget *torna atras* (restore to original)

and so on (Morner 1967:58). A complicated racial mixture earned the names of *ahi te estas* (there you stay) or *sal si puedes* (get out if you can)! Hybrid racial types were placed on the colonial socioeconomic ladder in this manner (van den Berghe 1967:49).

Effects of racism

Aside from its role in class relations, the mestizo phenomenon also produced sociopsychological difficulties. Thus, "the mestizo offers a richer opportunity for psychological interpretation than the phlegmatic, subordinated Indian" (Gibson 1966:116). Cultural marginality was now joined by racial marginality, a mixture of the Old and New World, and often a strange and exotic combination at that (Helms 1975:172). In addition to valuing assimilation into Spanish culture, subordinate members of colonial society got ahead by honoring the color and appearance of Spaniards. Indians and mestizos became traitors to themselves (Wagley and Harris 1958:260). Paradoxically, female mestizos were considered excellent mistresses. As the colonial elite used to say, white women for marriage and home, black women for work, and brown women for amorous adventures.

In addition to these psychological burdens, feelings of racial inferiority further oppressed the majority. Many became ashamed of their racial countenance, thinking it disgusting and unworthy. Clearly, this desire to change one's face for another reflects an insecure self-image.

This inferiority complex hindered the advancement of both natives and mestizos. They were taught to dislike their faces so that their minds would remain troubled and uncertain about their self-identity. Meanwhile those responsible for this attitude went unchallenged. Although this method of rule is unjust, vicious, and unscientific, it assured dominance over the majority population. Unfortunately, native action to remove that burden was generally disorganized and sporadic, and efforts to unite with others who suffered a similar condition failed because of this. This proves how crippling its effect really was (Wolf 1959:233-256; Ramos 1962:54-72; Paz 1961:65; Hewes 1954:216-218).

Racism and group conflicts

While they shared many problems, mestizos and Indians also underwent experiences that set one group against the other. For example, many mestizos copied Spanish cultural habits, which often meant oppressing Indians. As is often the case in a system based on inequality, they probably tried to identify with the more powerful, "superior" race. As a result, whenever the opportunity arose, these mestizos harassed and exploited Indians (Zorita 1963:250). Prodded by protective clerics, colonial administrators shielded Indian communities. Thus, mestizos were harmed by being excluded from both Spanish and Indian towns (Helms 1975:171). This maneuvering taught them to survive in a relentlessly stubborn way. Nevertheless, Indians were still worse off because they were regarded by both Spaniards and mestizos as a despicable, inferior race. "They ascribe to Indians inferior traits and scorn many of their customs and beliefs as backward, infantile or gross, befitting primitive or rude people" (de la Fuente 1967:435).

Sociopsychological constraints were only partially effective, and the Spaniards maintained native subjugation by taking other actions. For example, any area that rebelled against racist practices and conditions was quelled by military force. If resistance intensified, stronger coercive measures were taken, such as punishment or death for the instigators. Native backwardness and underdevelopment were necessary for the success of the colonial empire, and racism, the emphasis on color and facial features, supported this arrangement.

5

Breakup and transformation of the social order

CONTACT *(Enlightenment)*

While military contact usually receives more attention, it must be remembered that human thoughts shape and move those physical actions. The childhood colonial period began with pressure from the Spanish sword, an externally derived force, and yet there was a motive behind the sword. In the breakup of the colonial social order actions and thoughts again intertwine (Romanell 1967:30-31), but it is ideas that dominate because the most crucial forces of change come from within.

Human social actions are usually based on conditions that require some type of adjustment. Often the necessary changes bring improvements; in the case of Mexico, another step toward maturity. These ideas were slow to unfold but eventually caught the imagination of every disenchanted person in the New World. "If the effect of the Enlightenment was less pronounced in Latin America than in Europe, it nevertheless created a climate favorable to progress and reform. It dominated the thinking of nearly all of the men who led the independence movement and, often, that of their opponents" (Fagg 1977:304).

Background to the Enlightenment

Such writers as Rousseau and Locke questioned European thought, and these and other efforts to redefine the nature of society led to the Age of Enlightenment. According to its philosophy, humankind directly shaped sociohistorical conditions and institutions, and events were not accidental. Whatever humans built they could also dismantle and rearrange according to their whim. Previously humans were taught from infancy what to do and whom to serve, living and dying without questioning the teachings. The Enlightenment undermined this indoctrination by emphasizing the plasticity and malleability of humankind. A person's concept of self or society depended on what authority figures placed in his mind. The mind was a *tabula rasa*, or blank board, that reflected what was written on it.

Europeans who were unhappy with existing social conditions gained inspiration from Enlightenment thought. Monarchical European countries led by the top-heavy aristocratic elite—landed gentry, nobility, and clergy—were challenged. They could no longer rule absolutely as they had for centuries. A new image of society was emerging. European upheavals toppled regimes and stimulated the breakup of colonial territories.

Revolutionary beginnings

"The ideals of the Enlightment were transmitted to the Spanish colonies in many ways. Spanish Americans who travelled or studied in Europe, and officials and merchants who came out from Spain, brought with them the progressive ideas current abroad" (Haring 1963:224) (Rydjord 1935:272). An idea born in one time and place must undergo a process of revision in a new setting, and this happened in the New World. Latin American criollo intellectuals and dissidents rapidly learned from the revolutions in the Old World and applied the knowledge to their conditions—thus developing finer nuances to the theories. The rise and spread of literary clubs carried these new doctrines far and wide, and the pen surpassed the sword in its ability to subvert the political regime (Diffie 1945:551).

This assertive program took time to gain momentum, since ideas are never enough; humans must always implement them. "Once the importance of the ideas of the Enlightenment as a cause of revolution was accepted, it followed that the popularization of these ideas in the previous revolutionary movements in the United States and in France was a significant means by which the fundamental ideas came to be transmitted to Latin America" (Griffith 1961:120-121).

The United States Revolution in 1776, especially as the first successful one in the New World, and the French Revolution in 1789 greatly influenced the Spanish colonial social structure. "That which resulted in the United States provided an example to Latin America no less than to Europe. . . . That was by far the greatest, and in a sense the only important contribution of the United States to the independence of Latin America" (Webster 1965:75-76). The effect of the French Revolution was more indirect. Napoleon's armies spread the doctrine of "liberty, equality, and fraternity," throughout Europe, eventually loosening the hold the aristocrat elite had on their subjects. Almost immediately, the Spanish people felt the impact of the French slogans, especially after Napoleon took control of Spain. The political debate and struggle around socioeconomic issues that began in the mother country necessarily involved the colonies and led to dissolution of the empire. "They [Spaniards] had imbibed many of the concepts of the French Revolution and British liberalism, and planned a new and liberal Spain" (Simpson 1967:233). Eager participants began proposing social theories to correct unjust and unequal conditions (Bazant 1977:6-7). In the end, "what Spanish bureaucrats had long dreaded materialized: the collapse of central authority, rebellion, and the refractioning of the Spains into competing regions, and the possibility that colonial areas in America would follow the path of the Spains toward local administration or juntas" (Stein and Stein 1970:110).

Enlightenment legacy

These years of Enlightenment ferment set the tone for subsequent world history. For example, the question of left against right (the terms originated in the French National Assembly, where change-oriented representatives were seated to the left and the status quo elements to the right), or Jacobins vs. reactionary conservatives, was initiated by the French. In the New World the process of taking sides—whether to create a new political system or to retain and strengthen the old one—was repeated, though the ideological lines were less sharp. The struggle reached some of the most isolated regions and affected many oppressed Mexican people.

Other issues increased the revolutionary momentum of the Enlightenment period. Among them: (1) European nations, particularly England, were interested in breaking the Spanish colonial commercial stranglehold and advocated a freer trade policy; and (2) much like North American colonists, the criollos were tired of oppressive colonial rule and sought independence and home rule. Both were economic issues and, in combination with ideas of social justice and examples of revolutionary activity, they made a heavy impact on the New World (Sierra 1969:136-141; Robertson 1961:28-30). "It may even be that Spain's inability to defend her place in the world's debate was due in part to her tendency to enjoy it while it lasted" (de Madariaga 1947:319).

The Chicano childhood years were altered by the Enlightenment, open-door trade, and home rule. Ideas stimulated the movement toward dissolution of the colonies. But this was only the first stage, because in a childhood that lasted three hundred years the people had to undergo even more innovative thought and action to overcome deep scars. Many years passed before the ideas took hold and eventually flourished. It took a long time to erase the colonial thumbprint. As might be expected, confusion reigned after this contact period, as everything and everyone was in flux.

CONFLICT *(Independence)*

"The Creole [criollo] never gave up his conviction that the American countries belonged . . . to but one class of Spaniard, to the Creole . . . as an aristocrat, a noble: with famous ancestors and a family tree, he despised the recently arrived Spaniard . . . as an upstart unsurping positions that rightfully should belong to the Creole" (Sierra 1969:100-101). Thus, the criollo challenge to gachupine rule ignited a full-scale conflict and brought other smoldering issues out into the open. Because of disastrous financial conditions in Spain, a result of costly European wars, the colonists were pressured into paying more to the mother country. This excessive burden further drove criollos to seek home rule. During the first years of the struggle, active participation and dialogue centered on nationalism, because political parties were ill defined and loosely organized (Turner 1968:28). Later, after the Spanish expulsion, political definitions and distinctions were made, sides chosen, and political and military battles fought.

Before ideological conflicts take root, there must be a receptive soil to nourish them. Hence, "the colonial elite found natural allies in the mestizos, mulattoes, and castas in general; the Indians they handled gingerly . . . if mobilized intelligently, [Indians] could be controlled to aid in the elimination of the handful of Spanish bureaucrats and merchants" (Stein and Stein 1970:114-115). Mestizo discontent resulted from the Spanish policy that disdained mixed bloods. Consequently, the persisting socioeconomic and racial problems of the mestizos and Indians provided fertile ground for colonial unrest, even though these problems were ignored after liberation. Undoubtedly, the discontent of the majority mestizos and Indians contributed heavily to the mounting revolutionary dissent.

Liberals vs. conservatives

"Mexico's independence, then, was the achievement of two opposed sectors, each working toward a different immediate objective. One side wanted to separate from a liberal Spain and continue the system without the motherland. The other side wanted separation from Spain too, but it wanted to wipe out the colony and establish a new order" (Alba 1967:41-42). Those criollos who wanted separation and a home rule type of monarchy were known as conservatives. Liberal criollos followed a more humanist orientation and demanded a more extensive program of political reform. To a degree, they desired to improve socioeconomic conditions, basing their program on a constitutional parliamentary model. The conservatives were stronger; they held powerful positions in the Catholic Church and the military, groups that were highly supportive of their goals. The smaller criollo group of liberals championed reform issues, which included minor concessions to mestizos and Indians.

A further clarification of this political split must be made. Conservatives were usually members of the urban upper class who had developed a centralist political strategy. They believed that power should remain in the cities, the center of sociocultural life. In contrast, liberals favored a federalist plan that catered to provincial chieftains and the nascent middle class. Their plan emphasized regional input in decision-making processes (Bazant 1977:38). The numbers of the liberals were swelled by many mestizos, especially those with middle-class positions or aspirations.

During the first years of the independence struggle, both the conservative and liberal ideologies were refined under various leaders. Opportunism characterized the political philosophy of many of these self-serving leaders. Nevertheless, political wrangling over the nation's future direction generally found liberals addressing mestizo and Indian issues (Calvert 1973:26). It was necessary to include these groups in the political process, for they constituted the majority of the population whose oppressive conditions commanded attention. With tacit support from mestizos and Indians, the liberals more strongly argued for reform, if only giving it lip service (Simpson 1967:223).

A split in liberal ranks resulted. "Some wanted to 'go quickly,' to fulfill the aspirations of Liberalism at all cost and as soon as possible; others wanted to 'go slowly,' to achieve the same ideals at less cost and without haste. The former were called 'puros' or 'reds' and the latter 'moderados'" (Villegas et al. 1974:104). Although lines were not clearly drawn, the moderados were usually criollos and the puros mostly mestizos. One example of a criollo puro was Lorenzo de Zavala, who advocated a vast program of social revolution under the rubric of Mexican nationalism. However, he is the exception to the majority of upper- and middle-class criollos and mestizos; they protected their own interests, with little concern for the condition of the bulk of the population.

1810: El Grito de Dolores

By 1810 there were four million people in Mexico. They were divided into three groups: ten percent of Spanish lineage, thirty percent of mestizo and mulatto background, and the remaining sixty percent of Indian descent (Alba 1967:37). Dissident activity had already occurred throughout Mexico, but the cause célèbre of independence was *El Grito de Dolores* (The Cry of Pain), a proclamation made by Miguel Hidalgo, a parish priest, on September 16, 1810. Although a criollo and a Jesuit and fairly well-off, he felt concern for less fortunate members of society. He could be characterized as an activist puro. His goal was the liberation of Mexico, even if gachupines must be slaughtered. When the opportunity arose, he led the first large military forces against the gachupines. Shortly thereafter he was captured and executed by a firing squad. But in the aftermath the gates of revolution remained open.

Following in the footsteps of Hidalgo was another small-village priest, the poor mestizo, Jose Maria Morelos. Interestingly, both based their actions on the teachings of Jesus Christ and repudiated the reactionary position of the church. A farseeing political and military genius, barely five feet tall, Morelos rallied the revolutionary forces until his execution in 1815. He

Fig. 5-1. Balcony from which Hidalgo addressed masses, Dolores Hidalgo, Guanajuato, Mexico.

outlined radical propositions aimed toward a true social revolution. "The revolution was justified, Morelos insisted, because the perfidious gachupines were enemies of mankind, who for three centuries had enslaved and subjugated the native population, stifled the natural developments of the kingdom, squandered its wealth and resources, and violated the sacred cult" (Simpson 1967:218-219). Some of his goals were the nullification of internal tariffs, the division of the land, the burning of official archives, the elimination of slavery, and the convocation of a congress (Alba 1967:39).

By 1820 the people had tired of the struggle. The time was ripe for a compromise, despite the fact that both Hidalgo and Morelos had lost their lives for the radical cause. Augustin de Iturbide, a moderate leader, mediated the ideological conflicts between conservatives and liberals. He made a pact with the liberal rebel Vicente Guerrero. As the inheritor of the Hidalgo-Morelos tradition, Guerrero, along with other liberals, had eventually grown weary of the prolonged anarchy. The agreement between Iturbide and Guerrero was called the Plan of Iguala. "Mexico was to be an independent monarchy, governed by King Ferdinand or some other European prince; the Roman Catholic church was to retain its privileges; and Creoles and Gachupines were henceforth to be equal. These were known as the three guarantees" (Parkes 1969:170). The guarantees are symbolized by the colors of the modern Mexican flag: green for the monarchy, white for the Catholic Church, and red for the gachupines and criollos. Religion was the unifying feature of the plan. "It was necessary to defend the Catholic faith. With this issue, the author of the manifesto—whoever he was—found the common denominator for Spaniards and Mexicans, for landowners and landless, for whites, Mestizos, and Indians, for higher and lower clergy" (Bazant 1977:27).

1821: peace

Liberal-conservative ideological rivalries were temporarily put aside when the compromise was reached in 1821. However, they resurfaced shortly after the constitutional monarch, Iturbide, was overthrown and executed in 1824. In the wake of this event, Guadalupe Victoria, a liberal mestizo, became the first elected president of the Republic of Mexico. However, the liberal-conservative battle continued throughout the first half of the nineteenth century.

CHANGE *(Experimentation and nationalism)*
Age of the caudillo

"It is not easy to follow the thread of reason through the generation following the Independence of Mexico. The loosely cemented strata of colonial society had split apart in the cataclysm of 1810-1821, and their mending is still an uncertain and remote aspiration" (Simpson 1967:230). This time is best summarized as the age of the *caudillo* (strong, charismatic leader).

The setting for the rise of military and political strongmen was provided by the liberal-conservative conflict and by dissension among the liberals. There were so many coups, countercoups, intrigues, and palace guard incidents that political goals became secondary to personal motives. "The most dramatic representation of the supremacy of regional forces . . . is seen in the rise of Caudillos . . . they competed vigorously for the personal prestige and material rewards that could be derived from control of local and sometimes national power positions" (Helms 1975:221). General Antonio Lopez de Santa Ana was a fine practitioner of this art. Beginning as a supporter of liberal causes, he repeatedly switched sides to advance his own career. For over thirty years this comic pattern of usurpation and exile continued, while Mexico suffered under the vogue of personal aggrandizement. "From 1821 to 1850, Mexico was in a state of constant turmoil. In thirty years there were fifty governments, almost all the result of military coups and eleven of them presided over by General Santa Ana" (Villegas et al. 1974:97).

Early difficulties

Despite this instability, liberals made some sincere efforts to undermine church influence, a power amassed over 300 years. Anticlericalism rose during this time, and when Benito Juarez, the culturally assimilated Indian, took office in 1857, laws were implemented to curtail vested church power. Contrary to some interpretations, and perhaps as an unintended outcome, these Juarez-inspired laws also infringed on Indian land tenure practices (Bazant 1977:73-74).

Initial strivings toward Mexican nationalism had been made earlier, but after independence an incipient type of nationalism gradually took shape. At first efforts revolved around construction of an entirely new governmental model. In time nationalist sentiment produced a hybrid strategy derived from Spanish and Indian traditions (Romanell 1967:17). Furthermore, foreign nations coveted Mexican territory, recently won but poorly protected because of the political turmoil, and this helped the growth of nationalism (Rydjord 1935:307; Sierra 1969:192-193). "One of the forces that facilitates cohesion within a group is xenophobia, the common fear or hatred of foreigners outside the group" (Turner 1967:15). However, a cohesive nationalist ideology was still not fully formulated by the end of the nineteenth century. Another revolution in 1910 partially fulfilled this goal.

Events in the north

Within liberal ranks puros, pushing harder than moderados, became frustrated with the slowness of change. Their activity was a prelude to the 1910 revolution. One of them, Lorenzo de Zavala, migrated north to the borderlands, hoping to institute social experiments unwanted by central Mexican authorities (Alba 1967:51-52). He later predicted that this northern region (now the United States Southwest) would separate from the increasingly despotic conservative government. This prophecy would later come true, although under different circumstances (Bazant 1977:42-44).

Borderland settlement appeared imperative because the sparsely populated region required a more permanent body of residents to fend off foreign land-grabs, a threat that mounted after independence. However, Indians controlled most of the area, making settlement difficult, if not impossible. To counter foreign intervention, some Mexican leaders sought to establish a colony in the borderlands, inviting non-Mexicans (usually United States frontiersmen) to join them in an outpost of the new nation. Reasons for this varied. Some Mexicans simply wanted more whites there to offset Indian influence. Others, politically idealistic, wished to have the new society exposed to United States democratic traditions. This goal was only partially attained but nevertheless highlights the discontent and frustration of radical Mexican liberals toward conservative policies. One such liberal Mexican invited the well-known British utopian socialist, Robert Owen, to found a new Mexican social order (Alba 1967:54). Instead Owen brought the experiment to the United States, where it failed.

These and other incidents reflect the Mexican unhappiness with a government unwilling to chart a new political course. Some, in short, refused to wait for change.

Conflict over Indian program

On several issues political ideologies were mixed. For example, a goal of the nationalist program was the granting of citizenship and other rights to all residents of Mexican territory. This primarily meant the Indian population, who traditionally had been kept outside the mainstream of social and political life. The conservatives supported Indian national integration because Indians still were closely allied with the church, one of the conservatives' interest groups. The liberals also agreed with the integration policy, hoping to improve opportunities for mestizos as well, but they alienated the natives through lack of an effective liaison with them. Most significantly, the natives showed lukewarm acceptance of the program. Their well-founded wariness was based on history, because further integration was often associated with more complete native exploitation and oppression.

Behaving like their Spanish forefathers, the Mexican nationalists refused to acknowledge the basis of native distrust. In fact, the leaders shaping policy ignored the overriding issue of that time: "The struggle between the privileged classes and the masses of the people has been the hub around which all the troubles of the country have revolved throughout its whole history" (Loya 1958:199). Using force and punishment, all with "the good of natives" in mind, Mexican leaders rushed headlong into accommodation programs without assuring the people of their good intentions. For example, liberals broke up Indian communal lands and villages with the idea of helping them. Instead, as noted previously, it created more problems for the Indians, who were made unhappy for their own good.

"In the first twelve years of independence, Mexico had experimented with monarchy, moderate constitutional republic, radical populist regime, conservative government, and liberal government; each in turn failed to produce stability" (Bazant 1977:61). Lacking this foundation, or perhaps because of its tenuousness, the native and mestizo population remained backward. It did not matter whether the social planners were gachupines, criollos, mestizos, or culturally assimilated Indians; the majority of the people, mostly Indian in this period, continued as before—on the receiving end. Eventually change took place, but not before much bloodshed had occurred and many years had passed.

REFERENCES

Alba, V.: *The Mexicans: the making of a nation*, New York, 1967, Praeger Publishers.

Bazant, J.: *A concise history of Mexico: from Hidalgo to Cardenas, 1805-1940*, New York, 1977, Cambridge University Press.

Bolton, H.: *The Spanish borderlands*, New Haven, Conn., 1921, Yale University Press.

Borah, W., and Cook, S. F.: *The population of central Mexico in 1548*, Berkeley, 1960, University of California Press.

Brading, D. A.: *Haciendas and ranchos in Mexican Bajio: Leon 1700-1860*, 1979, New York, Cambridge University Press.

Calvert, P.: *Mexico*, New York, 1973, Praeger Publishers.

Cancian, F.: Political and religious organization. In Wauchope, R., editor: *Handbook of Middle American Indians*, vol. 6, Austin, 1967, University of Texas Press.

Carrasco, P.: The Mesoamerican Indian during the colonial period. In Bell, B., editor: *Indian Mexico: past and present*, Los Angeles, 1965, The University of California, Latin American Center.

Chance, J. K.: *Race and class in colonial Oaxaca*, Stanford, Calif., 1978, Stanford University Press.

Chevalier, F.: *Land and society in colonial Mexico*, Berkeley, 1966, University of California Press.

Cox, O. C.: *Caste, class, and race*, New York, 1970, Monthly Review Press.

de la Fuente, J.: Ethnic relationships. In Wauchope, R., editor: *Handbook of Middle American Indians*, vol. 6, Austin, 1967, University of Texas Press.

de Madariaga, S.: *The rise of the Spanish American empire*, New York, 1947, Macmillan Inc.

Diffie, B. W.: *Latin-America civilization: colonial period*, Boston, 1945, Charles River Books, Inc.

Dusenberry, W. H.: *The Mexican mesta*, Urbana, 1963, University of Illinois Press.

Edmonson, M. S.: Nativism, syncretism, and anthropological science. In Edmonson, M. S., editor: *Nativism and syncretism*, Middle America Research Institution Pub.

No. 9, New Orleans, 1960, Tulane University.

Elliott, J. H.: *Imperial Spain: 1469-1716*, New York, 1963, The New American Library, Inc.

Fagg, J. E.: *Latin America: a general history*, New York, 1977, Macmillan, Inc.

Foster, G: *Culture and conquest*, New York, 1960, Quadrangle Books Inc.

Foster, G.: Peasant society and the image of limited good, *American Anthropologist* **67**:293-315, 1965.

Frank, A. G.: *Capitalism and underdevelopment in Latin America*, New York, 1969, Monthly Review Press.

Gibson, C.: *Aztecs under Spanish rule*, Stanford, Calif., 1964, Stanford University Press.

Gibson, C.: *Spain in America*, New York, 1966, Harper & Row, Publishers.

Gillin, J.: Mestizo America. In Linton, R., editor: *Most of the world: the peoples of Africa, Latin America and the East today*, New York, 1957, Columbia University Press.

Gist, N. P., and Dworkin, A. G., editors: *The blending of races: marginality and identity in world perspective*, 1972, John Wiley & Sons, Inc.

Griffith, C. C.: The Enlightenment and Latin America. In Whitaker, A. P., editor: *Latin America and the Enlightenment*, Ithaca, N.Y., 1961, Cornell University Press.

Haring, C. H.: *The Spanish empire in America*, New York, 1963, Harcourt Brace Jovanovich, Inc.

Helms, M. W.: *Middle America: a culture history of heartland and frontiers*, Englewood Cliffs, N.J., 1975, Prentice-Hall, Inc.

Hewes, G. W.: Mexicans in search of the Mexican: notes on Mexican national character studies, *American Journal of Economics and Sociology* **13**:209, 1954.

Johnson, C. S.: The economic basis of race relations. In Locke, A. and Stern, B. J., editors: *When peoples meet: a study in race and culture contacts*, New York, 1946, Hinds, Hayden and Eldredge Inc.

Leon-Portilla, M.: *Aztec thought and culture*, Norman, 1963, University of Oklahoma Press.

Leiris, M.: *Race and culture*, Paris, France, 1958, UNESCO.

Link, H. G.: *The rediscovery of morals*, New York, 1947, American Elsevier Publishers, Inc.

Loya, D. G.: Mosaic of Mexican history, Mexico, D.F.: Editorial CVLTVRA, T.G., S.A. 1958.

Madsen, W.: Religious syncretism. In Wauchope, R., editor: *Handbook of Middle American Indians*, vol. 6, Austin, 1967, University of Texas Press.

McWilliams, C.: *North from Mexico: the Spanish-speaking people of the United States*, Westport, Conn., 1969, Greenwood Press, Inc.

Morner, M.: *Race mixture in the history of Latin America*, Boston, 1967, Little, Brown & Co.

Nicholson, H. B.: The efflorescence of Mesoamerican civilization: a resume. In Bell, B., editor: *Indian Mexico: past and present*, Los Angeles, 1967, The University of California, Latin America Center.

Padden, R. C.: *The hummingbird and the hawk: conquest and sovereignty in the Valley of Mexico, 1503-1541*, Columbus, 1967, Ohio State University Press.

Parkes, H. B.: *A history of Mexico*, Boston, 1969, Houghton Mifflin Co.

Paz, O.: *The labyrinth of solitude*, New York, 1961, Grove Press, Inc.

Picon-Salas, M.: *A cultural history of Spanish America*, Berkeley, 1965, University of California Press.

Ramos, S.: *Profile of man and culture in Mexico*, Austin, 1962, University of Texas Press.

Ricard, R.: *The spiritual conquest of Mexico*, Berkeley, 1966, University of California Press.

Romanell, P.: *Making of the Mexican mind*, Notre Dame, Ind., 1967, University of Notre Dame Press.

Robertson, W. S.: *Rise of the Spanish-American republics*, New York, 1961, Macmillan, Inc.

Rydjord, J.: *Foreign interest in the independence of New Spain*, Durham, N.C., 1935, Duke University Press.

Schurz, W. H.: *This new world*, New York, 1964, American Elsevier Publishers, Inc.

Sierra, J.: *The political evolution of the Mexican people*, Austin, 1969, University of Texas Press.

Simpson, L. B.: *The encomienda in New Spain*, Berkeley, 1966, University of California Press.

Simpson, L. B.: *Many Mexicos*, Berkeley, 1967, University of California Press.

Spicer, E.: *Cycles of conquest*, Tucson, 1962, The University of Arizona Press.

Stein, S., and Stein, B.: *The colonial heritage of Latin America*, New York, 1970, Oxford University Press, Inc.

Turner, F. C.: *The dynamic of Mexican nationalism*, Chapel Hill, N.C., 1968, The University of North Carolina Press.

van den Berghe, P. L.: *Race and racism: a comparative perspective*, New York, 1967, John Wiley & Sons, Inc.

Vasconcelos, J., and Gamio, M.: *Aspects of Mexican civilization*, Chicago, 1926, University of Chicago Press.

Villegas, D. C., et al.: *A compact history of Mexico*, Los Angeles, 1974, The University of California, Latin American Center.

Vives, J.V.: *An economic history of Spain*, Princeton, N.J., 1969, Princeton University Press.

Wagley, C., and Harris, M.: *Minorities in the New World: six case studies*, New York, 1958, Columbia University Press.

Waters, F.: *Mexico mystique: the coming sixth world of consciousness*, Chicago, 1975, The Swallow Press, Inc.

Whetten, N.L.: *Rural Mexico*, Chicago, 1969, University of Chicago Press.

Wolf, E.: *Sons of the shaking earth*, Chicago, 1959, University of Chicago Press.

Zavala, S.: *The Spanish colonization of America*, Philadelphia, 1943, University of Pennsylvania Press.

MEXICAN INDEPENDENCE AND NATIONALISM
1821 to 1846

Adolescence is a time of increased autonomy and often strident demands for still more independence. It is frequently characterized by bold experimentation, by excursions further and further from one's home base. And yet it is also a time of great confusion. While part of the adolescent seems driven toward vaguely defined future goals, another part yearns for the security (not necessarily the comforts) of childhood. In addition to these internal sources of ambiguity, the external environment often imposes sharp limits on adolescent experimentation and even inflicts sometimes harsh punishment for youthful errors and miscalculations.

"Parts" of a nation, of course, are much more concrete than are the competing aspects of an individual personality. Nevertheless, the metaphor can provide insights into the events that followed Mexican independence from Spain. The Mexican nation during this period was characterized by the storm and stress that psychologists attribute to adolescence. At times reformist leaders attempted to move the country toward major (if ill-defined) social and economic changes. As often occurs, more conservative elements thwarted such change, turning the society and economy back toward institutional forms established during the colonial period (childhood). As these reform and counterreform contests continued, many people left the centers of political strife to colonize the frontier regions of Mexico. In these new locales they often patterned their social establishments on those that predominated in the land of their origin. Amid this activity Mexico was also threatened by the expansionist tendencies of powerful foreign nations, the United States and France in particular.

Adolescence often includes major turning points in one's life, and such is the case with the history of the Chicano people. The Anglo-American acquisition of Mexico's northern provinces was one of the more severe blows suffered by Mexico in the years between its independence in 1821 and the

1910 revolution. For the Chicano people within the territories annexed by the United States, however, it was even more: An abrupt end had come to their adolescence. While Chicanos in the United States continued to be affected by events in metropolitan Mexico, other social environments became overwhelmingly important in their everyday postadolescent lives.

In anticipation of that importance, our study of the adolescent period will focus considerably more attention on events in the Mexican frontier regions than has been the case in previous chapters. Because the adolescent period lasted until the 1910 revolution for Mexicans living in Mexico, this stage includes some discussion of late nineteenth century events in Mexico, such as the role of land tenure under the regimes of Benito Juarez and Porfirio Diaz.

6

Intact and stable social order

CLASS *(Ideological struggle between liberals and conservatives)*

Mexico under criollos

"As far as popular liberties were concerned, independence thus seemed to have brought little change. Political power passed from the officials of the Crown to the Creole oligarchy, but the nature of society remained as before" (Clissold 1966:82). The socioeconomic structure was rid of the gachupines, but they were replaced by the criollos. Nevertheless, some opportunities were also allotted to mestizos and culturally assimilated Indians (Cline 1963:13). Barriers to social mobility still remained after decades of struggle, but isolated breaches of the barriers did occur.

Political confrontations between conservative and liberal leaders and their followers dominated the scene, and even within liberal ranks debate continued. "These 'pure' liberals (puros), as the radicals called themselves, were firmly dogmatic, whereas the more flexible moderates (moderados) preferred to come to an 'understanding' with the Church" (Alba 1967:56). At the center of this political discord was the issue of how to reconstruct the social and economic sectors to best enhance Mexico's future. Liberals accepted both the event and the spiritual promise of independence, while conservatives only acknowledged that it had happened and believed that no significant social alterations were needed (Hale 1968:22).

"Contending forces within the small groups striving for leadership were relatively evenly balanced but often diametrically opposed on large and small issues, and quite unwilling or unable to compromise. The results provided Mexico with a grim and tragic history for the first fifty years following independence" (Cline 1963:16). During this period of strife, haciendas, debt peonage, and sharply defined class differences continued.

Condition of masses

Indeed, before the end of the nineteenth century, under the dictatorship of the mestizo Porfirio Diaz, the situation deteriorated: "the hacendados took advantage of the lapse of the colonial protective legislation and enlarged their properties by expropriating the lands of the villagers [with] 11,000 hacendados controlling some 57 per cent of the national territory. . . . At the other end of the scale, some fifteen million persons were landless" (Singer 1969:49). The liberal Benito Juarez had initiated the sale of Indian communal and mission lands to promote reform (Bazant 1977:75), but the holdings instead "passed unbroken . . . into the hands of private individuals" (Whetten 1948:98). The expansion of haciendas required more cheap labor, supplied by dispossessed Indians, and further broadened the power of the hacendados. In the meantime, the nation's affairs and international reputation suffered: "the government stumbled from one financial crisis to the next" (Cumberland 1968:147).

In the political arena, the liberal and conservative viewpoints represented a wide contrast; yet when the time for policy implementation arrived, liberals also followed self-interest motives. As a result, the majority Indians and mestizos remained exploited and powerless; there was perhaps even greater socioeconomic inequality. One assessment suggests that modern peasantry is caused by earlier colonial practices: "most analysts recognize that, at least in backward, underdeveloped, or dependent areas of the globe, the heritage of the past has shaped and is shaping current widespread poverty there" (Stein and Stein 1970:189). Leaders of all persuasions fol-

Fig. 6-1. Nineteenth century communal Indian village. (From Starr, F.: *Indians of Southern Mexico*, Chicago, 1899, published by the author.)

lowed the customs of a former age, while the majority, despite changes in their formal legal status, continued to suffer (Glade and Anderson 1968:23).

"Nearly all classes and groups experienced the delight of being free, of regarding themselves as masters of their own destinies" (Fagg 1977:375). Indians and mestizos participated in the struggle for independence but were unable to enjoy its fruits. "Half the population, the Indians, played no conscious part in the public life of the new nation. They continued to labor as peons or to live in the missions. Many of them withdrew almost entirely from contact with the white man" (Fagg 1977:391). After the revolution criollos were in control, but "issues in early Mexican politics were debated within a very small circle of predominantly mestizo (mixed blood) leaders, with the locus of power in the alarmingly large Mexican army" (Cline 1963:17).

Events in northern Mexico

Debate on the future of Mexico also occurred in the northern territories. Although the issues took on a different complexion and were discussed within a smaller circle of participants, there appeared to be a clear tendency toward a liberal solution. Some leaders even went so far as to suggest that a Mexican nationalist program should be patterned after the United States. This was particularly true in California and New Mexico, two

Fig. 6-2. Modern mural of Benito Juarez in Chapultepec Castle, Mexico City.

fully established settlements. California's situation (not forgetting the importance of New Mexico and later, Texas) serves to increase our understanding of important social class patterns, especially in light of the 1846 war, its
aftermath, and modern historical developments.

Conditions in the borderlands, especially California, were similar
to those in Mexico. A smaller-scale hacienda system prevailed, with land
ownership again determining social rank and role. "Once the Spanish empire was overthrown, the Colonization Act and the Reglamento of 1828
opened up the land for private settlement" (Nava and Barger 1976:128).
Landowners were known as *gente de razon* (people of reason), and social life
revolved around their privileged circle. Some worked their ranchos, but
most preferred the traditional hacendado role. "They themselves were anything but industrious. Captain Jose Bandini reported in 1828 that most of
them did nothing. Their days were spent in dancing, riding, and gambling.
They had neither profession nor trade. . . . Behind this sad state of affairs . . .
lay the fact that the Californians [gente de razon] were seldom without Indians to do their work" (Hutchinson 1969:138). Mestizo and Indian *pobladores* (settlers) usually worked as *vaqueros* (cowboys) and foremen, but if
independent, often operated *ranchitos* (small ranches) for themselves. Many
also served gente de razon as household domestics (McWilliams 1968:89;
Vigil 1974:26-27).

"In many respects, the social structure of Spanish California resembled that of the Deep South: the gente de razon were the plantation-
owners; the Indians [California natives] were the slaves; and the Mexicans
were the California equivalent of 'poor white trash'" (McWilliams 1968:90).
Later mestizo and Indian immigrants became semiemployed, unskilled laborers. They spoke poor Spanish, and their lot was often little better than
that of the California Indian, except that they had hopes of future improvement. They were known as *cholos* (half-breeds; Indians in transition from
one culture to another and somewhat marginal to both). "In Mexico, they
would have been in the lower social strata. But in California they were in a
new area where they could hope to rise in the social scale, for there were
other people who could be pushed into the lowest places in society" (Borah
1970:13). The lowest group, of course, were California Indians: "Caught in a
vicious circle of ignorance, poverty, vice, prejudice, and oppression, most
Indians never escaped their low status. The 'sale' of Indians by [the city officials of] pueblos like Los Angeles illustrates the condition of many" (Nava
and Barger 1976:129).

Economic enterprises in the north

Gente de razon, pobladores, cholos, and California Indians comprised the class system. Other borderland regions used different class labels,

but essentially the same unequal system obtained. For example, in New Mexico two classes existed: *ricos* (rich) and *pobres* (poor) (McWilliams 1968:68, 84-86). In contrast to California, New Mexican Indians were much less integrated into Mexican society because they had more effectively resisted total Spanish subjugation. The central government of that era had tried to improve opportunities for all Indians (Hutchinson 1969:109), but the program that sought to integrate them into the national culture was poorly implemented.

Before Mexico's independence, California Indians were widely dispersed geographically, and the Spanish soldiers had to locate and capture them to force them to work on colonial enterprises and accept Christianity. According to a British observer of those events: "If . . . any of the captured Indians show a repugnance to conversion, it is the practice to imprison them for a few days . . . and thus they continue to be incarcerated until they declare their readiness to renounce the religion of their forefathers" (Moquin and Van Doren 1971:133). With Indian aid, twenty-one missions had been founded in California, each strategically located one day's ride from another. While the missionary goal was native religious conversion and training, much energy was also expended on making the socioeconomic unit self-sufficient. This scheme mirrored Mexico's hacienda system in thoroughness and severity. "The main instrumentality for the Spanish policy was the mission. The term had acquired a very special meaning in Spanish usage. Over a period of more than two centuries, the Spanish in America had worked out a theory of the mission as an instrument for handling Indians and harnessing aboriginal societies to the Spanish state" (Borah 1970:7).

Housing over 30,000 Indians and with holdings valued in millions of dollars, the missions flourished as religious-economic centers. The colonists introduced Spanish and Mexican technology and products, making them the mainstays of economic and social life (Samora and Simon 1977:53). Some of the new subsistence products were cattle, sheep, pigs, grapes (both wine and raisin), citrus fruits, avocados, olives, pomegranates, pears, wheat, flax, alfalfa, beans, and cotton. Indian labor cared for and produced them. Indians were also trained for various occupations, such as vaquero, shepherd, blacksmith, horticulturist, brick and tile maker, irrigator, miner, and church attendant (Nava and Barger 1976:106). As noted previously, Hispanicized Indians were given better jobs, and after the secularization of mission lands they served the gente de razon.

Breakup of California missions

After Mexican independence the anticlerical movement affected colonists in the northern region. Many wealthy Californians, including both long-time criollo settlers and newcomers, sought to weaken church power.

Since the seat of religious authority was so far away, making administration nearly impossible, gente de razon stepped in to improve their fortunes. Secularization of the missions took place in 1834 to 1843, resulting in "the fashioning of a society in which religious values and the church as an institution would be of little consequence in the action of individuals" (Hale 1968:160) (Moquin and Van Doren 1971:153; Hutchinson 1969:128). Church land came under civil control and was redistributed by government grants.

Immediately after secularization, nearly 500 land grants created from the former mission lands were distributed to newcomers. Many of the earlier land-grant residents also benefited by adding more land to their estates. Land grants were of two types: individually owned, or controlled in common by a community of residents, usually as a grazing range for livestock. In California the primary unit was the individual estate. Within their land-grant boundaries, some patron Californians allotted smaller parcels, ranchitos, to their faithful workers and supporters.

System in New Mexico

The New Mexico land system developed along different lines. After 1598 settlers had carved out large land units and often set aside communal landed estates (more here than in California) for settlers engaged in raising sheep. As a result of this early beginning, socioeconomic life flourished, and despite the persistent conflicts with neighboring dissident Indians, some degree of stability (and some racial mixture) had been established by the time Mexico became independent.

In 250 years the Spanish-speaking population of New Mexico swelled to 60,000, the largest colony in the north. A rico/pobre dichotomy prevailed, with Indians in the lowest position of course, but intense conflict had subsided as the social relations between the groups became established. Within this relatively quiet setting, the large and small rancheros and their workers carried on an independent, self-sufficient life. Many surrounding Indian groups, however, had resisted full Hispanic control and maintained a semblance of autonomy in the region, although there was some diffusion of Hispanic culture.

Rancho life

Much of the rancho life in California resembled that of the missions before them, but with some variations and important additions. Almost nation-sized in extent, the ranchos became centers of cattle-raising, which soon mushroomed into a lucrative commercial network. All of the activities and paraphernalia associated with this industry surfaced here: rodeos, vaqueros, branding, and so on. Trade with New England merchants developed, in which hides and tallow (used in the manufacture of soap and candles) were exchanged for manufactured products from the Eastern Seaboard. Cattle hides became popularly known as "California bank notes," and the United States leather industry flourished. Mexicans who carried the balls of tallow to the waiting clipper ships were left with a slick mess of grease on their backs. They came to be known as "greasers," an opprobrious label eventually used toward all things Mexican.

Interestingly, the early Yankee settlers (mountain men, traders, seamen, and adventurers) were readily accepted by gente de razon. "The first Anglos to arrive . . . inter-married with the Mexicans and lived in peace. The Californios, therefore, did not view the Anglos as enemies" (Acuna 1972:102). Most of the immigrants became Hispanicized and acquired their own land grants. Afterward, as a result of intermarriage, many Yankees inherited large parcels of land that gente de razon had willed to their daughters. Assimilated Yankees became the social equals of Californios, with the cholos and Indians remaining in the lowest position (Samora and Simon 1977:76).

CULTURE *(Budding Mexicanismo)*
First steps toward national unity

With the exception of the trend toward a national Mexican culture, most institutions remained the same during this period. Patterns of language, religion, family structure, and many other traditions persisted. The overriding societal theme was "that all citizens should be 'incorporated' into the nationality economically as well as spiritually in order to aid the process of breaking down the 'artificial and antipatriotic barriers to national unity'" (Turner 1968:74). While liberals and conservatives were locked in a power struggle, with the issue in doubt for decades, the liberals sought educational reform for natives. "But the laws on education were soon abrogated by Santa Ana, the 'Attila of Mexican Civilization'" (Hale 1968:175), who became president of Mexico in 1832 and later gained notoriety in the Texas war of secession from Mexico.

The conservatives adamantly opposed social transformations. Neither political group's policies clearly dominated before 1860, with the exception of the mid-1850's liberal reforms. A last-ditch conservative effort to reassert control ended disastrously. By inviting the French archduke Maximillian to establish a Mexican monarchy in 1864, some conservatives incurred the animosity of patriotic Mexicans of all political shades (Helms 1975:227; Bazant 1977:85). After the foreign intervention failed, liberals took over national leadership. Porfirio Diaz, a liberal mestizo who had been a top general under Juarez in the defense against the French, ruled as dictator of

Mexico until 1910. At the beginning of his regime the liberal reform movement had already waned, as the national mood moved toward peace and
away from confrontation and chaos.

If one were to examine the writings of reformers of this period, it
would appear that a tremendous social upheaval was taking place. However,
these "ink-and-paper" innovations were never implemented. Indians and
mestizos were consistently barred from joining the mainstream. Current
practices are surely derived from these earlier conditions: "Neither the children of mixed unions nor Indians who have become completely acculturated
both linguistically and culturally are accepted as Mexicans. . . . Local society
remembers the Indian origin of these people, and by a rule of descent places
them in the lowly Indian category. Only by moving to another region and
into a town where one's genealogy is not known may such people 'pass' as
Mexicans" (Wagley and Harris 1958:81). Mexican leaders were concerned
more with shaping a national identity and establishing an entrepreneurial
class than with improving conditions for the masses (Turner 1968:9).

As mentioned previously, national reconstruction was blocked by
political turmoil. "With the mass of the population hungry, ill-clothed, and
illiterate, and with few public institutions concerned with its improvement,
with class cleavages as sharp in 1850 as in 1750, and with little concern on
the part of the political and social leaders for its implications, with, in short,
an apparently stultified and static society and little evidence of any real
change in the offing, small wonder it is that both the economy and the society suffered" (Cumberland 1968:173).

Decline of cultural imperialism

Increasingly concerned with their national image, Mexican leaders sought to build on Enlightenment thinking. They did this by applying
European concepts to the nation's evolving cultural style (Hale 1968:148).
Efforts at emulation, however, added to the divergence already prevalent,
with each individual or group championing one European attribute or another, all equally detrimental to a nation built on an indigenous base. The
comment of one liberal spokesman, Jose Maria Luis Mora, highlights an attitude that ran counter to the needs of the people of that time. "He asserted
that 'the glory of the legislator does not consist in being an inventor, but in
guiding his subjects (comitentes) toward happiness.' The only aim of society . . . is the happiness of the individual members" (Hale 1968:155). As it
turns out, these "individual members" were the liberal elite. However, a few
leaders continued to strive toward shaping a truly national culture.

The outstanding cultural themes of this period were the evolution
of a political philosophy and the rise of a nationalist consciousness (Cline

1963:18). Internal military upheavals affected the direction of these goals, sometimes helping them and other times slowing or stopping them altogether (Sierra 1969:201). "The chaos which was to fill Mexico for nearly seventy years found its origin in the struggle for national freedom, and in the interval from the end of the colonial administration to the beginning of the Diaz regime all [stable] government may be said to have disappeared in Mexico" (Tannenbaum 1933:73).

Eventually Mexico stopped mimicking other nations and charted a course of its own making (Romanell 1967:18), but not without severe difficulties. For example, the weakness shown by a fledgling nation such as Mexico created the opportunity for foreign intervention. The previously mentioned French-imposed monarchy was one example. The Mexican-American war of 1846 was even more disastrous and ended with over half of Mexico's territory lost to the United States. Both affairs, coming at a vulnerable time for Mexico, increased public support for nationalism (Turner 1968:35-36; Sierra 1969:212). Furthermore, the growing sense of cultural and racial homogeneity encouraged nationalist awareness (Turner 1968:74). The 1910 revolution would bring this about much faster.

Cultural variant in northern Mexico

Settlers in the northern reaches of Mexico mirrored many of the shifts in attitude in higher social circles.

Government and military officials had been sent to rule and maintain order, thus complementing missions in the religious sphere (Pitt 1968:2). The missions, *pueblo* (civil rule), and *presidio* (military defense) affected cultural life. The pueblo and presidio ensured that native laborers would be kept in check and that foreign intruders would be resisted.

Even at this early date, California and other parts of northern Mexico represented a dual heritage. The syncretic experience that shaped Mexico was repeated here, but, as might be expected, with different causes and results. "The people who brought Hispanic culture to California were mostly Mexicans rather than Spaniards born in Spain" (Borah 1970:4). Also, "the Spanish in the eighteenth century were having serious trouble with the Indians of what is today northern Mexico and our Southwest. In that area, during the late sixteenth and seventeenth centuries, there developed a resurgent Indian culture, an effective Indian response to a European challenge" (Borah 1970:5).

A combination of Spanish and Indian vocabulary and names for rivers, mountains, deserts, and other geographical features resulted. The names of the southwestern states are a carry-over from this period. California, New Mexico (a syncretic name), Nevada, and Colorado are from Spanish words, and Arizona, Texas, and Utah are named after Indian tribes. In California many place names originated from Indian sources, including Lompoc, Malibu, Pacoima, and Pismo.

In colonial California Indian laborers had built many buildings following a syncretic style, for instance, Indian adobe bricks with Spanish tile roofs (Samora and Simon 1977:54). Much of the terminology identified with the United States Southwest, such as that used in agriculture, livestock-raising, and mining, is borrowed from the Spanish and Mexicans.

Economic influences on cultural patterns

The Spanish-Mexican legacy includes more than words alone. "The vineyards that developed so rapidly in California after 1848 were planted in or near the original vineyards which the Spanish had laid out . . . the state's thirty million vines were producing upwards of seven million gallons of wine. The Spanish introduced raisin culture . . . wheat . . . flax . . . cotton seeds" (McWilliams 1969:32-33), and the many other resources noted previously. Indian labor contributed greatly to agricultural expansion and maintenance. Spaniards, Mexicans, and later other groups benefited from plentiful, cheap Indian labor, which made labor-saving technology unnecessary. "The plan was that the Indians should raise their own food and supply themselves with all the necessary items. . . . They were also to maintain the missionaries and furnish much of the food needed in the presidios" (Borah 1970:11).

As a result of native labor, rancho social life bustled in the postcolonial period, especially for richer criollos and mestizos. In the lucrative livestock industry, for instance, the cattle roundup season involved several weeks of work, followed by a time of feasting and drinking. "Men did not prepare for the future, as such. They did do hard work when it was necessary and did take pride in it, but more in anticipation of the fun that came right at the end of it, rather than for any anticipated distant need. Owing to a happy combination of good climate, ample land, and cheap Indian labor, the rancho order worked smoothly on the basis of this value system" (Pitt 1968:12-13).

Even the work was designed for entertainment and included numerous contests of roping and bull-dogging. Fiestas for religious, marital, baptismal, and other important occasions were common and sometimes lasted a week. Often rancheros throughout California were invited to the affair. Hired hands, vaqueros, and some domestic servants also participated, though they might celebrate in separate rancho buildings.

Like politics and philosophy, ranchero social habits were patterned on those of upper-class Mexico City residents. A formal social etiquette prevailed, which seems pretentious or bizarre in a region far removed from sophisticated civilization. A rustic environment had generally not prevented criollos and mestizos from life's enjoyments. They maintained the social rituals of their antecedents in spite of the difficult circumstances. This was less true of New Mexicans, who over two centuries had fashioned a sociocultural life more suited to their environment (Sanchez 1967:4).

COLOR (*Mestizaje and lingering racism*)
First challenges to racism

"In Mexico 'race' mixture had proceeded even more rapidly since independence than it did in colonial days. . . . Although legal distinctions as to race were terminated in 1822, in many cases racial terminology continued to be applied in official documents" (Navarro 1970:145). The race question became even more important with the spread of mestizaje. "The process of miscegenation by which the Indian and white races intermarried to form the mestizo group greatly changed the racial composition of Mexico during the nineteenth century" (Turner 1967:72). According to census figures, mestizos

Fig. 6-3. Criollo couple. (Drawing by Mary Nunez.)

rose from 27.3% of the population in 1824 to 53% in 1900, becoming the majority group in Mexico. Criollos and some mestizos who passed for white were the first to challenge racism. Motives for their actions varied, but racial tolerance was the primary reason for many; also, enlightened philosophical viewpoints had become fashionable. Equally significant was the fact that criollos linked their egalitarianism with the notion of human progress (Bazant 1977:65).

Problems of redefinition

The hidden motive for the criollos' nondeprecating view of mestizos may have been that they too were of mixed racial background. Perhaps they felt guilty about hiding this fact, but more likely they wanted to eliminate the barriers that had kept them from advancement. Unfortunately they were not motivated enough to nullify the conditioned psychological effects of the colonial past. Even radical liberals such as Zavala continued to support racist practices, as his argument for the expulsion of Indians shows: "he urged them to 'force the barbarians to organize themselves into regular societies or leave the national territory, as the North Americans are doing with their Indians'" (Navarro 1970:147).

Although criollos became more inclined to reevaluate the effects of racism, they were too imbued with the past to break with it completely. While seeking improvements, they still agreed that the lower classes prevented full national development. "In searching for the causes of backwardness, the Latin American elite conveniently pinpointed . . . the 'apathy, indolence and improvidence' of the masses" (Stein and Stein 1970: 183).

Role of mestizos

Mestizos generally fell in with this attitude, and thus "independence turned the Mexicans into the 'Gachupines of the Indians'" (Navarro 1970:148). They created even more suspicion among Indians by mistreating them in order to obtain more favorable positions for themselves. As previously noted, social conditions forced mestizos into this path. "Alongside the Indian villages and the entrepreneurial communities located near haciendas, mines, or mills, there developed loosely structured settlements of casual farmers and workers, middlemen and 'lumpenproletarians' who had no legal place in the colonial order . . . the very marginality of their origins and social position forced them to develop [antisocial] patterns of behavior" (Wolf 1965:89). "Restrictions on economic activity and the dead-end street which confronted the rejected castas [half-breeds] created urban slums, which in turn spawned an indigent population always ready for any situation which might bring profit" (Cumberland 1968:57).

In addition, despite a national mood bent on curbing racism, mestizos attempted to pass as whites and became repressive fixtures of the social order (Stein and Stein 1970:115; van den Berghe 1967:45). The masses still were affected by the social mobility barrier, which emphasized facial features and the color of one's skin. An exception to that centuries-old social rule was rare indeed—although one exception was the presidency of the assimilated Indian Benito Juarez.

Race and class linkages

Individuals were ranked in the social class system on the basis of their racial appearance; race and class were tied together. Generally, the darker and more Indian-appearing one was, the lower the social class position, and the whiter, the higher. "The same age that witnessed the high bourgeoisie's rise and prosperity in Latin America also witnessed deterioration in the living conditions of the working masses, most of them people of darker skin" (Morner 1967:106). Furthermore, many leaders sought "to 'whiten' the population by encouraging European immigration and prohibiting the entrance of Asians and Negroes. [For example] Mora's [a prominent liberal politician] mid-nineteenth-century plan for the population of the country by white foreigners who should be given preference over the 'colored' races in everything that did not constitute a 'clear violation of justice'" (Navarro 1970:154).

The modifications that occurred were mostly in people's awareness of racism, not in any substantive changes that were made concerning it. Previously, a closed class sytem existed. "Opaque partitions" kept colonial classes separate, blocking out the vision one class had of another. Very few were publicly aware that the social class system was based on racial differences. With independence, the opaque partitions were exchanged for transparent (or maybe merely translucent) ones. Classes still were separate, but now people realized that the white Europeans were on top, the medium-hued mestizos in the middle, and the dark Indians at the bottom. The people on top or in the middle would not break the partitions, and as a result, racist ideology and practices persisted. "Legally, the use of racist terminology in official documents was ended in 1822. However, it continued until 1832 in certain remote or heavily Indian areas. In some states, the practice went on irregularly throughout the nineteenth century; indeed, with regard to marriage statistics, it extended until 1940" (Navarro 1970:155).

Indians in the north

These words of a Franciscan missionary illustrate native conditions in California and generally throughout the northern region: "The Indians of California may be compared to a species of monkey . . . and particularly in copying the ways of the 'razon' or white men, whom they respect as being much superior to themselves; but in so doing, they are careful to select vice, in preference to virtue. This is the result, undoubtedly, of their corrupt, and natural disposition" (Heizer and Almquist 1971:4). Taking into account the experiences of the Mexican Indians and mestizos, it is no wonder that those who were racially different became ingrained with an inferiority complex and negative self-image.

7

Breakup and transformation of the social order

CONTACT *(Anglo-American expansionism)*
Roots of contact

While Mexico was struggling with internal problems, increased contacts with foreigners—particularly Anglo-Americans—led to further disruptions. Initial contacts with the Anglo-American north introduced to Mexico concepts of democracy and social revolution far different from the Spanish social and ideological heritage. These helped to expand the adolescent horizons of emergent Mexico. However, further contacts soon introduced a decidedly less favorable concept: "In the mid 1840's a form of expansionism novel in name, appeal, and theory made its appearance in the United States. It was 'Manifest Destiny.' The term was not wholly new. . . . It meant expansion prearranged by Heaven . . . to the Pacific . . . or even over the hemisphere" (Merk 1963:24). To Mexico's misfortune, the "whole thrust of America's physical and cultural growth carried her inexorably westward. . . . Thrust in the way were three sparsely settled and inadequately protected Mexican provinces: Alta California, New Mexico, and Texas" (Bauer 1974:xix).

The notion that some superhuman power has ordained imperial expansion is not new; such ideas often motivate those who carry forth the flag of conquest. It is perhaps true that the underlying goal of expansion is to obtain new land and wealth for the victors. Thus, the Moorish and Christian conquests and the spread of Spanish Catholicism to the New World were accompanied by both idealistic motives and material rewards. Modern-day Marxian governments have fallen into similar patterns (Merk 1963:Preface). The expansionism of the United States in the nineteenth century also plainly exhibits a desire for land and resources (Ulibarri 1963: 169).

Expansionist tradition in the United States

The United States had barely come into being when the doctrine of Manifest Destiny was formulated. Americans felt an obligation "to over-spread the continent from the Atlantic to the Pacific" (Bauer 1974:2). Thomas Jefferson moved American boundaries toward Mexico by maintaining that the 1803 Louisiana Purchase included territory extending to the Rio Grande (Ulibarri 1963:9). Even before Mexican independence, Americans had settled in Texas and in some cases had participated in attempts to seize control of the region (Hollon 1961:96). As noted in Chapter 6, American merchants in the same time period had established a major commercial presence in California. Many had settled there, intermarried with the local aristocracy, and added their own antipathy to Mexican control to the Californios' desires for greater automony (Pitt 1966:4). At the same time, the flourishing fur trade in the United States had motivated hundreds of trappers and traders—often known as "mountain men"—to roam throughout the territories from California to Texas in search of furs (Horgan 1954:462).

Background to American takeover

The years following Mexico's independence from Spain were marked by increased American immigration into the Mexican frontier provinces. Many—perhaps most—of the immigrants carried with them the conviction that their new homes would eventually become part of the United States, and their activities helped to promote that idea. Americans in Texas and New Mexico chafed under Mexican government polices and spread their discontent among the local aristocracy (Weber 1973:83-84, 125-131). Communications from Hispanicized Yankees in California further whetted the Eastern entrepreneurs' desire for good seaports and expanded trade and also—whether intentionally or unwittingly—provided important strategic military information (Pitt 1968:12; Bauer 1974:12).

Mexican authorities attempted to secure the northern provinces by developing land-grant policies to encourage Mexican citizens to settle in the frontier regions. American immigrants were also given land and citizenship rights in an effort to win their loyalty to the Mexican government. While these policies led to prosperity for many settlers, some Americans viewed them as an expression of the government's weakness, and they continued their efforts to subvert Mexican rule. As one Mexican author has written: "We made a present of Texas to the Americans of the North, sometimes freely granting them our territory and sometimes giving it to Mexicans without resources or wealth for the ostensible purpose of colonizing it. With a few honorable exceptions the real object of the Mexicans in obtaining these grants was to sell at the lowest price and to the citizens of the United States the land thus acquired" (Castaneda 1976:310).

Officials of the American government encouraged intrusions into Mexican territory and sought, both openly and surreptitiously, to promote American incorporation of Texas, New Mexico, and California. As early as 1825, the government sent Joel Poinsett (whose name is now remembered for the Mexican flower he brought back) to Mexico with instructions to attempt to purchase Texas (Price 1967:16; Rippy 1926:5). A later envoy from President Andrew Jackson offered Mexico five million dollars for the territory (Acuna 1972:12). In California the United States consul Thomas Larkin "kept prodding the Californians to cast off Mexican government in name as well as in deed. As a longstanding friend . . . and as the government's leading money lender, he had their ear . . . and was reasonably confident that no blood need be shed in converting California into Yankee territory" (Pitt 1968:21). Some observers have likened these events to American dealings with the Indians. For example, Price writes: "The diplomacy of the United States with Mexico reflected the prevailing judgement of the American people on Mexicans. The attitude was that there was very little difference between an Indian and a Mexican; serious and respectful diplomacy was out of place in either case" (Price 1967:17).

Repercussions of annexation

In time these developments led to open warfare and, despite fierce if disorganized resistance by Mexico and forceful opposition in the United States Congress, to American annexation of the territories that comprise the present southwestern states. In Mexico these losses set the stage for further instability, another major foreign intrusion, continuing hostilities along the northern border, and still-prevalent bitterness and suspicion toward the American government. For Chicanos living in the newly American territories, the annexation brought a new layer of oppression. What one author has said of early American immigrants to Texas proved to be true throughout the Southwest: "many of the new arrivals were aggressive, opinionated, domineering, and intolerant. They made little effort to disguise their feeling of racial superiority and their belief that their democratic institutions were God's bequest to a select few. The frontier spirit of equality was admirable, but it applied only to the white race" (Hollon 1961:107).

CONFLICT *(End of the Mexican-American War, continuation of strife)*
Texas as prelude

Texas was the first battleground in the Mexican-Anglo conflict. "Though the plan of operations was conceived in Washington, Mexico contributed directly to its execution. The colonization of Texas, thrown open to adventurers from the United States, afforded them the best means for gaining that territory without the disregard, the violation, or the infringement of existing treaties" (Castaneda 1976:308). Anglo settlers had no intention of listening to a Mexican authority whom they considered inferior. Moreover, Mexican control was tenuous; the center of power was hundreds of miles from this outpost, which made political and military directives nearly inoperative. When Mexico sent in troops to stop the generous Anglo colonization program, it was too late. The clamor for a free and independent nation was led by influential Anglo leaders and dissident Mexicans (Connor and Faulk 1971:31). After a major, if bloody, Mexican victory in 1835 in which General Santa Ana demolished the Alamo defenders, an army led by Sam Houston caught Santa Ana napping at San Jacinto. The defeat of Santa Ana's forces necessitated his acceptance of Texas independence (Meier and Rivera 1972:61), and the Lone Star Republic was born in 1836.

The loss of Texas led almost directly to Mexican military conflicts with the United States (Fuller 1936:38). For ten years (1836 to 1846) there were constant battles, forays, and skirmishes between the rebel Texans and the Mexicans, most ending in a stalemate. "It was fortunate for the Texans

Fig. 7-1. Mexican cavalryman. (Drawing by Mary Nunez.)

that Mexico had too much trouble at home to send any considerable force to Texas for several years after the defeat of Santa Ana at San Jacinto . . . some leaders undertook to make a general war along the frontier until such time as the Mexicans would be prepared to make good their claims to the struggling young republic" (Webb 1935:48). The Mexican congress never legally ratified a treaty to give Texas an independent status. Although the United States remained publicly neutral to placate domestic political enmity, Texas was admitted to the union as soon as approval could be secured. This annexation occurred despite congressional opposition based on fears for trade relations with Mexico and on northern antislavery sentiment (for Texas was admitted as a slave state).

Texas annexation and intrigue

By annexing Texas, "the United States inherited this state of smoldering war. Indeed, according to announcements by the Mexican Government made while various propositions for annexation were under consideration, the mere fact of annexation was to be regarded by Mexico as a declaration of war" (Henry 1950:17). By following the 1844 Democratic Party platform, which advocated western expansion and Texas annexation, the newly elected President James K. Polk placed the United States on a collision course with Mexico (Hollon 1961:154-157; Price 1967:114-115). However, a new dimension was added to the acquisition of Texas: Polk's emissaries were instructed to offer anywhere from fifteen to forty million dollars for the territories of New Mexico and California! In the eyes of the Mexicans, this overture added insult to injury. The Mexicans considered the American annexation of Texas illegal because Mexico had never ratified Texas independence. Moreover, the annexation of Texas was in violation of the terms of the 1819 Adams-Onis American treaty with Spain, which specified that the western boundary of the United States was to be the Sabine River, the present-day border of Louisiana. This line was clearly outside the area of Mexican Texas (Horgan 1954:475; Livermore 1969:24). To complicate matters further, the United States government accepted the Texas claim of the Rio Grande as the boundary between the alleged independent Texas and Mexico proper. "In an effort to encourage Texas to accept annexation, he [Polk] assured leaders of the Lone Star Republic that the administration would uphold their exaggerated claims to the Rio Grande, even though the Nueces River, about 150 miles to the north, had been the traditional border of Texas and had been widely recognized as such by both the United States and Mexico. . . . Here Polk was on shaky ground because the Rio Grande had never been the recognized border of Texas, and the area between the Rio Grande and Nueces was, at best, disputed territory" (Schroeder 1973:8, 11). The American offer to purchase additional territory (without negotiating the status of Texas) was viewed as a subterfuge, for it seemed plain that the United States intended to take it anyway. "Inexorably, it seemed, the nation moved its boundaries westward, often by provoking its neighbors into war. In the mid-1840's, Mexico was the target. Anglo-Americans could not resist expansion into territory that seemed so lucrative—in this case, the unused land of the Mexican-held Southwest" (Acuna 1972:19).

Declaration of war

Polk was prepared for war in any event. An engagement involving the American and Mexican armies that took place between the two rivers was the excuse he needed. His May 11, 1846, declaration of war message to Congress stressed that "American blood was shed on American soil" (Merk 1963:88). This stands out as one of the most duplicitous phrases ever spoken by a president. War was declared—even though Mexican soldiers had lawfully defended Mexican territory from foreign aggression.

The Mexican-American War was speedily brought to a conclusion. By 1848 the United States had forced its version of the disputed Texas boundary on Mexico and had seized additional Mexican lands extending be-

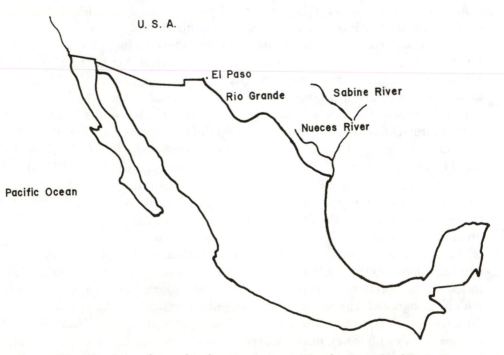

Fig. 7-2. Area of river border controversy. (Map by Jesus Medina.)

yond the Rocky Mountains. With Yankee victory upon victory, expansionist enthusiasm flourished. What Castaneda (1976:307) has described as American "plans to acquire what belongs to their neighbors" and Livermore (1969:13) labels "this lust for territory" was publicly proclaimed in many circles. "Prompt excuses have been discovered for this boa-constrictor appetite of swallowing states and provinces, in the glory of free institutions, the blessings of civil and religious liberty, and the extension of our industrial and commercial [enterprises]" (Livermore 1969:12). "Gatherings which assumed the character of revival meetings created enthusiasm for the idea of 'rescuing' the Mexicans" (Fuller 1936:81). Northern congressional opposition—whose ranks included the young politician, Abraham Lincoln—could not reduce this fervor.

Skirmishes and resistance

In spite of the seeming rapidity of the war, much Mexican resistance was encountered in both Mexico and the borderlands. Several incidents in California show that the Mexicans fought bravely and successfully (Pitt 1968:34). The revolt in Los Angeles, a skirmish at Chino (just south of Los Angeles), and the Battle of San Pasqual (near San Diego) are three examples of well-organized and -executed victories over American forces. The affair at San Pasqual was a humiliating defeat for United States forces, who lost over twenty men with more wounded, particularly since it involved the General of Western Operations, Steven Kearney, and his scout, the famous Kit Carson. Furthermore, not one Mexican casualty was suffered (Bancroft 1889:344-345). In New Mexico the revolt of 1847 by disgruntled *pobres* (peons and Indians) further underscores native resistance (Zeleny 1974:105-108; Weber 1973:125). However, Anglo numerical and technological superiority won out in the end.

The battle was lost, the war formally ended, but fighting raged on. There has been "a pattern of conflict which has prevailed from Brownsville to Los Angeles since 1846 . . . it becomes quite apparent that the Mexican-American War was merely an incident in a conflict which arose some years before and survived long after the Treaty of Guadalupe Hidalgo" (McWilliams 1969:98). The Mexican elite, gente de razon and ricos, who believed they would benefit from the new rule, were surprised when in only a few years their land was taken from them. As they soon discovered, the spoils of war go to the victors.

Unfortunately, those who caught the initial onslaught were the poorer Mexicans, the pobres, peons, and cholos. Since they were on the first line of defense, they were brought into contact and conflict much sooner. The few ranchitos they possessed were occupied immediately. Unlike the more

Fig. 7-3. A, General Winfield Scott's entry into Mexico City during the invasion of Mexico. **B,** Chapultepec, the fortress defended by young Mexican cadets. (Courtesy of the Library of Congress.)

affluent members of Mexican society, the owners of large ranchos whose land was stripped away piecemeal, the poorer classes were the first to react against these transgressions.

Outlaws or "social bandits"?

Although the actions taken by these Mexicans were sporadic and disorganized, the conflict sometimes reached a revolutionary level. Instead of fighting against soldiers in full military uniform, the rebels battled law enforcement officers such as Texas Rangers and sheriffs in the towns and hinterland (Webb 1935:177). "It seems to be a law of history, or of human relationships, that when two peoples of widely differing cultural traditions and technological development come into contact with each other, they are mutually hostile for a long time. Consequently, the borderlands between different people are the historic scenes of violence and disorder" (Clendenen 1969:1). In addition to this, there was the frontier violence that marked the period, in which outlaws of all races made life miserable for settlers and entrepreneurs. One writer referred to them as "prairie pirates, seizing any property that comes in their way, murdering travellers, and making descents upon trains and border villages" (Taylor 1934:31). Such conditions only worsened Mexican-Anglo relations.

Mexican guerrilla or resistance activity persisted through the nineteenth century. Anglos vehemently maintained that the Mexican rebels were nothing but common, ordinary bandits (Acuna 1975:43; Webb 1935:178). However, many became folk heroes to the oppressed Mexicans, and some observers maintain that this *social banditry* was revolutionary in character (Hobsbawn 1959:13-29; Vigil 1974:1-2). Social bandits usually flourish after a war, when their group has been subjected to a subordinate status. Native resistance mounts because the whole social order is changed in favor of the victor (Pitt 1968:75). It is noteworthy, however, that in the theater of agrarian unrest that central Mexico became at this time, the rebellious laborers and peasants who attacked haciendas also were labeled criminals.

There were dozens of social bandits in the border regions. Joaquin Murietta and Tiburcio Vasquez in California, Sostenes L'Archeveque in New Mexico, and Cheno Cortina in Texas are only a few of the more famous ones. Murietta's career apparently began because of the abuse he and his family received (Vigil 1974:34-37). Furthermore, he had resisted the discriminatory treatment Mexicans received in the mining region of California, where gold had recently been discovered (Ridge 1969). His spree of antisocial acts lasted from 1851 to 1853. Accounts as to his death (or escape?) vary, but one fact stands out: Resistance on the part of others continued afterward.

Fig. 7-4. A, Joaquin Murietta. **B,** Tiburcio Vasquez. **C,** Juan "Cheno" Cortina. (**A** and **B** courtesy of The Bancroft Library, University of California, Berkeley. **C** drawn by Mary Nunez.)

Another social bandit was Tiburcio Vasquez. Some accounts have him riding with Murietta, but it is certain that by 1854 he was branded an outlaw by Anglo justice (Greenwood 1960). Before he was captured and hanged in 1876, he said: "Given $60,000.00 I would be able to recruit enough arms and men to revolutionize Southern California" (Greenwood 1960:13).

The situation in New Mexico was somewhat different because many Indians joined the Mexican resistance (Swadesh 1974:64). "The law-less aspect in inter-group relations was due to influence [sic] of the Anglo-Americans, rather than the Spanish-Americans. . . . Many of the Anglo-Americans . . . were unscrupulous fortune-seekers who took advantage of the fact that the American system of law and order had not been extended as yet in any effective form in the area" (Zeleny 1974:150-151). The career of Sostenes L'Archeveque, one among many who resisted, is illustrative. "After his father was shot down by Anglo-Americans in . . . eastern New Mexico, the young man lost little time in acquiring twenty-three 'gringo' notches on his gun" (McWilliams 1969:120-121). Later, a group known as *Las Gorras Blancas* (The White Caps) became famous when they stood up against land barons, particularly since they escaped capture and punishment (Weber 1973:234).

Juan "Cheno" Cortina, the *Tejano* (Texan), was another Mexican who fought injustice and inequality. His life exemplifies the widespread resistance of the period and also the continued ties of Chicanos in the United States with Mexico. Cortina has been praised (Paredes 1958) and condemned (Webb 1935; Clendenen 1969). His career was an unusual one. He survived all attempts to stop him, finally ending up as a top official in the northern Mexican state of Tamaulipas (Acuna 1972:49; Vigil 1974:41). Early in his life, Americans labeled him the "Red Robber of the Rio Grande"; later, fellow government officials in Mexico distrusted him and there were apparent conspiracies involving him (Bazant 1977). He even fought on the Union side during the Civil War, clearly an instance of political expediency. "Throughout his life he betrayed, changed sides without hesitation, murdered and stole . . . and his lack of any moral foundation made it impossible for him ever to be more than a glorified bandit" (Clendenen 1969:42). So went the pattern of conflict—some claimed that resistance was pure and simple criminality, while others argued that it was based on a just cause.

Conflict as pattern

The Mexican people generally supported the individual acts of social bandits. "One thing, however, was greatly in his [Vasquez] favor, as was also the case with Murietta; in all those counties where he operated, he had the moral support and physical aid of his countrymen" (*Evening Free Lance* 1927:Preface). Frequent crowd protests occurred in which accusations were

made about the dual system of law enforcement—Mexicans were punished
and Anglos went free. The solidarity of the Mexican people was reflected in
countless incidents during the 1850's and 1860's (Vigil 1974:41-42; Mc-
Williams 1969:129-132). Opposition to the courts mounted when a similar
double standard was practiced: "after 1848 the Mexican was 'victimized by
the law,' . . . 'the old landholding families found their titles in jeopardy and
if they did not lose in the courts they lost to their American lawyers' . . . the
'Mexicans suffered not only in their persons but in their property'" (Paredes
1958:31).

In the former Mexican territory there were many adventurers
(mostly Anglos but some Mexicans) who planned and carried out filibuster-
ing missions against Mexico (Rippy 1926:90). Some even attempted to conquer Central American republics (Rippy 1926:93, 177). An undeclared war
pervaded the entire border region, and this state of affairs continued until
well into the twentieth century (Clendenen 1969:xv).

These and other notable events increased Mexican awareness of
their station in society. One avowed champion of the people in Los Angeles
was Francisco P. Ramirez, the editor of the newspaper *El Clamor Publico* (The
Public Voice). His coverage of events and personalities of the 1850's attests
to a tension-filled climate (Pitt 1968:189-193; Vigil 1974:42-48). While the
newspaper carried the usual fare, it also took up the cultural, economic, and
political problems of the Mexican people. An especially newsworthy item on
September 16, 1856, concerned the United States government's refusal or
reluctance to live up to the Treaty of 1848, a document that was clearly intended to protect Mexican rights (Vigil 1974:23).

CHANGE *(New system for Mexican-Americans)*
Treaty of 1848

"It should never be forgotten that, with the exception of the Indians, Mexicans are the only minority in the United States who were annexed
by conquest; the only minority, Indians again excepted, whose rights were
specifically safeguarded by treaty provision" (McWilliams 1968:103). The
Treaty of Guadalupe Hidalgo (1848) resolved several issues and established
a political boundary; through it, a huge region "was suddenly changed from
the northern-most province of New Spain to the southwestern province of a
new transcontinental nation" (Meinig 1971:17). The most noteworthy ar-
ticles concerned the protection of land grants and cultural rights, especially
the protocol added later, which referred to the Louisiana Purchase stipula-
tion of 1803 (Telefact Foundation 1968:23-24; Ross 1928:22-23). According to
this treaty, some Mexican practices would be protected. Land grants and

tenure rights established during the Mexican period would be respected on the basis of international law (Ross 1928:22). "The treaty . . . can and should be regarded as containing a guarantee for the valid and legitimate land grants in Texas, New Mexico, Arizona, and California" (Mawn 1975:61).

Furthermore, Mexican cultural customs and patterns were to be given equal consideration with Anglo culture; this meant recognition and accommodation of the Spanish language and Catholic religion. For example, in California the first state constitution was written in Spanish and English (Pitt 1968:46). In other regions there was a definite trend, at least initially, toward respect for the Spanish language (Zeleny 1974:274). This policy came to an end somewhat abruptly when a backlash occurred on several fronts. In addition to the conflict conditions already noted, "the worst violence has been the unrelenting discrimination against the cultural heritage—the language and customs—of the Mexican Americans" (Moquin and Van Doren 1971:181).

Ethnic rivalry and hostility

It was not mere coincidence that land rights and cultural accommodation declined sharply at the same time. There is clear evidence of Anglo encroachments and eventual absorption of both small and large parcels of Mexican property (Zeleny 1974:147-148; McWilliams 1968:120). One ob-

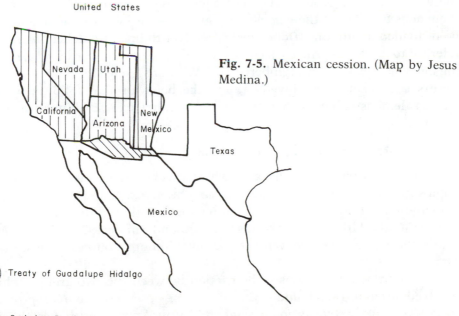

Fig. 7-5. Mexican cession. (Map by Jesus Medina.)

server of Texas says: "But it is certain that the traditional belief in unfair deprivation of private property in land remains an element in the background of Mexican emotional hostility to Americans. Both Mexicans and Americans told me their versions of what happened, the Americans often corroborating the Mexicans" (Taylor 1934:188).

Moreover, the dominant Anglos became increasingly convinced that socioeconomic and cultural privileges should not belong to a "culturally and racially inferior" people. For example, Anglos complained that the large ranchos were poorly developed by the Mexicans (Moquin and Van Doren 1971:190; Ross 1928:48). They also believed that Mexican customs retarded the full use of land and natural resources; that is, too many fiestas hindered large-scale development. The new leaders maintained that the cause of civilization would advance with land control in Anglo-American hands.

In this era of Anglo-Mexican relations, Manifest Destiny provided a cultural reason to expropriate land. During the war hostile attitudes were sown and nurtured by each ethnic group (Acuna 1972:19). When competition over land intensified, there was an increase in invective on both sides. During the war Anglo soldiers, many of them rowdy backwoodsmen, took special joy in killing "greasers," desecrating Mexican churches, and raping the women. The word "greaser" became a commonly used derogatory term for Mexicans. According to one writer, it referred to their greasy food (Paredes 1978:69). To Jeremiah Clemens, an 1840's observer, the ethnic label described the whole Mexican group: "The people look greasy, their clothes are greasy, their dogs are greasy, their houses are greasy—everywhere grease and filth hold divided dominion" (Dobie 1969:179). Not to be outmatched, Mexicans referred to Anglos as *gringos*, a corruption of the Spanish word *griego*, meaning one who speaks Greek (gibberish) (McWilliams 1968:115). Thus attitudes were set, epiphets were invented, and the behavior that followed was a vicious demonstration of how territorial conflict can set human against human.

Roots of friction: economic competition

The first target was land, which was gradually taken over by the Anglos. Soon after, Mexican labor was sought, secured, and exploited. With land and labor under Anglo control, it obviously followed that wealth (capital) would also fall into their hands (Samora and Simon 1977:177-118). As a result, the Mexican people were left largely without resources, almost destitute.

As noted previously, the friction between the two groups, which revolved around racial and cultural issues, obscured the real problem source—*economic competition*. Racial and cultural practices that establish a dominant/subordinate relationship are often obvious, but there is a reason why one group discriminates against another racially or culturally (Price 1967:18; Acuna 1972:7). The Anglo discrimination only added to the previous burden of racial and cultural oppression experienced by the Mexican people.

Variance in treatment of Mexicans

A complex situation arose. Those Mexicans who could not look and act the part of Europeans were accorded a subordinate status. Generally speaking, gente de razon had a somewhat easier time because of their Latin background. It was the poor, darker individuals unassimilated to the European model who suffered more abuse. In the words of a modern writer: "One cannot understand the discrimination that has been visited upon Mexican-Americans without taking into account the color of their skin and the fact that they look like Native Americans or part Native Americans" (Forbes 1964:4). The treatment received by the socially immobile, dark-looking, and Indian-acting Mexicans further emphasized the Anglo attitude that "the only good Indian is a dead Indian" (Price 1967:17). Many of the lighter-hued, Spanish types felt superior to the other Mexicans and "to this day, the don's [gente de razon, rico] descendants refuse to acknowledge their Mestizo ancestry or to recognize that their grandfathers acquired Mexican, not Spanish, land grants" (Pitt 1968:290). They were simply practicing an earlier form of inequality.

A Mexican intragroup split resulted. Because the more oppressed elements suffered considerably, they tended to group together against those who were above them on the social scale. To protect their interests (McWilliams 1968:121-122), many of the gente de razon joined Anglos in opposing the resistance acts of the Mexican masses (*Evening Free Lance* 1927:Preface). Despite this uneasy alliance, they too lost out in the end, becoming bankrupt and poverty-stricken in some instances. For "despite the division between the two groups, . . . Anglo-Americans regard them as one— as Mexican—except for ceremonial occasions when elements of the native-born become 'Spanish'" (McWilliams 1968:209).

The European-appearing "Latins" only had to worry about an inferiority complex based on cultural traits. If they desired acceptance, a cultural change was at least possible. However, a racial changeover was out of the question, further underlining the difficulties encountered by the low-status Mexicans.

New dimension to a sense of inferiority

The Mexicans' subordinate status instilled in them a strong sense of inferiority. Their racial makeup was the primary obstacle placed in the path of socioeconomic mobility. If that barrier was not enough, then cultural criteria were used to undermine their advancement. For many, it was truly a perplexing situation, since they were only beginning to master the Spanish language when a new dominant one was substituted for it. However, the new social structure was not so new after all, since it generally resembled the old colonial one.

Basis of new cultural blending

The native cultural style was being replaced by a new one. There was some trepidation among natives concerning this "time is money" and "cold materialism" ethic (Pitt 1968:23-24). Although some features of the Anglo social structure contrasted sharply with earlier systems, enough remained to remind natives of past experiences and adjustments. For example, natives were introduced to a new language, customs, beliefs, and values. "The Nuevo-Mejicano in Santa Fe, the Californio in Los Angeles, and the Tejano in San Antonio were swallowed whole into the North American political body. . . . The immediate change in customs . . . was from that of regional subcultures of Mexico to occupied territories within the United States" (Paredes 1978:73). Many Mexican traditions, such as Catholicism, were altered, and this further added to the confusion and growing sense of powerlessness. "The taking over of all administrative, trade, and cultural activities by the incoming Anglo-American naturally meant that the original settlers, in the new role of conquered and governed people, took a secondary role with minimum participation in decision making" (Campa 1973:19). Obviously, certain beliefs concerning the family, work, child-rearing, and the nature of individual and group life had to change if the Mexicans were to survive. Unfortunately, aside from concessions made to the "Spanish" elite (some of whom had participated in the development of the new society), and these only of short duration, most of the natives fared poorly because the Anglos made few efforts at cultural accommodation. In the words of one writer, "he mourns the destruction of Mexican culture in the Southwest at the hands of American arrogance and commercialism and declares the Mexicans in that area to be in a state of total moral defeat" (Robinson 1963:296). This "somewhat pessimistic view is an accurate assessment of the early years of domination, but eventually there arose positive cultural reintegration—but it took time" (Robinson 1963:300-301). As noted before, many Anglo-Americans were Hispanicized or mestizacized, thus taking the lead in cultural integration.

Cultural accommodation or disintegration

For most natives, a successful life was based on their adoption of new norms; refusal to do so often meant failure. In some respects the earlier Spanish experience had prepared them for such choices. Perhaps it is universally true that subjugated native peoples must shift and readjust to changing sociocultural conditions. In this prevailing Anglo world numerous types of native reactions were possible, and most occurred.

More and more Anglo-Americans and European immigrants poured into the Southwest, especially California. This was especially true after the gold rush (1850's) in the north and the completion of the railroads (1870's and after) in the south. Almost immediately the Mexicans, finding themselves in the way, began to establish their own communities. Since they played such an important role in the growing economy, they remained close to fertile land, jobs, and the homes of the wealthy. This choice was made in order to survive (McWilliams 1968:217-218).

It was necessary for Mexicans to integrate themselves somehow into United States society, even if only partially. All-out resistance was futile. Some reasoned that if this route were selected and held to, they would surely suffer the fate of the American Indians. One avenue eventually taken, the era of social bandit activity notwithstanding, was for Mexicans to group together for defense. Many Mexicans were still being abused without provocation. Suspicion and distrust characterized the Anglo attitude, for Mexicans were perceived as deceitful, treacherous people. Therefore, staying within their own spatial and social boundaries, both groups became isolated from each other (Grebler et al. 1970:82-89; Camarillo 1979:53).

Growth of economy

During this time the Anglos built a great economic empire. As mentioned previously, many Indian-Spanish-Mexican practices were borrowed by Anglo entrepreneurs. These traditions, readapted by the Anglos, became the mainstays of the Southwest—mining, irrigation and riparian rights, ranching and cattle-raising, and so on (Richardson and Rister 1934:363, 443-447; McWilliams 1968:133-161; Blackmar 1891:275).

In keeping with the dominant/subordinate system of economic relations, the Mexicans were employed in and contributed to many enterprises (Forbes 1964:80-86). Often they did not receive equal pay for equal work (Taylor 1934:116; Paul 1947:351-352). Although initially ethnic conflicts drove Mexicans out of the mining industry, when Anglos eventually gained control, they began to enlist Mexican workers. This was only the first of many occupational adjustments. "If this process of change bore heavily upon the gente de razon, it had a simply crushing effect upon the Mexicans. One after another the economic functions for which they had been trained were taken from them. . . . The Mexican then reappears in the local annals as a farm worker and livery-stable hand" (McWilliams 1968:93). Since Mexicans had to eat, they worked at any job, which usually meant the lowest.

Fig. 7-6. A, Decaying rancho in the late nineteenth century. **B,** Fieldhands at old mission in the 1880's. **C,** Adobe brick makers. (Photographs reproduced by permission of The Huntington Library, San Marino, California.)

Farm work as fieldhand peons was not new to Mexicans; it was similar in some respects to the Spanish colonial pattern. The difference here was that *campesinos* (fieldhands) participated in the building of an agricultural empire; in California, it later became unequaled in the world. In addition, when railroads spread throughout the Southwest, section laborers were needed to lay and care for the tracks. For this purpose towns owned and supervised by the railroads sprang up, inhabited mostly by Mexicans.

Adaptation strategies

As noted before, there were several types of reactions to these changes. According to one writer on California: "Submergence of the Spanish-speaking thus entailed various possibilities: for some, an irrational armed resistance through crime; for a few, assimilation into the mainstream of Yankee culture; and for still others, assimilation into the Mexican community" (Pitt 1968:262). Many variations of these reactions were possible. For example, some followed a separatist route and escaped into the hinterland. Eventually, though, the Anglo-Americans settled there, making the respite short-lived. Those who wished to protect and maintain ethnic traditions

Fig. 7-6, cont'd. For legend see opposite page.

founded town *barrios* (ethnic enclaves) or rural *colonias* (colonies). The colonias evolved from small ranchito settlements. When hostilities ran high, Mexican resisters or social outlaws found sanctuary in such places.

Although assimilation was difficult, especially for Indian-appearing Mexicans, many selected that approach. In large measure, the lighter the skin and the better the English, the smoother the change.

For some, "life . . . was not always a matter of conflicting cultures; there was often cooperation of a sort, between ordinary people of both cultures; since life had to be lived as an everyday affair" (Paredes 1978:72). Recognizing the benefits of the dominant culture, many Mexicans learned the English language and Anglo customs. And yet, particularly in border regions such as Texas, they also retained important Mexican language and sociocultural traits. Unlike assimilationists, they adopted a nativist type of acculturation—learning the dominant culture but not unlearning the native one (Vigil and Long 1978). For some the adjustment was shaky, especially since dominant group institutions worked against cultural accommodation. In many instances the result was a sense of marginality to both cultures. This was a repetition of the native experience in the colonial period, which sometimes had a positive result (a new, hybrid culture), and sometimes ended in confusion.

Thus, some rejected separatism, assimilation, and acculturation—or were forced out of these patterns by poor treatment—and continued a life of resistance. Obviously, there were serious problems for those who took this militant path. Resisters faced death or jail, both endings being poor examples of adjustment to the newly imposed social order. All of these reactions to change became integrated into the already broadly based Mexican sociocultural character. As the years passed, a new cultural synthesis developed.

REFERENCES

Acuna, R.: *Occupied America*, San Francisco, 1972, Canfield Press.

Acuna, R.: Mexican American history: a reply. In Hundley, N., editor: *The Chicano*, Santa Barbara, Calif., 1975, ABC-CLIO, Inc.

Alba, V.: *The Mexicans: the making of a nation*, New York, 1967, Praeger Publishers.

Bancroft, H. H.: *California pastoral*, vol. 34, San Francisco, 1888, The History Co.

Bauer, K. J.: *The Mexican War 1846-1848*, New York, 1974, Macmillan, Inc.

Bazant, J.: *A concise history of Mexico: from Hidalgo to Cardenas, 1805-1940*, New York, 1977, Cambridge University Press.

Blackmar, F.: *Spanish institutions of the Southwest*, Baltimore, 1891, The Johns Hopkins University Press.

Borah, W.: The California mission. In Wollenberg, C., editor: *Ethnic conflict in California history*, Los Angeles; 1970, Tinnon-Brown, Inc.

Camarillo, A.: *Chicanos in a changing society: from Mexican pueblos to American barrios in Santa Barbara and Southern California, 1848–1930*, Cambridge, Mass., 1979, Harvard University Press.

Campa, A.: The Mexican American in historical perspective. In Rosaldo, R., Calvert, R. A., and Siligmann, G. L., editors: *Chi-*

cano: the evolution of a people, Minneapolis, 1973, Winston Press, Inc.

Castaneda, C. E.: *The Mexican side of the Texan revolution (1836) by the chief Mexican participants*, New York, 1976, Arno Press, Inc.

Clendenen, C. C.: *Blood on the border. The United States Army and the Mexican irregulars*, New York, 1969, Macmillan, Inc.

Cline, H. F.: *Mexico: revolution to evolution, 1940-1960*, New York, 1963, Oxford University Press.

Clissold, S.: *Latin America: a cultural outline*, New York, 1966, Harper & Row, Publishers.

Connor, S. V., and Faulk, O. B.: *North America divided: the Mexican War, 1846-1848*, New York, 1971, Oxford University Press.

Cumberland, C. C.: *Mexico: the struggle for modernity*, New York, 1968, Oxford University Press.

Dobie, F. J.: *Guide to life and literature of the Southwest*, Dallas, 1969, Southern Methodist University Press.

Evening Free Lance: Crimes and career of Tiburcio Vasquez: the bandit of San Benito County, and notorious early California outlaws, Hollister, Calif., 1927.

Fagg, J. E.: *Latin America: a general history*, New York, 1977, Macmillan, Inc.

Forbes, J. D.: *The Indian in America's past*, Englewood Cliffs, N. J., 1964, Prentice-Hall, Inc.

Fuller, J. D. P.: *The movement for the acquisition of all Mexico, 1846-1848*, Baltimore, 1936, The Johns Hopkins University Press.

Glade, W. P., Jr., and Anderson, C. W.: *Political economy of Mexico*, Madison, 1968, University of Wisconsin Press.

Grebler, L., Moore, J., and Guzman, R.: *The Mexican American people*, New York, 1970, The Free Press.

Greenwood, R.: *The California outlaw: Tiburcio Vasquez*, Los Gatos, Calif., 1960, Talisman Press.

Hale, C. A.: *Mexican liberalism in the age of Mora*, New Haven, Conn., 1968, Yale University Press.

Heizer, R. T., and Almquist, A. J.: *The other Californians: prejudice and discrimination under Spain, Mexico, and the United States to 1920*, Berkeley, 1971, University of California Press.

Helms, M. W.: *Middle America: a culture history of heartland and frontiers*, Englewood Cliffs, N. J., 1975, Prentice-Hall, Inc.

Henry, R. S.: *The story of the Mexican War*, New York, 1950, Unger Publications.

Hobsbawn, E. J.: *Primitive rebels*, New York, 1959, W. W. Norton & Co., Inc.

Hollon, W. E.: *The Southwest: old and new*, Lincoln, 1961, University of Nebraska Press.

Horgan, P.: *Great river. The Rio Grande in North American history*, New York, 1954, Lippincott & Crowell.

Hutchinson, C. A.: *Frontier settlement in Mexican California*, New Haven, Conn., 1969, Yale University Press.

Livermore, A. A.: *The war with Mexico*, New York, 1969, Arno Press, Inc.

Mawn, G. P.: A land-grant guarantee: the Treaty of Guadalupe Hidalgo or the Protocol of Queretaro? *Journal of the West* 10:49, 1975.

McWilliams, C.: *North from Mexico: the Spanish-speaking people of the United States*, Westport, Conn., 1968, Greenwood Press, Inc.

Meier, M. S., and Rivera, F.: *The Chicanos: a history of Mexican Americans*, New York, 1972, Hill & Wang.

Meinig, D. W.: *Southwest: three peoples in geographical change 1600-1970*, New York, 1971, Oxford University Press.

Merk, F.: *Manifest Destiny and mission in American history*, New York, 1963, Random House, Inc.

Meyer, M. C., and Sherman, W. L.: *The course of Mexican history*, New York, 1979, Oxford University Press.

Moquin, W., and Van Doren, C., editors: *A documentary history of the Mexican American*, New York, 1971, Praeger Publishers.

Nava, J., and Barger, B.: *California: five centuries of cultural contrasts*, Encino, Calif., 1976, Glencoe Publishing Co., Inc.

Navarro, M. G.: Mestizaje in Mexico during the national period. In Morner, M., editor: *Race and class in Latin America*, New York, 1970, Columbia University Press.

Paredes, A.: *With his pistol in his hand: a border ballad and its hero*, Austin, 1958, University of Texas Press.

Paredes, A.: The problem of identity in a changing culture: popular expressions of culture conflict along the lower Rio Grande border. In Ross, R. S., editor: *Views across the border: the United States and Mexico*, Albuquerque, 1978, University of New Mexico Press.

Paul, R. W.: *California gold*, Cambridge, Mass., 1947, Harvard University Press.

Pitt, L.: *The decline of the Californios: A social history of the Spanish-speaking Californios: 1846-1890*, Berkeley, 1968, University of California Press.

Price, G. W.: *Origins of the war with Mexico: the Polk-Stockton intrigue*, Austin, 1967, University of Texas Press.

Richardson, R. N., and Rister, C. L.: *The Greater Southwest*, Glendale, Calif., 1934, The Arthur H. Clark Co.

Ridge, J. R.: *The life and adventures of Joaquin Murrieta*, Norman, 1969, University of Oklahoma Press.

Rippy, J. F.: *The United States and Mexico*, New York, 1926, Alfred A. Knopf, Inc.

Robinson, C.: *With the ears of strangers: the Mexican in American literature*, Tucson, 1963, The University of Arizona Press.

Romanell, P.: *Making of the Mexican mind*, Notre Dame, Ind., 1967, University of Notre Dame Press.

Ross, I. B.: *The confirmation of Spanish and Mexican land grants in California*, Berkeley, 1928, University of California Press.

Samora, J., and Simon, P. V.: *A history of the Mexican American people*, Notre Dame, Ind., 1977, University of Notre Dame Press.

Sanchez, G. I.: *Forgotten people: a study of New Mexicans*, Albuquerque, 1967, Calvin Horn Pub., Inc.

Schroeder, J. H.: *Mr. Polk's war: American opposition and dissent, 1846-1848*, Milwaukee, 1973, University of Wisconsin Press.

Sierra, J.: *The political evolution of the Mexican people*, Austin, 1969, University of Texas Press.

Singer, M.: *Growth, equality and the Mexican experience*, Austin, 1969, University of Texas Press.

Stein, S., and Stein, B.: *The colonial heritage of Latin America*, New York, 1970, Oxford University Press.

Swadesh, F. L.: *Los primeros pobladores: Hispanic Americans of the Ute frontier*, Notre Dame, Ind., 1974, University of Notre Dame Press.

Tannenbaum, F.: *Peace by revolution: Mexico after 1910*, New York, 1966, Columbia University Press.

Taylor, P. S.: *An American Mexican frontier*, Chapel Hill, 1934, The University of North Carolina Press.

Telefact Foundation: *El Tratado de Guadalupe Hidalgo, 1848*, Sacramento, 1968, California State Department of Education.

Turner, F. C.: *The dynamics of Mexican nationalism*, Chapel Hill, 1968, The University of North Carolina Press.

Ulibarri, R. O.: *American interest in the Spanish-Mexican Southwest, 1803-1848*, Salt Lake City, 1963, University of Utah, Ph.D. dissertation.

van den Berghe, P. I.: *Race and racism: a comparative perspective*, New York, 1967, John Wiley & Sons, Inc.

Vigil, D.: *Early Chicano guerrilla fighters*, La Mirada, Calif., 1974, Advanced Graphics.

Vigil, D., and Long, J. M.: Unidirectional or nativist acculturation? A case for bilingual education, Unpublished paper, Chaffey College, Alta Loma, Calif., 1978.

Wagley, C. and Harris, M.: *Minorities in the New World*, New York, 1958, Columbia University Press.

Webb, W. P.: *The Texas Rangers: a century of frontier defense*, Austin, 1935, University of Texas Press.

Weber, D. J.: *Foreigners in their native land*, Albuquerque, 1973, University of New Mexico Press.

Whetten, N. L.: *Rural Mexico*, Chicago, 1948, University of Chicago Press.

Wolf, E. R.: Aspects of group relations in a complex society. In Heath, D. B., and Adams, R. N., editors: *Contemporary cultures and societies of Latin America*, New York, 1965, Random House, Inc.

Zeleny, C.: *Relations between the Spanish-Americans and Anglo-Americans in New Mexico*, New York, 1974, Arno Press, Inc.

ANGLO-AMERICAN PERIOD
1846 to 1960's

The complex historical adolescent period in Mexico came to an end only with the civil war of the early twentieth century. For those Mexicans living in the northern territories annexed by the United States, it came much earlier, and with equal force, at the end of the Mexican-American War. The period of early adulthood in both countries and in both time periods was a highly variable process of maturation. During this period in the United States, the resident Chicano population confronted a society that passed through a major civil war, abrupt and strife-ridden industrialization and urbanization, two world wars and several lesser wars, and periods of capitalistic expansion and depression. Throughout this time, Chicanos in the United States were also affected—primarily through the continuing northward migration of Mexicans into the region—by the turmoil of the latter stages of Mexico's adolescent period, the civil war that transformed that society, and the markedly different but no less decisive modernization efforts that marked the early adulthood stage in Mexico. Considerations of time and place are thus integral elements in understanding this historical growth stage.

The transition from adolescence to early adulthood is characterized by strains and stresses. On entering adulthood, many people view the future with uncertainty. Because of this perspective they remain transfixed and cautious and make unnecessary mistakes. Whether the errors stem from poor judgment or lack of experience, it is clear that maturation usually occurs only with trial and error. Maturation was a very uneven affair for both Mexicans in the United States and those in Mexico.

In the United States the postindependence adolescent striving for maturity was abruptly moved in new directions. Imposition of a new Anglo-American order made Mexicans aware of other groups and other social systems, especially in regard to important human links to the environment— jobs, homes, and health. However, earlier struggles and successes had already given Mexicans a sense of confidence. As a result, the momentum to make decisions, learn from mistakes, and, within limits, plan a new life course was definitely under way.

The factors affecting human migration, especially after the 1910 Mexican revolution, are an obvious illustration of this stage of growth. Although begun during the adolescent stage, before 1848, the pattern of settlement in the southwestern United States is a demonstration of the energy that causes people to seek out the new and unknown.

The Mexican people were like the nearly full-grown youth who has won some autonomy but must reassert his independence in the face of new demands of obedience and conformity. For some Mexicans the event took place after 1846, and for many more it occurred after the 1910 civil war. The Mexican people were dedicated to taking control of their destiny. Too much blood had been spilled, too many lives had been lost, and too many centuries had passed for them to acquiesce quietly to the new authority. Freedom whets the appetite for more of the same, and it also encourages defiance of anyone who wishes to curb or eliminate what already has been gained. Numerous setbacks characterize this age, but the Mexican people continued to move ahead.

8

Intact and stable social order

CLASS *(Industrialism and urbanization)*
Background to capitalism, roots of inequality

As the Chicano people entered their early adulthood stage, the economies of the United States and Western Europe were becoming full-blown capitalist systems. Capitalism is a system in which the means of production and distribution (that is, land, factories, mines, railroads, and so on) are privately owned and operated—more or less competitively—for profit. Capitalism is the culmination of previous systems such as mercantilism, colonialism, and racial/cultural imperialism. The contemporary social class structure and its problems are strongly rooted in these origins. Soon after 1860 (when intense Mexican ethnic resistance subsided) the United States moved into this new age of commerce, investment, and speculation (Rippy 1926:361). Mexico, too, was caught in the web of late nineteenth-century economic expansion, as United States capitalists (also known as captains of industry or robber barons) invested hundreds of millions of dollars in railroads, mines, oil-wells, and agricultural enterprises (Rippy 1926:313-318).

It was an age characterized by intense class conflict in both the industrial and agricultural sectors of the United States. Strikes, bombings, arrests, and intervention by government troops regularly appeared on the front page of newspapers. These developments were closely linked to the rise of industrialism and the increasing urbanization of the population. Under these conditions various types of laborers were employed in varying settings. For a few the economic expansion, industrialization, and growth of cities brought great wealth, for others a comfortable living, and for many poverty. The Chicanos, along with other minorities, were more often found in the last category. As a result of this system, by the mid–twentieth century one fifth (twenty percent) of America's families controlled three fourths (seventy-six percent) of the wealth, which means that the remaining eighty percent of the people were left with twenty-four percent of the wealth (Spencer 1977:65).

Obviously, this method of resource acquisition and distribution causes problems.

One result was that thirty or forty million United States citizens in the 1950's were poor, or below the poverty line of a $3200 income for a family of four (Harrington 1962:177). Within this category, the percentage of Chicanos was disproportionate to their total population. "The inordinately high incidence of poverty is one of the most serious problems confronting Chicanos. In 1960, 32.8 percent of the Chicano population in the Southwest were officially classified as being poor (1,082,000 persons in families)" (Briggs 1973:14). The figure was really higher because many individuals were uncounted, especially unmarried immigrant males.

Still, the largest number of poor people in the United States have always been white (Harrington 1962:181-183): "more than 12 million Caucasians are poor, over half of the American poor" (Pillisuk and Pillisuk 1971:3). Despite the significance of ethnic connotations, as verified by the

Fig. 8-1. Foreign-owned oil field in late nineteenth century Mexico. (From *A History of Mexico*, by Henry Bamford Parkes. Copyright © 1938, 1950, 1960, 1966, 1969, by Henry B. Parkes. Reprinted by permission of Houghton Mifflin Company.)

high incidence of poverty among Chicanos, the fact that white people also experience inequality and deprivation emphasizes the importance of the *class* factor. This fact cannot be overstated. As noted previously, the wealthiest families are comparatively few, but commensurate with their resources they have a considerable influence on social and political sectors of American life. However, positions of privilege and power have evaded most citizens, including millions of whites. Inequality (lack of wealth and thus limited social and political resources) is a fact of life for many citizens and especially for minorities such as Chicanos, who comprise a higher proportion of those in the lower socioeconomic strata.

The national class structure that evolved in this period can be divided into three main categories, each one having two subcategories: upper (upper-upper, lower-upper), middle (upper-middle, lower-middle), and lower (upper-lower, lower-lower) (Gordon 1963:90). These strata were based on income, occupation, housing, and various other factors. One's location within the system determined power, esteem, and prestige (or lack of them, in the lower levels). Most people were somewhere in the middle sectors.

It is this middle sector (following the lead of earlier bourgeois conventions) that set the pattern for national thought and action. Cultural membership notwithstanding, "Mexican middle class persons are more like American middle class persons in their general way of life and basic outlook than they are like lower class persons from their own country" (Penalosa 1973a:258). It is this life-style that many lower-class, socially mobile people strive to emulate. However, because of their typically lower-class standing, Chicanos have had to reach higher to attain that level. One statistical study of selected workers, which controlled for education and occupation, found that the total income difference in 1959 between Anglo and Mexican male workers was $2,050. "Of this total difference $1,141 are attributable to the different occupational and educational distributions of Anglos and Mexican Americans. The remaining portion of the difference, $900 can be [mainly] attributed to minority membership" (Poston and Alvirez 1976:107).

Chicano role in the economy

The foundation for Chicano poverty was set in the last century. Chicanos in several regions played a major role in building up the capitalist economy. When mining enterprises dwindled, for example, many mineworkers joined farm laborers who were already toiling in the fields. Besides the contributions made in the cattle industry as vaqueros and, later, the railroad industry, there were many other unskilled occupations filled by Chicanos (Gomez-Quinones 1977:29; Galarza, Gallegos, and Samora 1969:viii). According to one writer of the 1920's: "Today we are as a nation building a great empire in our Southwest, and we are building it, to a large extent, out of stones quarried from the human quarries of Old Mexico" (Stowell 1974:122). The same author notes that at that time millions of dollars of investment capital were "dependent for their productiveness upon Mexican labor" (Stowell 1974:40). Once again, the Chicano masses (Indians, mestizos, and other lower-echelon ranchers), who in earlier stages of their history had participated in building up other empires, did not appreciably benefit from the new wealth.

As these conditions were emerging in the United States, significant events were occurring in Mexico during the regime of Porfirio Diaz. The Indians and mestizos, mostly peons and low-paid urban workers, remained in a postcolonial state even though a degree of liberation had occurred. "Social inequality was taken for granted by both hacendados on the one hand and peons (mostly southeastern Mexico), tenants, and sharecroppers (Central and Northern Mexico, in a semi-servile state) on the other" (Bazant 1977:128). The hacendados, comprising approximately 1000 families, controlled ninety percent of the land, while eighty-five percent of the rural popu-

Fig. 8-2. Farm worker in the United States and peon in Mexico. (Drawing by Mary Nunez.)

lation was landless (Cumberland 1968:202). "The peasants felt that the hacendados had stolen their land. . . . They felt it was only just to demand that
their ancestral lands be restored to them" (Bazant 1977:129). Thus, conditions were ripe for revolt. While "the conservatives and the liberals of the
earlier conflicts had made their peace under Diaz and were content with the
fruits of the bargain [this] compromise was ruptured by the common people,
the peasants, the Indians, the city laborers" (Tannenbaum 1933:115).

The 1910 Mexican revolution, then, had the earmarks of a common people's revolt. Before the civil war erupted, however, there were recur-
ring attempts by opposition leaders to unseat Diaz. The sentiment against
him mounted, and eventually a coalition overthrew his rule. One member of
the opposition, Diaz Soto y Gama, had this to say in 1910: "Mexico was ruled
by a narrow, unpatriotic, dictatorial clique, which catered to the interests of
foreigners and especially the Catholic Church, [and] were conspiring to take
over the nation and destroy every last remnant of earlier revolutionary reforms. . . . The ultimate target of . . . the attack was Porfirio Diaz: the Caudillo who betrayed democracy" (Cockcroft 1968:98).

The Mexican civil war lasted throughout the decade and even into
the 1920's. Agrarian reform was a key issue for the masses. "The military
leaders who have achieved fame in the movement were children of the upheaval: Pancho Villa, Obregon, Zapata, Calles, Amaro, and others like them.
They were all unknown, unheralded, children of peasants, of Indians, bare-
footed in their childhood. The Revolution made them, gave them means and
support" (Tannenbaum 1933:115-116). Many of their demands were granted
totally, others only partially, and still others not at all. Like most revolutions,
the Mexican revolution broke the bondage of earlier ages, bringing Mexicans
more fully through adolescence and on to early adulthood. But, again like
many revolutions, unresolved questions remain to this day.

Few would disagree that the Mexican masses generally benefited
from the upheaval. Although other observers (Villegas et al. 1974:151) have
used different frameworks in discussing postrevolutionary Mexico, the following summary will suffice here. The Institutional Revolutionary Party
(PRI) is the ruling party of contemporary Mexico, and its spokesmen maintain that every presidential regime (each one lasting six years) is part of a
"continuing, permanent revolution." After the PRI was instituted in the
1920's, political turmoil quieted. During the 1930's President Lazaro Carde-
mas led the nation toward improving social conditions. From 1940 to 1960
the Mexican government emphasized economic and technological development, but after 1960 there was a turn to a "balanced revolution" (a pragmatic mix of political, social, and economic reforms as needed, according to
the leaders) (Cline 1963:191).

Fig. 8-3. A, Mexican urban workers at the time of the revolution. (From Turner, J. K.: *Barbarous Mexico*, Austin, 1969, University of Texas Press.) **B,** Street vendor in central Mexico.

Fig. 8-3, cont'd. C, Unemployed urban nomad. **D,** Modern southern Mexican Indians.

Fig. 8-4. Principal figures behind the Mexican revolution. (Drawing by Jeffrey Huereque.)

Fig. 8-5. Both sexes showed a fighting spirit. (Drawing by Mary Nunez.)

Effects of 1910 revolution on the United States: the push-pull factor

Mexico was profoundly transformed by the 1910 revolution, resulting in a definite maturation. However, the revolution also had a significant impact on the United States. For one thing, social unrest in Mexico and the destruction of human ties to the land brought internal and external migration. Most adult Chicanos presently living in the United States have a parent or grandparent who migrated to the United States during that time. While it is important to note that the presence of immigrants reinvigorated the Mexican culture in the United States and added a more determined, militant element to the labor struggle, it is the immediate features of immigration that concern us here.

Along with the "push" factor stemming from the strife in Mexico, an economic "pull" force was simultaneously operating in the United States (Nelson-Cisneros 1975:240). "The movement of Mexican workers to the

United States was inextricably linked to the economic development of the American Southwest" (Reisler 1976:3). This push/pull reciprocity in large part explains why Mexicans immigrated, some with permission papers and others without them. But there are also other reasons. The United States had closed the door to Asian immigration and soon after, in 1924, placed immigration quotas on southern and eastern Europeans, who had served as the United States labor reservoir for over fifty years. As a result, a new pool of workers was needed, and the Mexicans filled this need. Because of previous problems with Mexicans (conflict, resistance, hostility, economic competition, and so on), there was a general reluctance to admit this new "brown horde"; there was even a movement to include them in the 1924 quotas. "It was acknowledged that Mexican labor was desired, but that the Mexican was not. A migration policy that permitted, or otherwise made possible, temporary use of Mexican labor with minimal settlement of Mexican people was advocated" (Cardenas 1977:165-166). However, economic motives won out over social attitudes, and "farmers and ranchers in the Border states have been very glad to welcome Mexican laborers regardless of the path by which they may have arrived" (Stowell 1974:33), and regardless if legal or not.

The ebb and flow of immigration continued for decades. "In order to explain the origin and cyclical influx of illegal Mexican aliens attention must focus on the desire and recruitment practices of agribusiness with regard to Mexican labor . . . agribusiness has been influential in the outcome of state and federal legislation, which means that its influence has affected immigration policy. It is in such a manner that immigration restrictions have been periodically relaxed and special migration treaties enacted. The relaxation of immigration restrictions permitting the entrance of Mexican labor during World War I and the Bracero [literally "arms" or fieldhand] Program, initiated during World War II, are two outstanding examples" (Samora 1971:33).

Living conditions for these workers were poor, with no appreciable changes forthcoming for many years. Even when the situation was brought to public attention, few forceful efforts at improvement were made. The Mexican immigrant was paid lower wages than other local labor (Galarza 1964:31). "His wages were barely at the subsistence level, and his job was always in jeopardy. His housing and hygienic conditions were substandard. While wages were more favorable in factories than on farms, persistent job insecurity prevented the Mexican's community in industrial centers from becoming highly structured and organized" (Reisler 1976:117). As one study showed, agricultural communities are varied in their social reality, some more complex than others, especially with the rise of agribusiness (Goldschmidt 1947).

Life in an urban environment

The influx of immigration occurred at the end of the United States' rise to industrial prominence. A concomitant development was the gathering of more workers in urban areas. Mexicans were a part of this process. Some businessmen went so far as to state "that were immigration to cease, or be cut much below the present average by a quota, they would be left on the verge of bankruptcy" (Gamio 1969:30; Alvarez 1976:43). As Mexicans became increasingly urbanized, they were additionally affected by the problems of urban life. In 1931 one authoritative source reported: "In California manufacturing industries there are about eleven Mexicans in every one hundred wage earners. In factories where there are both Mexicans and other workers, the Mexicans constitute 17 per cent of all the employees. The proportion of Mexicans in a number of industries ranges from 2.4 to 66.3 per cent" (*Monthly Labor Review* 1974:56).

Participation in this transition affected Mexicans in several ways. "As an example, the work environment provided a new experience. . . . In the city the worker must contend with time and punctuality, transportation, machines, office buildings, crowds of people of different backgrounds, unions, bureaucracies and a whole host of other factors that might be quite strange

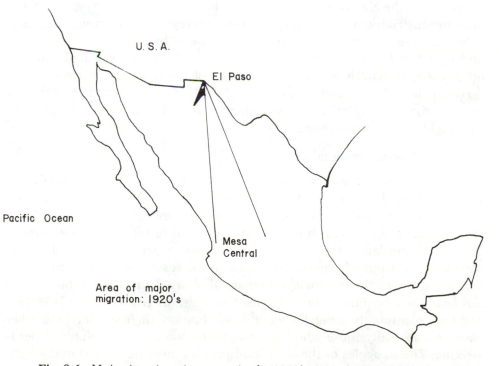

Fig. 8-6. Major immigration route in the 1920's. (Map by Jesus Medina.)

and different. Not all people have been able to adjust well to an urban set-ting" (Samora and Simon 1977:153). While a rural-urban transformation is in itself portentous, the Chicano case must be viewed in a magnified form because it also involved a shift across national and cultural lines. For this reason, the Chicano tendency to establish ethnic neighborhoods (colonias and barrios, which were similar to other immigrants' housing patterns) was continued and even enlarged.

As previously mentioned, this settlement pattern functioned in two basic ways: it protected and preserved cultural lifeways, and it pro-tected groups from social abuse and discrimination. Many social problems that originated with the first groups were, in turn, transmitted to the new arrivals. Accordingly, "a group of Mexican laborers, therefore, means at once a new Mexican settlement in the United States or an old one enlarged, and since an overwhelming proportion of the Mexicans who come into the coun-try are very poor, various social problems are more or less inevitable in every Mexican colony" (Stowell 1974:42; Samora 1971:17). Besides suffering from an oppressive labor position, Mexicans became victims to serious social ills that further undermined their development and well-being.

If this were not enough, dominant Anglo institutions attempted to thoroughly reenculturate the populace. In this the Chicano experience par-allels that of the Native American. "The political values and attributes of the urban-industrial way are propagated through regular contact with the out-side, they are taught by the educational system, by the outside observers, and by those Indians [or Chicanos] who have been acculturated into the other value system. Nonetheless, remnants of the Indian way are still pre-served, primarily in the private culture of the home" (Krueger 1973:89). This process significantly affected class placement and will be discussed more thoroughly later in this chapter.

Internal colonialism

Economic and social problems have existed internationally as well as nationally. For example, today thirty-five percent of the world's popu-lation earns ninety-three percent of the total income, leaving the remaining seven percent of the wealth for sixty-five percent of the population, figures shockingly similar to the national proportions (Starr 1978:354). These in-equities stem from who possesses and controls resources, both natural and human, and how the products of human labor are distributed. While Chica-nos have their own unique role in this world drama (Bustamante 1978:186) and have continually struggled against domination, their similarity to other peoples (especially those who have undergone some sort of colonial rule) is striking. The struggles of these colonial peoples must be viewed in the light of global history, especially in regard to the recent wars of national self-determination.

It is clear that the United States benefited because of the land, labor, and wealth of Native American people. The Chicano variant of this experience has been called "internal colonialism" (Barrera, Munoz, and Ornelas 1974:282). Acuna's summarization of this dominant/subordinate system highlights economic, cultural, and racial inequalities and injustices that occur after a war of conquest in which the victors thoroughly subjugate the vanquished (Acuna 1972:3). This model can be applied to other national ethnic minorities (primarily blacks and Indians) in several ways: (1) isolation in separate ethnic communities (barrios, ghettos, reservations); (2) poor educational preparation; (3) lack of political power; and (4) as a function of the first three, inability to improve their social and economic conditions.

Early in their American experience, Chicanos had begun to exercise their rights as workers. "The discrimination which they encountered . . . had the effect of stimulating them to organize in self-protection" (McWilliams 1968:190). Many strikes occurred because Chicanos were unhappy that they received a lower wage than whites for similar work. In fact, "there were Mexican trade union responses to class oppression and conflict. These are plagued with difficulty, and met at best with partial success. . . . Trends toward spontaneous resistance movements and participation in radical and organized labor increased with the consolidation and expansion of industrial capitalism during the early twentieth century. . . . Throughout the United States [however] Mexican union activity was negatively affected by language discrimination in union proceedings, and by the preferential treatment given to the Anglo workers in job assignments at the work place and by general prejudice practiced by Anglo workers against Mexicans" (Gomez-Quinones 1977:62-64).

Chicanos led a series of farm worker strikes beginning in the early twentieth century (Arroyo 1975:139). In most cases they were the majority of the workers. Throughout this century they have repeatedly challenged agribusinessmen because of the large proportion of Chicanos in agriculture. "Nationally, 586,000 Spanish-speaking Americans were listed as part of the civilian labor force in 1960. Nearly half were engaged in agricultural labor" (Glick 1966:100). Improvements were slow in coming, however, for in some areas Chicanos were held in low esteem. For example, in Texas, "Many expressed the views that Mexicanos were a poor, simple, childlike group that needed guidance and close supervision. . . . Both patron and worker accepted the belief that the natural order of things was the superior-subordinate relationships of the rancho" (Foley et al. 1977:15). Similar attitudes prevailed in California, despite the union activity. "A large grower declares:

Mexicans are much to be preferred to whites. Once fixed, they are permanent and reliable. I do not think they are good for other types of labor'" (*Monthly Labor Review* 1973:181).

Strike activity soon occurred in other occupations, especially after urbanization (Lopez y Rivas 1973:42). The issues debated were based mainly on class interests: better wages, improved housing and sanitary conditions, a decent education for children, and many other improvements. This stance aroused the ire of Anglo employers and the general public and in many instances brought even more repressive counterattacks.

The inherent difficulties of a Mexican-Anglo cultural transformation were increased by the effects of urbanization (Penalosa 1973a:259). White workers in Western Europe and the United States had already experienced or were experiencing this endemic feature of the capitalist system. They suffered similar hardships and met repression when they sought to alleviate or eliminate such conditions. There were important differences for the Chicanos, however, because of their racial and cultural distinctiveness. This account from the Midwest explains an aspect of the difference: "Investigators found that rents charged Mexicans and blacks generally exceeded rents paid by European immigrants for comparable or even superior dwellings" (Reisler 1976:106). Other problems resulting from urbanization and severe economic inequality were poor sanitation and housing conditions, inadequate health services, crime and juvenile delinquency, breakup of the family structure, unemployment, and an overwhelming dependence on the capitalist elite for the means of livelihood (Price 1973:20; Moore 1970:145; Fuller 1974:9).

Depression, repatriation, and post–World War II mobility

Workers gradually left agricultural occupations for those in the city (Galarza 1964:41). During this transition, however, the United States was hit by one of its periodic economic crisis—the 1930's depression. "With the Great Depression of the 1930's, Mexicans bore the brunt of nativist hostilities and suffered massive deportations" (Betten and Mohl 1975:125). The public recognized the need for reform, but Mexicans were excluded from the widespread demands to improve living conditions. One irritant to the public was the Chicano migrant worker organizations and demonstrations against the usual poor working and living conditions. This was particularly true in the highly productive San Joaquin, Coachella, and Imperial Valleys of California.

By 1940 a New Deal compromise had been worked out with the Anglo majority workers. In contrast, Chicanos were deported wholesale. This deportation program, known by the less offensive word "repatriation," was originally initiated against dissident farm workers (McWilliams 1968:193). Eventually, "pressure mounted to remove aliens from the relief rolls and, almost paradoxically, from the jobs they were said to hold at the expense of American citizens. In the Southwest, immigration service officers searched for Mexican immigrants, while local welfare agencies sought to lighten their relief load by urging Mexican indigents to volunteer for repatriation" (Hoffman 1974:2). Under this program, several hundred thousand Chicanos, including thousands born in the United States, were "repatriated" to Mexico.

The government's failure to respond to the needs of agricultural workers only served to stiffen Chicano opposition. "The Mexican nationalism of immigrants often intensified in the United States. 'I would rather cut my throat before changing my Mexican nationality,' declared a laborer who had resided in the United States for twenty-five years. 'I prefer to lose with Mexico than win with the United States'" (Reisler 1976:114).

"But even throughout the years of setback, Mexicans were carried along with the tide. Increasing numbers moved into the middle class and out of the barrios" (Moore 1970:110). They did this "because of the nature of urban living and industrial production of the post World War II era of United States capitalism" (Alvarez 1976:47). In this "boom" period many Chicanos moved to the suburbs. Some even became lower middle class, with a few attaining a higher level after pursuing educational and professional career goals. In proportion to the total these were still a small number, but they reflect how aspirations of social mobility are joined with strategies of assimilation and acculturation. "Despite great obstacles, this population as a whole is clearly moving further away from lower-class Mexican traditional culture and toward Anglo-American middle-class culture, so that both its cultural status and its social-class status are changing" (Penalosa 1973a:257) (Lopez y Rivas 1973:63). This trend of making a cultural transformation a precondition to social mobility widened in the post–World War II years.

However, improvements during the post–World War II period can be easily exaggerated; since the previous "immigrant" generation started with nothing, any upward shift in the subsequent generation appears to be progress (Alvarez 1976:47). Chicano socioeconomic mobility had taken place, but the average family income in the Southwest was only $4164 in 1960. When contrasted with the average Anglo income of $6448, there was still a considerable gap. In addition, the figure of $4164 includes wages earned by all family members, not just the household head (Grebler, Moore, and Guzman 1970:126; Romero 1979:12). Other ethnic minorities, especially the American Indian, mirror these problems.

Trade unionism also benefited the urban working class, including some Chicanos. However, in 1960 "about 30 per cent of Spanish males [were] in the categories of 'farm laborers,' 'foremen,' and other 'laborers' . . . a considerable decline from 1950, when 42 per cent of Spanish-speaking males were laborers. An increase in the proportion of 'service' and 'operatives' workers is clear" (Barrett 1966:198). Service occupations tended to be low-paying and low in prestige (Grebler, Moore, and Guzman 1970:246). One of the most serious hindrances has been that "the Chicano is systematically deprived from earning a living by one of the most formidable forces in the country, the labor unions. Union discrimination and the general problems of unemployment are twin facets of a single evil which Chicanos face—special, often deliberately imposed social obstacles to their economic survival" (Romero 1979:69).

Failure of the political system

Chicanos have usually been nearly powerless in the political arena. The failure of the two-party system to provide adequate representation has created a sense of discouragement and apathy among them. "The obvious result of the political activities of the Spanish-speaking in the Southwest is the fact that they have three Congressmen and one United States Senator. . . . In fact, the phenomenon of the three Spanish-speaking Congressmen occurred only in the 1960's" (Martinez 1966:47). Democrats are popularly considered to be supporters of Chicano interests, but they direct most attention to the group only during election time. Between elections concrete programs have been notably lacking, and past promises are seldom kept.

Several methods were employed to effectively bar or limit Chicano political participation. One was the lack of a proper education, specifically in regard to political awareness and paths of action. "At the general level, then, the Mexican American people lack the education necessary to deal with the system effectively, and the community also lacks the college-trained leadership that could help them overcome this liability. Thus, the community does not have the educational resources to convert into political power" (Garcia and de la Garza 1977:68).

Gerrymandering (named after Elbridge Gerry, the Massachusetts politician who invented this partisan strategy) was used to redraw state and national legislative district boundary lines in order to favor one interest group, usually one of the two major political parties (Juarez 1974:305; Steiner 1969:189). The Chicano ethnic interest group was sliced, trimmed, and snipped into political oblivion. Greater East Los Angeles, with several hundred thousand Chicanos in 1960, was clearly an example of gerrymandering. The region was deliberately divided to ensure that no state assemblyman or senator would have to rely on a majority Chicano vote to win.

Chicanos were a minority in every district; only recently has this situation changed. Because they were unable to elect leaders who reflected their interests, their voice went unheeded. "It is because of such practices that the U.S. Commission on Civil Rights concluded that the Mexican American in California has been gerrymandered out of any real chance to elect his own representatives to the State legislature or the United States Congress in a proportion approaching his percentage of the State population" (Garcia and de la Garza 1977:144).

In districts that were mostly Chicano, other political methods became necessary. For example, in Texas "about 1915 it was charged that at Corpus Christi poll taxes of Mexicans were paid by Americans, the receipts for which were handed to the Mexicans just as they went to the polls to vote as directed by those who had paid their poll taxes" (Taylor 1934:234-235). In addition, where Chicanos comprised a clear majority (sometimes close to ninety percent of the populace), Anglo leaders would handpick Spanish-surnamed candidates to run in the election. When such candidates won, they followed Anglo instructions during their tenure. But even in their defeat the Anglos won, for their candidate took votes away from other Chicanos, who perhaps were running with the intention of serving the community.

Of late, Chicanos in Texas have moved to change this state of affairs, even if only on a small scale. "Thus the best publicized effort was the successful deposition of the Anglo political structure in Crystal City, Texas, in the early 1960's. In this venture, PASO [Political Association of Spanish-speaking Organizations] joined with some non-Mexican groups, notably the Teamsters and the Catholic Bishops Committee for the Spanish Speaking" (Cuellar 1973:568). This is a classic example of the reintroduction of democracy to the people, who in this case were ninety percent of the electorate.

It is no secret that the outcome of many United States elections is almost directly dependent on the amount of money spent. Money is a requisite for political power, and it is not one of the Chicanos' possessions. "By all these measures, then, Chicanos are lacking in economic resources. Therefore, Chicanos will enjoy very little political success if they must depend upon economic power to promote their political objectives" (Garcia and de la Garza 1977:67).

• • •

In summary, Chicanos have historically been members of the exploited laboring population, kept in a dependent, underdeveloped, and disadvantaged state. In the years between the 1848 Mexican-American War and 1960, those relatively few Chicanos who managed to escape such conditions usually had to abandon much of their cultural heritage to do so. In adopting Anglo-American patterns of success, they often willingly or grudgingly gave up Mexican ways. Many denied their heritage—claiming instead a Spanish background—to escape from economic and social disadvantages (Reisler 1976:105; Moore 1970:111). An awareness of Chicano acculturation and even assimilation to the dominant mode of thought and action is crucial in understanding this period. Was a cultural transformation a precondition to socioeconomic advancement (Vigil 1976; Moore 1968:25)? Did such a transition ensure material betterment? If so, has this changed? The answers will have significant implications for the continuing Chicano struggle.

CULTURE *(Assimilation vs. nativist acculturation)*
Rise of middle-class American culture and Mexican immigration

During the 130 years since the incorporation of the Chicano into the United States, American culture has undergone major shifts. Industrialization and urbanization transformed a primarily agrarian society into an international military and political power. Conflicts engendered by these processes led to the development of cultural differences among socioeconomic classes, but the prosperity born of industrialization also brought about a numerically and culturally dominant middle class. The core values of the middle class became widely accepted as typical of American culture, and the development of mass communications strengthened that predominance.

One element of this value system was the ethnocentric notion that "American" culture was superior to any other, and the frequent corollary that "American" people were superior to any other. As wave upon wave of immigrants poured into the country to farm the frontiers, man the factories, and build the railroads, the average American greeted them with disdain. Although the immigrant groups contributed greatly to the enrichment of American language, arts, philosophy, and cuisine, the "100 percent American"—as Linton (1975) noted satirically—refused to recognize that his daily life included the use of behavior, beliefs, and materials derived from hundreds of different cultural traditions.

Social and economic sanctions were therefore developed to impede the entrance of ethnically and culturally "different" people into the mainstream of American society (even though that society itself was changing rapidly). These created pressures on the newcomers to assimilate—to discard the "different" traditions of their countries of origin and accept the values and beliefs of the American middle class (including discrimination toward subsequent arrivals) (Hirsch 1973; Castaneda 1974). The sanctions, especially discrimination in employment and housing, also helped to create distinct ethnic enclaves within which old country traditions persisted and nativist revivals of traditional practices as a source of ethnic pride could more readily occur.

The decline of massive immigration from Europe and Asia after World War I was accompanied by a diminution of such enclaves and the cultural variation they presented. A distinctively Mexican tradition continued to flourish in the United States, however, owing to the continued immigration of large numbers of Mexicans. More obvious racial differences between the majority of Mexican immigrants and most Americans also contributed to the perseverance of Mexican culture; unlike the sons and daughters of European immigrants, who learned American ways at school, the children of most Mexican immigrants were noticeably different in appearance from the white majority and were less freely accepted by its members. (Similar constraints also operated with regard to Asians, American Indians, and blacks.)

Although retaining a distinctly Mexican flavor, the culture that developed among Mexican-Americans nevertheless was affected by the same processes at work in other cultural minorities. The result was a hybrid culture presenting a wide range of elements from both Mexican and American backgrounds (each of which is itself a complexity of various origins), as well as unique patterns created through a fusion of elements from both traditions. Language usage is one example. "Such a complex continuum has given rise to four types of cultural-linguistic personalities: the monolingual in Spanish, the monolingual in English, the bilingual, and then . . . there is the child who speaks a patois" (de Leon 1970:36).

The strength of Mexican-American culture lay in the fact that it could draw from these two rich cultural traditions, the mestizaje style of Indian and Spanish motifs and the entrepreneurial industrialism of modern life in the United States. And yet that opportunity also gave rise to grave problems, for important aspects of the two traditions were in conflict and many Chicanos found themselves unable to sort the valuable from the harmful traits successfully. A kind of cultural impoverishment sometimes resulted, an empty marginality, with young people in particular turning to self-destructive values and behavior.

The culture of the dominant majority in the United States was formed from many themes, partly because of the large size of American society (Arens and Montague 1976). Nevertheless, certain core values, rooted in what has been labeled a "white Anglo-Saxon Protestant ethic" (giving rise to the acronym "WASP" or, less commonly, "McWASP," to emphasize its middle-class identity), have been of particular importance (Gordon 1963:73).

Not least significant in this context was the value placed on physical distinctions: Irish, eastern European, and southern European immigrants were all once considered racially inferior by the average American, and that superior attitude persisted much longer toward people who were more racially distinct (Feldstein and Costello 1974:2).

In keeping with the rewards that the industrial state has produced, American middle-class society focuses much of its culture on work and on visible symbols of the value of work. "As with other workers in the American economic system, work plays a pervasive and powerful role in the psychological, social, and economic aspects of Chicano lives. . . . It has other profound, personal, and social attributes which influence . . . workers regardless of their occupational position or economic status" (Romero 1979:22). Cultural life was heavily influenced by this economic fact, as people were relatively secure with the necessities of life. In this atmosphere of material consumption they demanded a certain type of food, clothing, or shelter that they could select from a seemingly endless array. The necessary cultural accoutrements that accompany these possessions—words to describe them, values to guide human energy in obtaining them, customs and rituals involving them, and so on—provided cultural divisions to augment those based on class criteria. These standards motivated United States citizens, including Mexican-Americans. "The most important aspects of any 'culture' should be . . . the manner in which society organizes the productive labor of its members" (Fernandez 1977:157).

Contrast between American and Mexican culture

Not all people had the same attitudes toward motivations for success. The middle-class American ethic was an industrial society's reworking of western and northern European cultural traits that arrived with the early English-speaking immigrants to America. Besides the cultural customs, northwestern Europe contributed Protestantism, a tradition that subsequently evolved from a collection of religious beliefs and practices into a general philosophy of life emphasizing hard work and frugality (Gamio 1969:115). Implicit in that philosophy and explicitly stated by some of its proponents is the concept that material success is a sign of God's blessing and failure a sign of his displeasure. Several other points highlighted the culture. First, values emphasized a universe in which humankind had full mastery. Every person in society had an equal opportunity in all matters. If inequalities existed, it was because some people did not strive to reach their potential. In other words, it was one's own fault if he failed to achieve success. Furthermore, by work and achievement one could gain control over natural forces. Because of this optimistic opportunism, societal members conformed to a standard that would bring material advancement for each individual (Diaz-Guerrero 1975:111). If everyone adhered to this pattern, group success would be enhanced (Inkeles 1977; Diaz-Guerrero 1978:291-301; Kluckhom and Strodtbeck 1961:20-30).

One can perceive the technological orientation of this world view. The age of industrialism proved that machines could master tasks previously unheard of. This achievement infected the human spirit, causing humans to strive to make nature bend to their wishes. The Protestant ethic complemented this goal, for it "is based on the belief that those who work hard will be favored by God, and that those favored by God will be rewarded with material success on earth and spiritual salvation in heaven" (Foley et al. 1977:45) (Weber 1958). This is the legacy of the industrial revolution.

Traditional Mexican cultural characteristics contrast with those just cited in major respects, some sharply and others only slightly. The cultural contrasts between Mexico proper and its northern settlements in the nineteenth century were previously mentioned. This has continued to be true throughout this century (Moore 1970:130). Mexican culture has been extremely heterogeneous because of mestizaje, and the waves of immigrants varied in the cultural style each brought to the United States. They come from different regions of Mexico, and perhaps they represent a more urban-

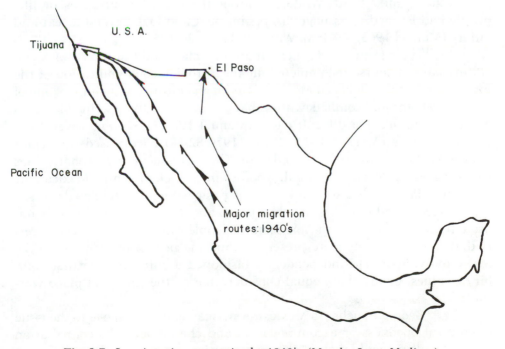

Fig. 8-7. Immigration routes in the 1940's. (Map by Jesus Medina.)

ized group recently in contrast to the rural people in earlier times. Also, of course, one must take into account the cultural changes that Mexicans underwent after several generations of exposure to United States customs. Thus, in over fifty years of immigration, numerous Mexican "cultures" were placed in the context of United States society.

Nonetheless, there are still some broad major features of Mexican culture worthy of consideration, at least to establish a basis for discussion. The family was of central importance, and work and the production of goods were for the group, not the individual. This fact deserves special mention because Mexicans also valued the "work ethic," but not for its own sake (Briggs 1973:43; Kluckholm and Strodtbeck 1961:207). Their past and present industry in agriculture has underscored this fact, despite former California Senator George Murphy's pejorative remark that "Mexicans are good farm workers because they are short and built low to the ground" (Servin 1970:140).

Generally, work organization and group cooperation were aimed toward fulfilling basic needs, with an emphasis on material gain. The present was valued more than future savings, and people were admired for what they were rather than what they did (Kluckholm and Strodtbeck 1961:30). Females were subordinate to males, and there was a clear preference for a patriarchal family head. While accepting the everyday struggles of life, people had learned to assuage disappointment and look beyond defeat and failure (Manuel 1965:34-44; McWilliams 1968:124-125).

These sketches of American middle-class and traditional Mexican cultures are of course incomplete, but they provide some indication of the major styles that influenced Mexican-American culture and point to some of the syncretisms and conflicts within that culture. To fully describe Mexican-American culture is a difficult chore (Manuel 1965:31-32), and several observers (Romano-V. 1973:43-56; Rocco 1970:82-88) have raised important questions challenging such an endeavor. The assessment of personal values would vary with each individual, whether middle-class, white, Mexican, or a mixture (Padilla 1971:67). However, the basic values of future goals versus present needs and doing rather than being are clear contrasts. What is unusual in the case of Mexican-Americans (a people who blend several cultures) is that these contrasts were present within one person (Arvizu 1974:127). Many individuals had independently fashioned a cultural style that combined values, giving them equal consideration as the time and place warranted.

George Sanchez, a Mexican-American educator, spoke to the issue of cultural openness or accommodation and championed the contribution Mexican culture could make. "That contribution might well embody worthy elements of his culture—language, music, folklore, architecture, foods, crafts, and customs. The New Mexican's filial respect, his love of home and of country, and his fortitude in the face of adversity are potential resources to Americanism" (Sanchez 1967:97-98). This viewpoint contrasts with the sometimes negative appraisal some critics have given to Mexican culture (Kluckholm and Strodtbeck 1961:237).

A few Mexican-Americans were able to syncretize aspects of both cultures; they learned to plan for the future and live the present fully. They enjoyed work for its own sake, remembering that work was only a means, not an end, and therefore they could benefit from the fruits of their labor immediately.

Strategies and problems of adaptation

Acceptance of aspects of both cultures was a positive response to the problem of adaptation. However, there was considerable variation in the types of reaction. Many Mexicans took the route of assimilation (Kluckholm and Strodtbeck 1961:26). This strategy began after the American annexation when Mexicans lost their land rights and began to familiarize themselves with the new cultural standards in order to improve their economic conditions (Zeleny 1974:157).

Assimilation usually occurred after long exposure to the dominant culture, but there were some who decided to accelerate the process. If they had lighter complexions, for example, they might first prefer to be called American, but if forced to commit themselves, they would claim a Spanish descent. Hence, "in order to differentiate themselves from those who had been subjugated into a lower caste, the so-called Hispanos in New Mexico [or California] started calling themselves Spanish Americans [or Californios] some time around the First World War, despite the fact that their anatomical features were those of Mexican mestizaje and did not resemble Spaniards" (Alvarez 1976:48-49). One work on the subject points out that some Mexicans differ intraculturally: "history shows that most of the successful Spanish-American patrones were far more individualistic in their behavior than average Spanish-Americans, and fairly ambitious planners" (Kluckholm and Strodtbeck 1961:31).

In some instances this assimilation reached extremes in which people became flag-waving superpatriots and worked to master perfect English. They socialized their offspring to this end. In their efforts to rid themselves of Mexican culture, however, they often aroused the wrath of fellow Mexicans. "No Mexican is so despised as he who denies his race" (Gamio 1969:93).

Assimilation entails the complete transformation from one culture to another (Castaneda 1974:23). There was no mistaking what assimilated Mexicans did politically, economically, religiously, and socially, even seeking marriage partners from the dominant group. Interestingly, in New Mexico the Hispanos were able to effect a coalition with the Anglos because of Mexican willingness to accept the new culture. This alliance, known as the Santa Fe Ring and patterned after East Coast political machines, dominated the state up to the present generation. In this case assimilation meant retention of political and economic power.

For many Mexican-Americans, however, assimilation was a sad experience because there were few accommodative mechanisms in the dominant social system to expedite the process. They were in limbo; they had changed but no one cared to find a place for them in middle-class white society. Many even changed their telltale Spanish surname: Martinez to Martin, Ramirez to Raymer, and Barajas (meaning cards) to Cards.

Another adaptive alternative for Mexicans was to change their secondary social allegiances while maintaining the primary ones. This meant functioning in all the important secondary Anglo areas to improve life's opportunities but keeping a primary Mexican ethnic identity, social relations, and cultural traditions (Gordon 1963:36). Such people would take the path of acculturation but maintain a primary, private life by speaking Spanish to their families and following Mexican customs. During work hours, at school, or in any place outside the primary area, they would adopt an appropriate English-speaking, Anglo-acting posture. According to a life-long advocate of this strategy, "Cultural buffer areas do exist and people living within their boundaries belong to both civilizations culturally" (de Leon 1970:43). Acculturation means living one's private life one way and public life another—or because of whim or need, mixing them up. Of course, there were "people . . . already selectively assimilating some positive functional aspects of the two cultures" (Diaz-Guerrero 1978:302). This dual process has been referred to as nativist acculturation: learning a new culture but not discarding the old one (Vigil and Long 1978).

Individuals who took this approach could refer to themselves as Mexicans if they wished; or, to reflect the bilingual and bicultural nature of their existence, as Mexican-Americans; or, to emphasize their secondary participatory rights, as Americans of Mexican descent. Whatever their choice of label, they still were equally (or almost equally) adequate in both cultural standards. As many other ethnic minorities in different times and places have discovered, there are psychological hazards for anyone who functions in both worlds.

What occurred in this regard was a continuation of the Chicano marginal syndrome that dated from colonial times. "For the basic conflict continues both in Mexico and in the thought of Chicanos in the Southwest United States. However, the original conflict, altered now by time and geography, has taken on a third dimension. . . . A triangular conflict has evolved" (Sanchez 1976:75). A person often found himself in a state of flux where first one trait was practiced and then a switch to another pattern was made. For example, one southern Texas Chicano noted: "I think like an Anglo and I act like an Anglo but I'll never look like an Anglo. Just looking at me, no one could tell if I am an American or one of those blasted Mexicans from across the river. It's hell to look like a foreigner in your own country" (Madsen 1964:8).

Drinking, fighting, anomie (normlessness), drugs (a modern way of escaping problems), and other forms of cultural disorientation were often exhibited by individuals who were unable to fashion a stable bilingual and bicultural world and who were not securely rooted in either Mexican or Anglo culture. This phenomenon sometimes involved cultural conflict between generations (Gamio 1969:94-96).

This dilemma had several sources. For some it was a personal choice resulting from the pressures of cultural conformity and discrimination. One of my former students once expressed it in this way:

> "I didn't know you were Mexican?" "I'm not, I'm Italian." I can actually remember saying this to my friends in school yards, dances and anywhere else the dreaded question would pop up. I tried as hard as possible not to be a Mexican, for that was the only way I thought I could be happy. Due to my light color and height I could easily pass for a white with the right clothes on. When the "surfer" craze was on I was right in there, wearing the latest surfer get-up I could find; but the funny thing was that I always felt so self-conscious, the fun was gone from acting this way. You must understand that at that age I never thought about who I really was, but just what I wanted to be, which changed from white fad to fad. In history class I remember being totally embarrassed when we studied Mexico. They would show films of old adobe huts with the mother patting tortillas and the father working in the fields. Everyone thought this was funny and I remember wishing that Mexico was all skyscrapers to show the others how great we really were.

Perhaps the most forceful factor stemmed from socioeconomic issues. As one investigator on ethnic identity stated, "It was extremely difficult to extricate psychological problems from environmental ones" (Bayard 1978:115). Frustration and discouragement often resulted when someone learned all he could about his occupation but was paid lower wages than the others doing the same work or was passed over when the time for promotion arrived. "The long history of discrimination against Chicanos coupled with the antagonism toward Mexican culture expressed by Anglos has only served to heighten the cultural alienation felt by many Chicanos" (Briggs, Fogel, and Schmidt 1977:23) (Moore 1970:369-370).

All this pressure grew in the individual, making him feel marginal in every respect to middle-class American life. Worse yet, "when one culture succeeds in socializing another to the extent that the other culture (usually an ethnic culture) believes in its own inferiority—and incapacity for political actions—it has succeeded in instilling a virulent form of self-racism" (Hirsch 1973:17). This accounted for much of the intragroup ethnic "sensitivity" to imagined and real slights, whether from language differences, surname changes, or a contrast in cultural life-styles and customs (Rubel 1966:244). One novel titled *Pocho* (a term for a Mexican-American with Anglo mannerisms) emphasizes the concern with resisting self-hate, when a father tells his son: "Only that, promise me—that you will be true unto yourself, unto what you honestly believe is right. And, if it does not stand in your way, do not ever forget that you are Mexican" (Villarreal 1970:169).

As mentioned before, a strong contributor to this self-hate was the social snubbing one received because of racial appearance. It was particularly offensive to those who had learned the new culture and were prepared to contribute but were unable to change their race or appearance. Of course, some elements within American society challenged such ethnocentric practices. For example, anthropologists were among those who advocated "cultural relativity," that is, a belief that each world culture is intrinisically worthy of respect and appreciation. Also, many humanitarian people and organizations accepted those who were ethnically different and sometimes offered aid in their defense.

Besides the negative individual experiences, discrimination against Mexican-Americans as a group also contributed to and exacerbated the situation. Law enforcement personnel, for instance, often mistreated and physically abused Mexican-Americans because they lived in the *barrio* or *colonia* community. This example from Arizona is reasonably reflective of the pattern throughout the Southwest: "Mexican Americans living in South Phoenix, a predominantly Mexican American area, will be picked up for questioning by the police, sooner or later, even though they may have no police record" (U.S. Commission on Civil Rights 1970:10). Residence in an area considered to have a high crime rate meant the increased possibility of police questioning and perhaps harrassment. One former Los Angeles police chief was frank about it: "Police deployment is heaviest in minority sections of the city because, based on statistical reasons [the police chief] believes *it to be a fact that racial minority groups commit more crime*" (Morales 1972:48). One can imagine the confusion caused among Anglicized Mexican-Americans who had willingly and obediently supported the dominant social agencies and yet were treated so shabbily.

New syncretism: pachucos

"Knowing that both as individuals and as a group they are not welcome in many parts of the city, they create their own world and try to make it as self-sufficient as possible" (McWilliams 1968:241). Thus was born a unique, defensive, and creative reaction to marginality. A new culture was invented to curb the confusion. No doubt this syncretic process began earlier, when "cattle culture was a union . . . of Northern Mexican ranchero culture . . . with new technological improvements brought in by Anglo Americans" (Paredes 1978:69). However, the variant that sprang up in the 1930's and 1940's following large-scale Mexican immigration was especially significant. It was the beginning of what later became known as Chicano culture (Barker 1972:21-22).

Pachucos was the name given to this generation of Mexicans who attended Anglo schools in large numbers. Their life-style was innovative. Some observers criticized this pattern: "Dressed outlandishly . . . they quickly undid the hard-earned reputation of the prewar Mexican. Rejecting their own culture, the bizarrely attired pachucos . . . gave the Mexican community . . . an undeserved reputation for lawlessness, cowardice, and disloyalty" (Servin 1974:117). "The pachuco does not want to become a Mexican again; at the same time he does not want to blend into the life of North America. His whole being is sheer negative impulse, a tangle of contradictions, an enigma. Even his very name is enigmatic" (Paz 1961:14). Others, while not championing the pachucos' cause, expressed a more sympathetic view: "The segregatory attitudes and practices, and the vicious economic exploitation directed against the 'Mexican' in California in the past . . . are responsible for the pachucos of today" (Sanchez 1974:123).

Even though much of what became recognized as *pachuquismos* (pachuco inventions) was actually *pochismos* (simple word mixing) (Galarza 1971:31), it is a fact that the pachuco style became more widespread at this time. The young student was caught in a cultural squeeze between school measures to induce students to adopt Anglo traits and home instruction to retain Mexican customs (Barker 1972:33). Rather than accept this state of confusion, many drew from both cultures to form a new one. Pachuco language symbolizes this trend. English was Hispanicized and Spanish was Anglicized, as these words attest: *Ay te watcho* (I'll be seeing you), *chante* (shanty), *daime* (dime), *brecas* (brakes), *bote* (jail, "can" translated into Spanish), and *ganga* (gang) (Griffith 1948:Glossary). In Texas a Tex-Mex argot has evolved, which often is created by adding a Spanish sound at the beginning or end of an English word (*cookiar, watchiar, parkiar, marketa*, and so on). Usually it happens this way rather than the reverse because Spanish-speakers are more pressured to adapt to English.

Other pachuco characteristics involved dress, manners, and social attitudes, for they took pride in their creations. For example, the zoot-suit (a suit that the "hip" urban crowd wore in the 1940's) became the pachuco uniform. It is interesting that the modern version of the pachuco, the low-riding *cholo** has also developed a peculiar life-style, much of which is borrowed from the pachuco innovators. However, their situation is noticeably different from that of the 1940's generation. A few have fashioned or adopted debilitating cultural patterns, including much more frequent drug use and gang killings.

The pachuco adaptation was an attempt to resolve the implicit contradictions of two cultural worlds. Many of the pachuco generation escaped the worst effects of marginality and, as a result, became fairly stable bilinguals. Furthermore, there was a long history behind the pachuco. The pachuco dialect, for example, was "mainly composed of Calo (the jargon of the Spanish gypsy much used by the bullfighters). It includes Hispanicized English, Anglicized Spanish and words of pure invention in Nahuatl and Archaic Spanish" (Hinojos 1975:58). Although the pachuco and his creations were castigated, over a period of time a more understanding assessment has replaced the earlier deprecating one.

Separatism

There were other cultural adaptive responses. Some Mexican-Americans took a separatist approach, turning their backs on assimilation, acculturation, marginality, and syncretism. Separatism entailed either returning to Mexico (Vigil 1974:45-46) or initiating the reconquest of the Southwest. Separatist ideology has been used throughout the twentieth century by those who advocated an aggressive, militant stand against the Anglo system. "To the south Mexicans were moving in rhythm with one of the surges for justice and the fulfillment of revolutionary ideals [1910-1917 period] which have periodically convulsed peoples throughout history. These ideals were not confined to Mexico, and there was a great deal of activity in the Southwest" (Gomez-Quinones 1970:125). During World War I a group of

---

*An earlier definition of this word throughout Latin America meant someone in cultural transition, such as a native acculturating to the Hispanic mode, but the word is now used to describe a Chicano subcultural, street-gang style; perhaps it is also indicative of the transition from Mexican to Anglo-American culture.

Mexican-Americans, led by a barber, formulated the San Diego Plan (named for a small town in Texas) (Gomez-Quinones 1970:124; Webb 1935:484-485). This plan aimed for the overthrow of the United States government and advocated the return of all territories once belonging to Mexico and freedom and land for similarly oppressed Indians, blacks, and Asians.

Another separatist scheme, the Sinarquista movement, was more widespread, especially in California. During World War II the group supported an Axis victory, with the goal of regaining sovereignty over the Southwest. "By 1942 the movement boasted of two thousand members in the United States and 'cells' were known to exist in such Southern California communities as Pacoima, San Fernando, San Bernardino, La Verne, Ontario, Watts, El Monte, Oxnard, Pomona, and Azusa; and, in Texas, at El Paso, McAllen, Mission, and Laredo" (McWilliams 1968:264). Despite the "falangist" (Spanish fascist party), right wing orientation of the Sinarquistas, Mexican-Americans of various political factions rallied behind this "nationalist" program. The party was based in Mexico, and until 1943 the maps used in some Mexican schools had the words "Territory temporarily in the hands of the United States" printed over the United States Southwest.

Mexican background: effect of time and place on culture and identity

The effect of Mexican immigration on the Southwest was mentioned previously (Briggs 1973:27). According to a 1930 study, three basic cultural traditions were prevalent in Mexico at that time: modern European, indigenous, and mestizo (a mixture of the first two). The indigenous and especially the mestizo traditions accompanied most Mexican immigrants to the United States (Gamio 1930:57-58). As a result, "The change from the aboriginal and mixed cultures to the highly modern civilization of the United States is . . . exceedingly abrupt" (Gamio 1930:64). Naturally, this created profound problems for cultural adaptation. Early immigrants usually settled in rural areas, but "by 1930, 57.5 percent of the national total were living in cities. This trend continued and became strong during World War II and the early postwar years" (Alverez 1973:38).

A review of the phenomena affecting cultural adaptation would necessarily begin with the *time* and *place* factors (N. L. Gonzales 1967:29; Moore 1970:100-101). Mexican immigrants brought a culture that reflected their *time* (historical or cultural tradition) and *place* (regional variations). Their new cultural life was strongly influenced by where they settled (what state in the Southwest, or in a rural or urban area) and how long they lived in the United States (generational distance from Mexico). One writer has stated that occupational differences "appear to be a consequence of the relative length of establishment" in the United States (Alverez 1973:41). Similarly, aspirations of social mobility and amount of income would operate to alter the cultural adaptation strategy.

One way to determine the changing strategies is by looking at cultural habits of the past and perhaps examining the motives behind a person's chosen ethnic label (Galarza, Gallegos, and Samora 1969:18-19). For example, two important Mexican cultural traditions are *compadrazgo* and, to a lesser degree, *machismo*. Machismo has been discussed already, so a brief comment will suffice. The changing work pattern caused by industrialization and urbanization has revised this cultural trait. In addition, urban problems have added to the disintegration of the positive aspects of machismo. In former times the patriarch dominated. In the city, where unemployment and street crime often undermined the male role, many women took over as household heads (Briggs, Fogel, and Schmidt 1977:23-24).

Likewise, compadrazgo—an intense bond of cooperation and friendship among parents and godparents (the word means "co-parenthood")—was affected by cultural changes. "We have suggested that in some respects the internal structure of family relationships has been reordered as Mexican Americans have moved more fully into the urban middle-class situation and culture" (Grebler, Moore, and Guzman 1973:327) (Moore 1970:104; Foley et al. 1977:52-62). Some writers characterize compadrazgo as a hindrance to full and successful participation in Anglo society (Briggs, Fogel, and Schmidt 1977:23). Others stress the positive, "adaptive qualities of this extended family unit, because it has braced the people during the hard times under various dominant social systems" (Grebler, Moore, and Guzman 1973:327). Several other socially valuable traits had been connected to this tradition. As an illustration, a person's role in the wider social system alone did not dictate how he should be treated. In addition to role status, his good, helpful, and humble familial actions could bring respect and devotion.

If deep-rooted cultural alterations occurred, what caused them? The factors of time and place were operating here. Investigators have found that the amount of time spent in the United States has a definite effect on cultural adaptation, especially because of discriminatory experiences (Dworkin 1976:139). One study on self-image found that Mexican "migrants had a more positive and in general a more favorable view of themselves than did the settled Mexican Americans" (Gecas 1976:150). In regard to compadrazgo and machismo, it is safe to state that after one or more generations a cultural value shift, or at least a type of modified readaptation, would occur (Grebler, Moore, and Guzman 1970:106). This is made likely by the fact that "the forces in the acculturating nation which require acculturating minorities to take on Anglo behavior at the expense of their own are at least as deeply rooted in history as the forces for persistence among the minorities" (Kutsche 1968:191) (Alvarez 1973:39).

In addition to these factors for change in the United States, there is the time element in Mexico. Mexican compadrazgo and machismo today are different from what was practiced even twenty years ago. "Mexican masses progressively have been abandoning the old traditions in favor of the new ones created and stimulated by the popular industrial culture [maintained mainly by] people who, at the middle-class level, want nothing more than to be like their American models" (Monsivais 1978:53) (Penalosa 1973a:257). The waves of immigration brought different "cultures" and thus an evolving pattern of compadrazgo and machismo (Lewis 1959).

Generally, there appears to have been a definite disavowal of these patterns by Mexicans who assimilated—some might even have been ashamed of their background. Many assimilated "Spanish-types" came to prefer the privacy of the nuclear family with perhaps a couple of children to care for. They often did not interact with other blood-relations because they were more concerned with stressing individuality and getting ahead (Diaz-Guerrero 1978:305; Penalosa 1973a:260). The fact that barrio dwellers, traditionally more Mexican culturally, were more family oriented than those who moved away further supports this assessment (Gilbert 1978:44). "The price for adapting to American society was high, and the traditional Mexican family system has changed" (Foley et al. 1977:131).

Acculturated Mexican-Americans showed a range of cultural response. Perhaps the ethnic label they selected is indicative of their attitude. If a preference was shown for the name "Mexican," they might favor that part of their cultural makeup; if they used "Mexican-American," they were somewhere in the middle; and if they called themselves "American of Mexican descent," they stressed the Anglo side. "Persons of Mexican descent who were not at one time enculturated into the subculture of some Mexican-American neighborhood are best labelled 'Americans of Mexican descent' rather than Mexican-Americans" (Penalosa 1973a:256). In other words, when Mexicans moved closer to the Anglo side, they tended to select a more Anglo ethnic identity. (When they moved instead to a new culture, as discussed before, the consequences were of course different, as was the usual word chosen to designate themselves). Thus, it is reasonable to assume that ethnic identification has been tied to cultural practices (Manuel 1965:40-41).

In the case of marginal individuals the variance is much more unpredictable. Without a set pattern, these people might at times be extremely Mexican and at other times very Anglo. A constant battle appears to have developed in their minds: sometimes Mexican, then Anglo, then a fleeting mixture of the two, and finally perhaps neither one. Their ethnic labels and cultural patterns were not deeply rooted in any well-defined cultural tradition.

Strengths and weaknesses of Mexican culture

In spite of the inherent difficulties in cultural transformation or the overall materially poor life of Mexican-Americans, there remained some outstanding cultural features. "What is it that Americans can learn from Mexicans? There are many things. The diffusion of the meaning of love for respect . . . most of the things that Americans can learn from Mexicans have to do with the business of how to live life better" (Diaz-Guerrero 1978:306), and also, perhaps, how to deal better with death. In general Anglos have always tended to avoid thoughts of death, living as though they had an endless amount of time. In contrast, Mexican-Americans have long accepted the everyday presence of death and, as a result, have lived each day as if it were their last. This could be a legacy from the Indian belief in the dual nature of life whereby one extreme cannot be understood, much less lived, unless its opposite is recognized as equally significant. Poverty may also have encouraged a total commitment to and involvement in each minute of life.

Another aspect of this contrast in patterns has been in the areas of work and recreation. It has been said that "Anglos work full time and enjoy life part time, and Mexican Americans work part time and enjoy life full time." This is not meant to disparage the work ethic previously discussed (Briggs 1973:43). However, for Mexicans "material objects are usually necessity things and not ends in themselves. In contrast to the Puritan ethic, work is viewed as a necessity for survival but not as a value itself" (Murillo 1976:17-18).

Many observers have remarked on the frequency of parties in Chicano life (Foley et al. 1977). This might be an inheritance from pre-Columbian times or from religious fiestas of the Spanish colonial period (Kluckholm and Strodtbeck 1961:237). In any case, when someone arranges a baptism, birthday party, wedding, or funeral wake, a great deal of effort goes into ensuring that the guests can drink and eat to their hearts' content. Although this custom has been criticized as too ostentatious for "poor people," it continues in a somewhat altered form. Similar customs are practiced among working-class people in other parts of the world. "The celebration of the Fiestas Patrias [patriotic fiestas] serves as a positive affirmation and reinforcement of Mexican ethnic identity. The elements and symbols of the ritual, such as music, dances, food, folk costumes, the Cura Hidalgo, the Virgen de Guadalupe, and the Grito de Dolores, have roots and meanings which are embedded in the unconscious through enculturation in early childhood" (Melville 1978:114).

Besides the symbolic significance, such events have a sound economic and historical basis. The habit "of providing security to [family] members, is sometimes expressed through a sharing of material things with other relatives even when there might be precious little to meet [the family's] own immediate needs" (Murillo 1976:20). Mesoamerican Indians still practice economic redistribution through civil-religious ceremonies. An affluent person extends an open invitation to the community to share in his good fortune as a demonstration of community involvement and dedication. This is more a sharing than a showing off of wealth. Great pleasure is derived from providing guests with an enjoyable relief from their daily, arduous work.

In contrast to these positive aspects, destructive features have continued to mark the culture of many Mexican-Americans. They have remained among the lowest-paid workers, living in substandard dwellings in the colonias and barrios and having limited opportunities to gain adequate jobs. They have been victimized by cultural imperialism on the part of the dominant white American society (Paredes 1978:68).

Aspects of cultural imperialism

Schools, which are next in importance to the family as a socializing agent, have generally failed to receive, prepare, and turn out well-educated Mexican-Americans. "Schools for 'Mexicans' and schools for 'Americans' have been the custom in many a Southern California city. It mattered not that the 'Mexicans' were born in the United States and that great numbers of them were sons and daughters of United States citizens" (Moquin and Van Doren 1971:326). This historical pattern is true for most of the Southwest (Grebler, Moore, and Guzman, 1970:156; Taylor 1934:215; U.S. Commission on Civil Rights 1971). Even today Mexican-Americans complete less schooling than any ethnic group of Americans except American Indians. In 1960 Anglos averaged twelve years of school; blacks, ten years; and Mexican-Americans, eight years (Grebler, Moore, and Guzman 1970:145). Furthermore, it is clear that many more Mexican-Americans start school than finish it, which means that parents send their children, but the schools cause them to drop out. Mexican-Americans themselves have often been blamed for their learning deficiencies, but "the mental capacity of the Mexican child is probably normal, although some investigators conclude that he is mentally inferior to an American child of the same age—a conclusion probably affected by racial attitudes of those in the dominant group and by a translation into terms of mental competence of differences in economic and cultural position" (Gamio 1969:72).

In conjunction with other factors, cultural imperialist programs have hindered Chicano educational advancement. After arriving at school, a young child's first lessons were in English, and if he spoke Spanish inside or outside the classroom, he was typically scolded (Briggs 1973:17). Often the mouth of the initially well-behaved was washed out with soap for speaking Spanish; many stopped talking to avoid such treatment. The school continually refused to recognize that the Mexican "is culturally different—and that he can be aided only by programs adjusted to his differences" (Sanchez 1967:85). This was not an unusual practice since Americanization programs have affected most ethnically different people (Sanchez 1966).

Many children were left behind academically because they could not understand the learning tasks given in English. "The Mexican American child was not a problem because he came to school speaking Spanish; the real problem was that no one in the school could understand him" (Guerra 1970:70). This linguistic difference made authorities think that students were mentally retarded, so they were placed in special classes (Carter 1973:451). By ignoring different cultural standards and educational needs, schools were shaping confused and disoriented students. The words of the student quoted earlier on marginality describe this problem:

> I remember in the fifth grade studying Spanish and when we had to do class conversations out loud it was always traumatic for me. Most of the kids in my class were Anglo, so when I spoke Spanish I was careful not to have an accent, so I would not be laughed at. Perhaps I should have showed more will power but it's awfully damned hard when even the teacher snickers. This kind of experience gave me a shyness I have never been able to get rid of. Instead of mastering the language, it was, instead, taken away from me and replaced by the knowledge that Columbus discovered America and that Indians were savages.

Steiner quotes a similar memory: "That teacher, she did not like us. . . . She was a good teacher, but for forty years she did not let children speak Spanish in her classroom. She made us ashamed" (Steiner 1969:209).

In time, as for millions of other members of minority groups, the cultural repertoire necessary to raise the educational level was learned. However, what sets Mexican-Americans apart from the others is the almost steady influx of Mexicans into the United States throughout this century. This regular "human infusion" has replenished fading Mexican cultural attributes; that is, Mexican culture spans the generations because there has been constant cultural immigration.

Insensitive educational practices

An integral aspect of cultural imperialism was the ethnocentric attitude of teachers, as the above quotations show. Many teachers believed that the positive benefits of learning American culture counterbalanced the negative teaching techniques. This insensitive attitude infected the classroom atmosphere and promoted a poor self-image among the students. How could anyone learn when made to feel slow, dirty, and deficient because someone else thought it was true? The imperialist basis of these attitudes was often explicit: "A teacher, asked why she had called on 'Johnny' to lead five Mexicans in orderly file out of a schoolroom, explained: 'His father owns one of the big farms in the area and . . . one day he will have to know how to handle the Mexicans.' Another teacher, following the general practice of calling on the Anglos to help Mexican pupils recite in class, said in praise of the system: 'It draws them (the Americans) out and gives them a feeling of importance'" (*School and Society* 1971:219).

The lack of a culturally sensitive program affected other areas of education as well. "Mexican-Americans are grossly underrepresented among teachers. Of approximately 325,000 teachers in the Southwest, only about 12,000 or four percent are Mexican-American while about seventeen percent of the enrollment is Mexican-American" (Casso 1975:145). In addition, the curriculum emphasized the value of the dominant group and denigrated the minority one. Many critics have questioned the lopsided nature of this identity-shaping. Coming from a different historical tradition, Mexican-Americans have found it difficult to identify with dominant cultural themes.

I'm sitting in my history class,
The instructor commences rapping,
I'm in my U.S. history class,
and I'm on the verge of napping,

The Mayflower landed on Plymouth Rock.
Tell me more! Tell me more!
Thirteen colonies were settled.
I've heard it all before.

What did he say?
Dare I ask him to reiterate?
Oh why bother.
It sounded like he said,
George Washington's my father.

I'm reluctant to believe it,
I suddenly raise my mano.
If George Washington's my father,
why wasn't he Chicano?

The preceding verse by Richard Olivas (Romano-V., 1968) shows that a well-established Mexican-American resistance to the monocultural educational experience has developed.

Those who overcame the learning barriers were usually very bright or lucky. However, there were additional obstacles that further restricted the development of their innate potential. For example, thousands of students have been counseled into vocational or trade courses, even if they were capable of professional career training. Congressman Edward Roybal and Dr. Julian Nava, two noted graduates of Roosevelt High School in East Los Angeles, were successful despite counseling advice to pursue careers as body-and-fender worker and auto mechanic, respectively. This advice, unfortunately, is rooted in the centuries-old belief that Mexicans (and Indians) are "good with their hands" and nothing else. This attitude was considered reasonable by some members of the dominant group, since few Chicanos were in higher professions before 1960.

COLOR *(Inter- and intragroup racism)*
Ethnocentrism

The young adulthood of the Chicano people's experience in the United States took place in the context of a society preoccupied with racial distinctions. Critics of the Mexican-American War noted the racist implications of the conquest (Acuna 1972), and soon thereafter the United States was almost dissolved in a war focused on slavery. A century after the Civil War, "people of color" were still subject to discrimination and social, economic, and even legal sanctions against their progress. This situation, of course, was not unique to the United States.

Ethnocentrism operates within most societies having a subordinate minority population. "The belief that one's own customs, language, religion, and physical characteristics are better or more 'natural' than those of others is termed ethnocentrism. Minor and minute cultural and physical differences may often be given exclusive attention to prove the inferiority of another people" (Wagley and Harris 1958:258). Economic competition is often the basis for this attitude (Barrera 1979:208-209).

Because of ethnocentrism, each racial minority has suffered a different yet similar experience. Methods of subjugation may vary, but the goal has been the same: to keep minorities down by all necessary means and specifically by emphasizing their racial inferiority (Lopez y Rivas 1973:54; Hughes and Hughes 1952:52).

Although the experience varied for each ethnic minority in the United States, there were some clear similarities. Emphasis on racial features is one of them. "Mexican ancestry, instead of being a source of pride, becomes a symbol of shame and inferiority . . . to the point that many dislike and resent being called 'Mexican,' preferring 'Spanish American,' 'Latin,' 'Latin American,' and similar euphemisms (Moore 1970:152-153; Forbes 1973). The use of racial standards as a justification for economic exploitation caused many individuals to suffer undue psychological hardship and stress (Padilla and Ruiz 1976:110). At first the goal was simple—one human group benefiting at the expense of another—but it soon grew, for "ethnocentrism is expressed in a variety of ways including mythology, condescension, and a double standard of morality in social relations" (Noel 1973:20). However, "the 'economic determinism' suggested here does not imply that people consciously formulated ideologies to justify their economically motivated actions" (Sowell 1975:30). Rather, the rationale is probably developed subconsciously to placate the dominant group's conscience. Responsibility for this state of affairs must be shared by Mexican-Americans because of attitudes remaining from the colonial period. Many downtrodden people carry racist perceptions of themselves, even without white people leading the way, and thus have a poor self-image.

Roots of prejudice and discrimination

Prejudicial attitudes gave rise to discriminatory behavior. To anchor Mexicans in the lowest positions, the dominant group prejudged their behavior negatively (prejudice) and set up social barriers (schools, housing, and so on) to impede their social mobility (discrimination). Thus, discrimination is prejudice turned into action. In a very short time, dominant group members believed Mexicans were "so obviously inferior, [that] their present subordinate status is appropriate and is really their own fault. There is a ready identification between Mexicans and menial labor, buttressed by an image of the Mexican worker as improvident, undependable, irresponsible, childlike and indolent" (Simmons 1973:390). Such imagery, similar to that used with regard to black slaves (and later sharecroppers), was widely disseminated in American society at the time of the Mexican-American War. Even white ethnic groups have had trouble overcoming barriers that for a long time prevented their advancement. Mexicans have had to wait even longer. Indeed, the problem was a dual one for Mexicans: the dominant group believed in their inferiority and rejected them, and worse yet, many Mexicans learned to agree with the dominant group's verdict and internalized a negative self-image. Few people understood that "racial ideologies developed as a consequence of the contacts of European peoples with the peoples of Africa, America, and Asia. . . . European economic and political control was justified on the ground that Europeans were dealing with inferior races" (Frazier 1957:269-271). As one observer has remarked, "Color is neutral; it is the mind that gives it meaning" (Bastide 1968:34). Unfortunately, this meaning has been far more sinister for Mexicans and other people of color than it has for European whites.

Class relationships were at the root of racial policies, eventually causing sociopsychological problems. The strain of gaining social acceptance made Mexicans in the United States work harder and longer than the average citizen. The Mexican experience was a continuation of a United States colonial pattern that began with the Indians. (For most, it was also a continuation of the discrimination suffered under the ethnic elite of Mexico.) During the Mexican-American War, Senator John C. Calhoun said: "I know further, sir, that we have never dreamt of incorporating into our union any but the Caucasian race—the free white race. To incorporate Mexico, would be the very first instance of the kind of incorporating an Indian race; for more than half of the Mexicans are Indians, and the other is composed chiefly of mixed tribes" (Weber 1973:135). The historical context of color discrimination against Chicanos thus began with the Indians but included subsequently the importation of African slaves, the inclusion of Mexicans after the 1846 war, the enticement of cheap Chinese labor from Asia, and large-scale southeastern European immigration in the late nineteenth century.

"Pigmentocracy"

"The Anglo conviction that Mexicans are very dark is so strong that when an Anglo meets a light-skinned Mexican who can be identified as Mexican on other counts he will often insist that the latter is Spanish rather than Mexican" (Simmons 1973:406). Anglo feelings of superiority were so pernicious that only lighter-hued Mexicans might escape the worst effects of racism, and even "swarthy" Spaniards were looked down upon (Heizer and Almquist 1971:139). According to Americo Paredes, a professor of folklore, the superiority syndrome is ethnocentrism perfected: "Nationalism becomes racism. The hero is always Anglo-Saxon, of course, and the cowards and 'bad guys' are men with darker skin than his" (Lopez y Rivas 1973:49).

While racism generally followed this pattern, it must be said that many American leaders and groups fought against this practice. There has always been a liberal faction that forced leaders to ameliorate the worst effects of discrimination. The 1964 Civil Rights Act is an example of this liberalism. Nonetheless, the overwhelming evidence shows that the results of their efforts were minuscule as compared to the effects of the majority's programs.

Cultural imperialism was easy to practice. One had merely to react to the racial features of a minority member by bringing out the ready attitudes and behavior of the dominant group (Gomez 1973:87). Sometimes just hearing the ethnic group's language (as in the case of lighter Mexicans) would be enough of a catalyst. In large part these identifying "marks" are responsible for hindering Mexican entrance into the social mainstream of the United States. Often the degree of assimilation or white appearance of the minority group member does not matter to the white middle class. A Mexican is still a Mexican no matter how refined in speaking English or stylishly dressed. "In too many quarters . . . 'a Mexican is a Mexican.' . . . Not that the Mexican is born with any particular moral deficiency, but rather that he has unfortunately been cursed with a political and a religious environment which has been largely responsible for making him what he is" (Stowell 1974:115).

Institutional racism

Branding with prejudicial words and labels might affect any minority group, but in the case of Mexican Americans it was accompanied by stronger discriminatory actions. No doubt this began in the period after the Mexican-American War (1848), when anti-Mexican feeling prevailed. In time these feelings and actions became institutionalized. Thus, the "authorities"— law enforcement officers particularly, but others too—did not wait for Mexicans to go wrong but acted precipitately to keep a tight rein on the population and asked questions afterward (Morales 1972:36-37). The struggle over resources (land, labor, and wealth) was an important reason for this behavior.

Racist ideology, and later, institutions, operated to prevent Mexican acquisition and retention of these material necessities. Their poverty was then frequently used to justify continued mistreatment. As recently as the early 1960's, a Los Angeles police chief remarked that "poor people who are of darker skin are under greater suspicion of committing crime—even more so if they communicate in a 'foreign' language. . . . It seems just, however, to say that Mexicans are unmoral rather than immoral since they lack a conception of morals as understood in this country. Their housing conditions are bad, crime is prevalent and their morals are a menace to our civilization. They are illiterate, ignorant and inefficient and have few firm religious beliefs" (Morales 1972:33).

Mexican-American efforts to obtain rights blocked by institutional racism had occasional success. Nevertheless, the well-structured program of suppression required only periodic supervision for maintenance (Simmons 1974:438-474). As mentioned earlier, schools and teachers were instruments that fostered this arrangement. Most other societal sectors were interwoven with racial standards that were implicitly or even explicitly aimed at the exclusion of ethnic minorities. Earlier generations who had learned these lessons socialized their children with the stain of second-class citizenship even before they might experience it themselves.

Public barriers

Racism continued in social realms outside the school. The community swimming pool might be especially reserved for Mexicans and blacks on a set day. The next day after they had used it, they witnessed the draining of the "color stain" from the pool, making the water pure again for white Anglo children for the remainder of the week. In addition, they observed that a lighter-hued Mexican might be welcomed during "white" pool days, affirming in their minds the superiority and inferiority of certain racial types. Even exceptions to these patterns served as reminders of the discriminatory attitudes of the general public. "In 1939, it was revealed that, although the swimming pool at Chaffey Junior College was used on an integrated basis during the academic year, when it was open to the general public during the summer, Chicanos were allowed to use it only on Mondays" (Acuna 1972:198).

A similar experience awaited Chicanos at the movie theater (Taylor 1934:252). One Texas town limited the types and amount of ice cream a minority person might buy. Even something as mundane as a haircut was touched by racism: "In 1945 a U.S. Senate Subcommittee on Education learned that Chicanos from McCarney, Texas, traveled forty-five miles to Fort Stockton for a haircut because Anglo barbers would not cut Chicano hair and Chicanos could not legally become barbers in McCarney" (Guzman 1974:269). A Texas barber explained why: "'No, we don't wait on Mexicans here. They are dirty and have lice, and we would lose our white trade. The Mexicans also have venereal diseases, most of them, but of course some whites do too. The Mexicans go to their own barber shop. The Negroes barber each other'" (Taylor 1934:250).

Reactions to mistreatment

Social discrimination, along with inadequate education and political practices such as poll taxes and gerrymandering, built up a backlog of negativity among Chicanos. This experience failed to prepare Chicanos for the better jobs and almost ensured that the sequence would continue with the next generation. Many Chicanos developed acute self-hatred and came to despise their ethnicity and all that it seemed to signify. However, the resistance and resilience of many more is of at least equal importance.

Chicano reactions against racism occurred in the nineteenth century in such forms as social banditry and have continued to the present. The

Fig. 8-8. Zooters and sailors battle. (Drawing by Jeffrey Huereque.)

so-called pachuco riots of the early 1940's in Los Angeles (one of several major race riots in American cities in that time) exemplified this stand against racist persecution. On that occasion Mexican-Americans grouped together for defensive purposes, as the community was subjected to angry attacks by both authorities and civilians, and rioting continued for several days. "In order to provide a more explicit moral justification for racial discrimination an unambiguous, unfavorable symbol was needed. The zoot-suit label which technically applied across ethnic and class lines to all wearers of the garb, was simply equated to Chicanos" (Guzman 1974:28-29). At first only "zoot-suit pachuco" types were beaten by armed mobs, then anyone Mexican, and finally any other easily recognizable ethnic minority.

The attacks on members of the Chicano community met strong resistance and even counterattacks over several days. The authorities, overlooking the actions of the predominantly white mobs, tended to blame the entire episode on the Mexican-Americans. Captain E. Duran Ayers, chief of the Foreign Relations Bureau (!) of the Los Angeles County Sheriff's Department, summed up the dominant public attitude toward the affair: "The biological basis is the main basis to work from. . . . This total disregard for human life has always been universal throughout the Americas among the Indian population" (Morales 1972:41). And yet both majority amd minority community members were forced to agree on one point: The events had proved that Chicanos were not docile in their reaction to unequal treatment and would fight back when pushed.

Returning Mexican veterans from World Wars I and II reinforced the battle against racist institutions. They were not content with first-class citizenship in the front lines and second-class citizenship at home. Discrimination was particularly resented since Mexican-Americans were the United States' most highly decorated ethnic minority (Morin 1966:11). Consequently, they steadily challenged the segregation policies of real estate operators, restaurant and movie theater owners, and other establishments that traditionally practiced ethnocentrism.

Negative imagery

The institutional discrimination was reinforced by the proliferation of derogatory images of Chicanos and labels such as "greaser" and "Mec-skin." One early book about Mexican travel has these words: "There are two things I could never understand, why the Lord made mosquitoes and Mexicans" (Stowell 1974:116). The vocabulary of insult was even expanded as the dominant group intensified efforts to fortify the legitimacy of its claims to superior status. The early labels were joined by "beaners," "wetbacks," "chili chokers," "tacos," "chukes," "half-breeds," and many others. Ironically, poorer whites who lived near Mexicans, often sharing similar underclass conditions, were usually the ones who used the labels. Although they were just as destitute, it made them feel better to have someone below them.

There were also more sophisticated ways of negatively portraying an ethnic minority. These carried more weight because social science writers and other academicians created them to rationalize the experiences of the ethnically defined underclass. Mexicans were described as lazy, dumb, dirty, bloodthirsty savages, immoral, breed-like-rats, culturally disadvantaged, and a host of other demeaning stereotypes. While social scientists now have purged their own remarks of such imagery, the legacy lives on elsewhere. One need only look to Hollywood movies and recent television programs to document the occurrence of stereotyping. In films, "Indians and Mexicans have been particularly distorted . . . whenever a character representing a Mexican appeared on the screen at all, he usually took the role of a bad-man. . . . Films helped spread notions that Mexicans were untrustworthy, vengeful, sadistic, and lustful. . . . For most citizens living in the population centers of the East and Midwest, the distorted caricatures on the moving picture screen served as their only contact with the culture of Mexican-Americans" (Lamb 1975:75-80).

Similarly distorted images were fed daily to national television audiences. "Advertising media that utilize Mexicans and Mexican-Americans have selectively presented and exaggerated racial and cultural characteristics. Not only are advertisers exhibiting racist thinking at the expense of everyone of Mexican descent, but they are also creating, in many cases, unfavorable racial and cultural stereotypes in minds that previously did not harbor them" (Martinez 1973:523-524). One blatant example was a deodorant commercial that depicted Mexicans as reeking of "foul-smelling" body odor.

Reverse racists

Chicanos have often reacted to this treatment by becoming "reverse racists," even toward other racial minorities. "Put-down" words such as "gringo," "paddy," "gavacho" (meaning foreigner, used initially toward the French), and "bolillo" (a hard-crusted loaf of white bread) were hurled back at whites. More sophisticated Chicanos have labeled Anglos as aggressive, competitive, money-hungry, exploitative, and insensitive. "The Mexican population in the United States has been subjected to a long process of ideological conversion, of having their attitudes molded by a capitalist system. They have been deliberately infected with all the values—including racism—

of the dominant society" (Lopez y Rivas 1973:59). In contrast, the lower classes in Mexico are much more tolerant of those who are racially different, possibly because that segment of the Mexican population is racially mixed.

Intragroup relationships have also been affected by reverse racism. To some degree, Mexicans in the United States have mistreated and verbally abused Mexican immigrants, calling them "chuntaros," "mojados" (wetbacks), "T. J.'s" (from Tijuana, or riffraff border residents), and so on. On occasion Mexican-American leaders have made an effort to reduce this animosity (Weber 1973:257-258). According to Samora, economic causes lay behind this friction: "the hiring of cheap alien labor has [had the effect] of pitting Mexican-Americans against Mexicans" (Samora 1971:130). Immigrant Mexicans reacted by calling Mexican-Americans "pochos," "agringados," and "cholos."

Although the labels aim at cultural phenomena, the terms are implicitly racist. The more Mexican-looking may resent those who are lighter and thus more employable by Anglo standards. "It is not unlikely that racial attitudes played a significant part in hiring practices in view of the favor given light-skinned Mexicans over dark-skinned Mexicans" (Reisler 1976:105). Another source of intraethnic conflict is the contrast in backgrounds. "The foreign born Mexican-American may compare his socioeconomic conditions with conditions in Mexico and note his relative advantage. But the native born Mexican-American may compare his socioeconomic condition with that of the Anglo and note his relative disadvantage. These perceptions may affect the stereotypes and self-image each holds" (Dworkin 1971:77).

Roots of intragroup racism

Not all Chicano racism is attributable to experiences in the United States. Families have been known to favor the *guero* (light-skinned) child over the darker *prieto* offspring. This appears to be a Spanish colonial practice that has carried over into the present day. In New Mexico, "although few Spanish Americans either can or do claim to be pure Spanish as their blood heritage, there is a highly defensive attitude about being part Indian. They frown upon intermarriage with Indians and, when it occurs, express their disapproval by stigmatizing the children of the union with the terms lobo or coyote" (Kluckholm and Strodtbeck 1961:205). Many who were lighter in color called themselves Spanish and sought to marry Anglos, often looking down on their own group in order to gain the allegiance and respect of Anglo acquaintances (Simmons 1974:406).

However, having a light skin did not guarantee that this would happen, for a light complexion was not necessarily equated with better socioeconomic conditions; many poor Mexicans were very white. In addition, darker-skinned Mexicans sometimes sought a status change through inter-marriage. Generally it is true that Mexicans have attempted to emulate whites, if only because opportunities for social mobility were increased in this way. Nevertheless, there was always a certain amount of pragmatic switching: "But it is patent that in any particular case, the distinction between Indian and Hispano may be difficult or impossible to make. Thus, individuals have been known to claim Spanish ancestry when dealing with other persons they believe to be of Spanish descent, and Indian when with members of that group" (N. L. Gonzales 1967:27).

Thus, at the end of the young adulthood period, the Chicano community still faced tremendous problems stemming from racial discrimination. Barriers to advancement in employment and social standing continued; the mass media ignored Chicanos at best and disparaged them at other times; and many within the community had incorporated an intrapsychic mode of self-repression. However, resistance to these conditions had also survived and even grown, and the stage was set for change.

Breakup and transformation of the social order

CONTACT *(Civil rights ferment)*
Shaping the Chicanos

From the time of its incorporation in the United States, the Mexican-American community has encountered forces that bred change in its lifeway and expectations. The Civil War and Reconstruction, the settling of the West, the rise of industrial capitalism and urbanization, labor unions and economic crises, and two world wars affected Chicanos along with other Americans (although in different ways). Social and economic discrimination and assimilationist policies afflicted them in common with other ethnic minorities (again, in different ways). Continuous contact with Mexico uniquely affected the Chicano people, at once affording more cultural stability and also exposing them (more than most other Americans) to the revolutionary ideas of the late nineteenth and early twentieth centuries (Knowlton 1975).

The Chicanos were not passively buffeted about by these social forces (Lopez-McKnight 1971; Lopez 1970). Many fought their way against great odds into the middle-class mainstream of American society. Others, with equal vigor, resisted the social pressures to "Americanize" and abandon traditional ways. Followers of both strategies won victories—large and small—in pushing for equality and justice. As Rendon (1971:2-3) has noted in rebutting the notion that the events of the 1960's were without precedent, "It is closer to the truth to say that there has always been a Chicano revolt. That is, the Mexican American, the Chicano, as he calls himself and his Carnales, brother and sister Chicanos, has never ceased to be a revolutionary all the while he has suffered repression."

Modern Chicano resistance to unequal treatment is rooted in the legacy left to the community from colonial times (Vigil 1978:23; Alvarez 1973:45-46). What Romano-V. has labeled the "seemingly endless decades" of Mexican and Mexican-American involvement in labor uprisings against unjust exploitation is an example of the continuity of the Chicano's quest for social justice, "conflict which involved literally tens of thousands of people of Mexican descent and which at one time spread to eight different states in the Union—conflict which was met with massive military counteraction" (Romano-V. 1973:54-55). Of course, not all these events were full-blown affairs like social banditry that captured the public eye. They were more often localized, sporadic, spontaneous eruptions, such as a group of people gathered around a jail, clamoring for release of a prisoner unjustly detained; workers from railroads, mines, or farms organizing to improve living conditions; or political rallies to support a candidate who reflects Chicano interests. Chicanos participated in many of these activities in unison with other members of American society.

In their own way Chicanos have carried a banner of protest throughout this century (Limon 1974:85-86). When repressive actions were stepped up, resistance issues and programs declined, and in some instances they were crushed completely. Nonetheless, despite temporary slowdowns, each revival of resistance brought on renewed discussion and planning in Chicano leadership circles (Romano-V. 1968:165). Early efforts at resolving basic contradictions were made, and many leaders worked to spread their insights, programs, and goals. Social and political recommendations varied from moderate to radical, but the main point is that "it is incorrect to assume . . . that previous generations of Mexican Americans passively accepted their social and economic status" (Lopez 1970:101). For example, one recent study of the Chicano youth movement mentions how those who started organizing in the 1930's later helped the present generation toward similar goals (Gomez-Quinones 1978:11).

Beginning in the late nineteenth century, *mutualistas* (mutual aid societies) were established for self-help purposes, often promoting the sense of ethnic unity and mission for other activities. "By pooling their meager resources the Mexican [people] learned they could provide each other with low cost funeral and insurance benefits, low interest loans and other forms of economic assistance" (Tirado 1970:54-55). Subsequent groups followed this lead and broadened the goals to encompass other external issues. Organizations such as the League of United Latin American Citizens (LULAC), organized primarily by World War I veterans to combat prejudice; the Community Service Organization (CSO), formed in Los Angeles in the 1940's; and G.I. Forum, an organization of World War II and Korean War veterans founded in the 1950's, are a few illustrations of this historical pattern (Alvarez 1971:72-73; Camarillo 1970:145-146). Such local and focused activities (when it was not yet possible or popular to organize on a larger scale) served a twofold purpose. First, they kept the light of protest burning during the

Fig. 9-1, A and **B.** Charter of the San Angelo Texas Fraternal Union, a *mutualista*. (Courtesy Adolfo Barela.)

quiet, incubating years. Second, these groups formed a core from which later organizations gained inspiration to continue the struggle.

Effects of modern urban industrial system

Despite the historical precedents, the modern period is unique for several reasons. Modern technological systems have brought traditional societies and peoples into the mainstream of work and urban growth. Previously most of the world's people were locally organized and nationally controlled. Now the spread of capitalist enterprises and networks has developed what is in many ways an international social system. In their drive to acquire raw resources and more workers, capitalist leaders have made a large part of the world's population more homogeneous; thus, modernization has also meant ideological revision and, perhaps, congruence and conformity in thought (Kahn 1979). This experience has tended to pull the interests, concerns, and needs of modernizing people into the same orbit. What happens to one group or in one part of the world generally has repercussions on other groups and regions (Almaquer 1974:27). Because of a system's macrolevel influences, observers are beginning to seek macrolevel solutions to conditions and problems. "Although there is no question that Chicanos must look after the interests of Chicanos, there are times when they can unite with other groups for a common purpose" (Florez 1971:85). Labor resistance to exploitation offers an example: Labor unions (which have a heavy Chicano representation) "are communicating with one another in trying to find the ways and means for long overdue social, economic, and political change" (Lopez-McKnight 1971:207).

Precursors of change

Three major developments helped to make the 1960's a watershed period within the Chicano movement and community. One was the inroads made by the black civil rights movement in the early 1960's (Rodriguez 1977:31; Heller 1971:251); another was the United States government's efforts under President Lyndon Baines Johnson to eliminate poverty in the nation (Harrington 1962; Florez 1971:78); and the third was the Vietnam War and its consequences. Each operated to restimulate the ethnic solidarity struggle, which at this time snowballed into the first relatively united national Chicano effort. The achievements of the black movement sparked renewed organization in the Chicano community, often modeled in large part on earlier black campaigns. The political power mustered by the civil rights campaigns also paved the way for stronger ties between Chicano leaders and national political organizations. The presidentially endorsed War on Poverty led to new job opportunities in the Chicano community and to the recruitment of Chicanos in government and the universities on a scale never previously reached. This, in turn, had two effects: It increased the number of highly visible middle-class Mexican-Americans, and it brought Chicano intellectuals into contact with the activist social reformers and revolutionists then concentrated in the universities. The war in Vietnam brought to the Chicano community the same dissension it sparked elsewhere in the nation. Newly radicalized Chicano students were quick to note the discrepancy between their community's underrepresentation in the social, political, and economic power structure and their overrepresentation in war casualty statistics.

Chicanos generated their own leadership and methods aimed at problems unique to them. "Late in the 1950's . . . political seismographers began to detect rumblings of discontent within the Mexican-American community. The sharpest tremors could be traced to the Community Service Organization [CSO] . . . in this case Mexican-Americans . . . already had by the sheer force of their numbers the primary instrument to effect social change" (Dunne 1967:53). Cesar Chavez was one Chicano who learned how to organize in the CSO. Chavez's successful attempt to organize farm workers was

Fig. 9-2. Union leader Cesar Chavez surrounded by farm workers. (Courtesy United Farm Workers.)

helped considerably after the United States' Mexican bracero program ended in 1964 (this had long been a goal of labor and liberal political forces). Under this program the United States government had officially recruited and sanctioned use of Mexican workers, which made it more difficult for Chavez to mount a unionization campaign. Thus, the United Farm Workers focused first on American-born or naturalized Chicanos. Generally they were more familiar with the union idea and working conditions in the United States, and presumably they were easier to organize. In addition, their extended exposure to conditions and consumer standards in the United States may have necessitated their drive to improve on their underclass role. The continued immigration of undocumented laborers and community opposition to suppression of the immigration later led Chavez to alter this strategy and attempt to organize the immigrant workers as well. A contemporary commentator noted: "It is a paradox that the termination of the Bracero Program is the only way in the long run of helping *Mexican* as well as American workers" (Nelson 1966:17). The farm workers' struggle continues to this day, with gradual success despite strife and many obstacles.

Another example of an idea put into practice was the Reis Lopez Tijerina land-grant movement, a collective demand for the return of a communal land grant. Historically, "the pueblo or community grant was given directly to a community of petitioners. More prevalent in northern Mexico than in most of the other colonies, it was made to a petitioning group of at least 10 village families for the purpose of establishing a rural farming community" (Gardner 1970:51). Following the takeover by the United States in the last century, such lands fell under new ownership. Tijerina and his followers had been active long before the nationally publicized incidents of 1966 and after (Nabokov 1969). Detailing the abrogation of Chicano land and cultural rights, and basing their program on the 1848 treaty ending the Mexican-American War, they went "to Mexico to turn over to President Lopez Mateos a memorial signed by thousands of Mexican-Americans. It asked that the Mexican government intervene with Washington to demand the fulfillment of the Treaty of Guadalupe Hidalgo" (Blawis 1973:522). Many Chicanos rallied behind these goals. The demonstrations led by Chavez, Tijerina, and others raised the social consciousness of Chicanos to the point where they planned further actions (Swadesh 1973).

As a result of exposure to urban life, many Chicanos were caught up in "rising expectations common to that segment of the population." This is best understood as a change in attitude to a desire to improve life's material rewards (Steiner 1969:157-158). Previous expectations were low, for the Chicano had inherited a meager standard of living with little hope for the

Fig. 9-3. Tijerina and followers petitioning Governor Fages of Arizona. (From Nabokov, P.: *Tijerina and the courthouse raid*, Albuquerque, 1969, University of New Mexico Press.)

future. The post–World War II years were good for the economy in general, and many Chicanos similarly benefited. Movement from the barrios and into a higher social status broke the pattern of low expectations (Heller 1971:251). "One middle-aged man dramatized the difference between the comparatively affluent poor today and his own youth by saying: 'Now you see bread lying in the streets. When I was a boy you never saw bread in the streets'" (Grebler, Moore, and Guzman 1970:343). Thus, with one dream fulfilled, there is a rising expectation for the satisfaction of previously unheard-of possibilities. Chicanos who experienced this feeling grouped together in order to have their wishes recognized and met (Wright, Salinas, and Kuvlesky 1973:43; Romero 1979:23-24).

   Contradictions were the fertile soil in which earlier Chicano organizational efforts, the example of the black civil rights movement, the War on Poverty, the Vietnam War protests, activist models such as Chavez and Tijerina, and the increasing need for overall improvements took root. The urbanization process was responsible for bringing Chicanos into the center stage of national life.

Nature of inequality

Urbanization brought Chicanos into contact with other people, some of whom had been similarly relegated to an underclass life. They quickly learned about the important differences among all of them, but there were some who began to perceive that strong threads held them together. Complementing this new mood of national interethnic awareness were the first attempts to draw parallels with colonized peoples in the Third World— the Americas, Africa, and Asia. Many Chicanos began to view their situation as that of an "internal colony."

Inherent in this assessment was the fact that colonial systems throughout the world share certain common features. Since Chicanos were either Indians (and thus the original inhabitants of this hemisphere) or Mexican settlers (before the United States expansion into Mexican territory), it was necessary to explain their presence in the United States in a framework other than that applicable to other immigrants or underclass ethnic minorities. Like so many people in other parts of the world, they were integrated into a new society by a war of conquest. Thus they became an internal colony. "Our view is that the barrio is best perceived as an internal colony, and that the problem of Chicano politics is essentially one of powerlessness. . . . To be colonized means to be affected in every aspect of one's life: political, economic, social, cultural, and psychological" (Barrera, Munoz, and Ornelas 1974:282) (Moore 1973:365). Although far from uniform throughout the southwestern states, the basis of such a belief is this: As indigenous residents of the area, Chicanos were involuntarily incorporated into the United States; thus, contemporary ethnic relationships are rooted in these beginnings.

In understanding this important fact, Chicano leaders began to develop new insights and gain increasing strength, with the goal of making alliances with other similarly affected peoples. Although some leaders never completely embraced this concept of human solidarity, preferring instead a strict La Raza nationalist program, many came to believe that similar conditions (or contradictions) necessitated coordination among the "powerless."

CONFLICT *(1960's Chicano movement)*
Movement background

What has become known as the Chicano movement was born, or at least was for the first time widely acknowledged, in the 1960's. "No one person can claim that his philosophy, technique, or charisma has been the cause of the ferment of revolution within the Mexican American Community. . . . There are too many varied aspects of the cultural and economic upheaval . . . to pinpoint any one cause or any one person as the root" (Rendon 1971:105) (Hernandez 1970:15). "Within the ferment created by changes in the ideological climate and material conditions of the early 1960's, there arose a variegated burst of activity, loosely identified as the 'Chicano Movement'. . . . It was a creative and revivalist cultural surge, it was a civil rights struggle, it was an effort for political recognition and economic rights by middle-class elements, and it had intimations of an incipient national liberation struggle" (Gomez-Quinones 1978:12, 29).

No single date marks the beginnings of the Chicano movement. One can safely state, however, that most of the widespread activity was unleashed in the mid-1960's as the Chavez farm workers and Tijerina *Alianza* (Alliance) gained momentum. In a remarkably short period of time many organizations and activities had blossomed (Meir and Rivera 1974). These groups focused their attention mostly on the issues and conditions that were discussed in the earlier stages. The farm union fought to correct injustices against workers, and the alianza sought the return of treaty-guaranteed land; both issues, land and labor, are at the center of this historical account. Other organizations brought attention to another core problem: the lack of resources and wealth among the Chicano population. Some groups narrowed the effort to a single sector, such as education or politics. Others, with some amount of success, attacked all social conditions that blocked Chicano development.

Groups and actions

The earlier reform groups were joined by others. The Crusade for Justice in Denver, led by Corky Gonzales, was a broadly based thrust for community control, mainly economic and political (Marin 1975:107-120). The Brown Berets (Sanchez 1978) and United Mexican American Students (UMAS), later MECHA (see p. 195), groups helped organize and participated in the Los Angeles high school walkouts in 1968 aimed at improving education (Gomez-Quinones 1978:30; Rosen 1973:159). The political goal of Angel Gutierrez's *La Raza Unida Partido* (United Peoples Party) in Texas was to build an independent third party throughout the country (Shockley 1974; Garcia and de la Garza 1977:163-168). The Chicano Moratoriums of the 1970's were nominally anti–Vietnam War but took on a broader platform involving the whole social system (Morales 1972:91; Camejo 1973:510). The *Catolicos Por La Raza* (Catholics for the People) demanded somewhat tumultuously that the church be made responsive to the needs of the Spanish-speaking poor (Acosta 1973:15).

An example of the momentous events of the period is provided by the 1968 Walkouts in which several thousand students boycotted classes.

Fig. 9-4. A, Student walkout in 1970 at Roosevelt High School in East Los Angeles.
B, Walkout at Excelsior High School in Norwalk, Calif.

This incident is important for several reasons: It was the first major urban confrontation in the largest Chicano-populated area in the nation. It was coordinated by numerous groups—teachers, students, and community activists—and afterward other individuals and organizations of various ideological shades rallied to their defense. Most importantly, the event and subsequent developments sparked debate and action not only on the educational front but on a number of different topics. However, education was the pivotal rallying issue. "Historically, the public educational system was a mechanism of cultural aggression and national and class oppression against the Mexican in the United States. Given this relationship, Mexican students recognized this antagonism and when this occurred they became part of the historical struggle for education and cultural rights" (Gomez-Quinones 1978:30). Two high school student leaders at that time wrote that "the situation created a climate . . . where students started questioning things. . . . Schools are supposed to service the community and they weren't. Rather, they were more like prisons in the community. They were just doing custodial things as far as keeping students together" (Santana and Esparza 1974:1).

Consciousness-raising

The reform activities show how far-reaching contacts brought many groups into conflict with the social system. Furthermore, these were not merely sporadic, apolitical confrontations, but well-organized challenges to the power-brokers. "Participation in such a movement offers the opportunity for positive identity formation in adults as well as adolescents. Indeed . . . such allegiance to an ideology is a part of the normal process of identity formation" (Martinez 1976:291). Protest activity served a psychological purpose in assuaging the effects of inferiority and marginality. Militancy became the rallying banner for those who confronted Anglo-American institutions. As noted previously, Chicanos challenged every sector. Generally, "at the present time, Mexican-American communities throughout the United States are in ferment. The intensity and form of the ferment vary from one section to another. New ideas, forces, and expectations are challenging old accommodations" (Knowlton 1975:55). Some groups even advocated taking up arms and went on a spree of terrorist bombings.

The ground swell also enveloped less militant organizations. One was the Association of Mexican-American Educators (AMAE), a moderate group that championed educational reform. Although accused of adhering to an "establishment" orientation, many in this group helped organize the students (Ericksen 1970:59). Some of the more radical teachers, such as Sal Castro, a major leader and spokesman of the walkouts, led the way for change. However, even the less-threatening suggestions of the AMAE moderates created suspicion in the eyes of the authorities. Both moderate and radical elements were in open conflict with the system at different levels. "In fact . . . the differences between them are less important than the similarities that bind them" (Garcia and de la Garza 1977:43).

An old-line (1959) political group, the Mexican-American Political Association (MAPA), steadily evolved under Bert Corona into a more militant organization as the movement spread (Garcia and de la Garza 1977:80; Gomez-Quinones 1978:14). Countless individuals and groups remained in the background but contributed immensely to the cause. The Mexican-American Action Committee (MAAC) was founded in 1966 in Los Angeles by young professionals who spanned the political spectrum but agreed on one goal: social action. Because of or despite this ideological diversity, by 1968 they were responsible for helping other groups and causes that caught the public eye. For example, members of the MAAC played instrumental roles in MECHA, the Brown Berets, the high school walkouts, and various educational and political reform actions.

Step-up in militancy: Aztlan nation

College and high school students eventually organized into a southwestern regional body known as *Movimiento Estudiantil Chicanos de Aztlan* (MECHA; The Chicano Student Movement of Aztlan). The use of the word "Aztlan," the ancient Aztec name for the Southwest, came to symbolize the Chicano destiny. Student groups, meeting in Denver in 1969, developed an historically based type of nationalism (El Plan Espiritual de Aztlan 1970:20-23). Their goal of an Aztlan nation was yet another instance of Chicano separatism. (Other examples are the Sonora Immigration in 1856, the San Diego Plan in 1914-1915, and the Sinarquistas in the 1940's.) However, separatism in this case meant more than a return to earlier, perhaps indigenous, sociocultural traditions. It also implied the use of modern resources and techniques for community control and development. One of the spokesmen, Rudolfo "Corky" Gonzales (1967:3), wrote an epic poem that explained an aspect of the Chicano dilemma, as this excerpt shows:

> I am Joaquin,
> Lost in a world of confusion,
> Caught up in a whirl of a
> gringo society
> Confused by the rules,
> Scorned by attitudes,
> Suppressed by manipulation,

And destroyed by modern society.
My fathers
have lost the economic battle
and won
the struggle of cultural survival
and now
I must choose.

Gonzales, the poet-politician, chose a separatist Aztlan. Others resolved the dilemma by working for cultural retention but a fairer economic integration, to obtain what they viewed as the best of two worlds. Still others sought total social and economic equality for Chicanos in the United States, with or without the retention of distinct cultural traditions. These reform movements were viewed with suspicion by much of the American public, who often misinterpreted the self-determination efforts of Chicanos as attacks on democracy, and by the political and economic elite, who correctly viewed them as a threat to some of the privileges they controlled.

August 29 Moratorium

Various actions were taken to stem the new wave of Chicano self-determination. Throughout the Southwest there were dozens of incidents, but one example will suffice here. On a hot summer day, August 29, 1970, the largest Chicano demonstration of the period took place. The peaceful marchers were protesting the Vietnam intervention policies of the United States, and in particular the high Chicano casualty rate there. Over 20,000 people from throughout the Southwest congregated at an East Los Angeles park for a rally. After a short time sheriff's deputies broke it up (Morales 1972:101; Sanchez 1978:4). When the police lined up to intimidate the protesters, some monitors attempted unsuccessfully to hold the crowd back. Nevertheless, several hundred policemen drove the people from the park. In the aftermath some people rioted, destroying over a million dollars in property on a main thoroughfare. Three people were killed and hundreds of others arrested. Scores of people were harassed, and one leader, Corky Gonzales, was apprehended and jailed because he "suspiciously" was carrying $300 in cash (Marin 1975:114).

A program of indoctrination was a major thrust of the countermeasures to this and other events. The media, politicians who preached "law and order," local and federal law enforcement officials, the court system, and other functionaries began to offer a negative assessment of the social ferment. At times their criticisms were correct. More often, however, they missed the mark. They characterized public protest as un-American and un-

Fig. 9-5. A, Low-riders at Moratorium. **B,** MECHA students from Long Beach, Calif.

Continued.

Fig. 9-5, cont'd. C, Marchers claiming racial pride. **D,** Moratorium monitors (in fore-ground) stand between crowds and police.

Fig. 9-6. Rioting after the Moratorium and the death of Ruben Salazar, a Chicano newspaper man, at the Silver Dollar. (Drawing by Mary Nunez.)

lawful, despite protest organizers' efforts to ensure legal compliance at rallies and meetings. Some government leaders considered even minor differences of opinion to be an attack on the United States. A Mexican-American congressman, generally regarded at the time as a liberal, nevertheless felt it necessary to disavow any ties to the protests: "It may well be that I agree with the goals stated by the militants; but whether I agree or disagree, I do not now nor have I ever believed that the end justifies the means" (Gonzalez 1974:260). That the protest organizers had never suggested otherwise and had in fact maintained discipline until police intervention was apparently lost on the national leadership.

Comparisons with other groups and counterreactions

Chicanos were not alone in their protests during this time, for other groups—blacks and Indians, in particular—were taking issue with similar features of the social structure. As a result, many minority group members began to perceive the social-class roots of inequality and injustice (Gomez-Quinones 1978:14). They were joined by white radicals in articulating and acting out their criticisms of government actions.

Developments tended to undermine the social movements. For example, many Chicanos, particularly those who were moderate or more conservative, were co-opted into various institutional networks, thus dulling the sharp edge of the movement. Some observers viewed this as a deliberate plan and pointed to the aftermath of the 1968 walkouts. "The school board established a community group, the Educational Issues Coordinating Committee (EICC), to represent Chicano parent and student interests, but it was structured to exclude the militants involved in the protests. With the establishment of this group and the repressive actions undertaken by the local law enforcement agencies against participants in the student walkouts, those who governed the schools solidified their position of power over the Chicano community" (Munoz 1974:135). In other situations authorities also supported Chicano groups favorable to the status quo in order to counter advocates of social change—thus creating intragroup fighting and slowing progress (Foley et al. 1977:224-225).

Furthermore, the Chicano organizations that were making the most headway attracted another type of law enforcement attention. Like other militant organizations, these groups were infiltrated by undercover agents, or agents provocateurs. "They made every effort to disrupt, misdirect, and discredit those organizations and to especially develop internal conflicts amongst the organizational leadership" (Munoz 1974:132). These provocateurs became full-time "militants" (with long hair, beards, and other visible paraphernalia) in order to redirect the movement into negative activities. David Sanchez (1978:6), former prime minister of the Brown Berets had this to say about the problem: "The infiltrators were one of the main reasons why the Brown Beret organization was so often misinterpreted and misrepresented. The infiltrators served as agitators of violence." Intimidation, harassment, and arrests characterized this period.

Factionalism and aftermath of the conflict

As in most historical periods of ferment, there were also intragroup struggles. In addition to the macrolevel contradictions, there were microlevel differences that set Chicano against Chicano. Sometimes these conflicts were as heated as those occurring in the national arena (Gomez-Quinones 1978:43). Not surprisingly, Chicanos argued with one another over the ideology and methods that would best effect change. Programs for change ranged from total assimilation to white middle-class America to separatism, and they were vociferously debated at national conferences or in smaller units such as college MECHA chapters. Almost as much energy was expended in these intragroup conflicts as in united actions. Many people and organizations were casualties as a result. Besides the disintegration of

some worthwhile organizations, the toll was often that Chicanos were alienated from each other and worse, from themselves. Intragroup conflicts had
some good aspects, though, as indicated by Gomez-Quinones (1978:5): "Factionalism is a part of development, positive or negative; if positive it
strengthens progressive ideological clarity and organizational coherence.
Negative factionalism causes confusion and weakens organization."

In summary, the 1960's movement made its mark. The process is
still unfolding, and so, of course, is a proper understanding of it. One interpretation is suggested by Negrete (1974:356): "Spectacular, dramatic changes
in the organizational structure by the establishment are not expected overnight. The view that mass protests do not succeed in producing structural
change . . . is just too limited in scope. It recognizes, but greatly minimizes,
the organizing skills that take root after each protest." However, Munoz
(1974:120) points out the movement's shortcomings: "The failure of the
Movement to contribute to fundamental changes in the barrios is to a large
extent attributable to the lack of a critical analysis on the part of Movement
leadership of the nature of Chicano oppression." Clearly, a careful assessment
of the impact of this conflict is in order.

CHANGE *(1970's and beyond)*
State of the people

It is difficult to speak of an aftermath of the Chicano movement
and the conflict surrounding it, for both the movement and the conflict continue in abated fashion. Many of the conditions that gave rise to the movement are still present—for example, underrepresentation of Chicanos in social, economic, and political positions of leadership; discord between the
community and local authorities; and lower average income and education.
The dramatic headlines of the 1960's are gone and an air of normality has
returned to the Chicano community. But the norms have changed, although
in many instances only subtly.

The movement has altered the consciousness of Mexican-Americans. The highly publicized assertions of Chicano rights and cultural legacies
have led some in the community to goals similar to those stemming from the
Mexican Revolution: that "the people refuse all outside help, every imported
scheme, every idea lacking some profound relationship to their intimate feelings, and that instead they turn to themselves" (Paz 1961:147). Others have
built on the earlier militancy in more traditionally American reform efforts,
directing their energies toward fuller Chicano participation in the benefits
of the larger society. As Samora and Simon noted (1977:227), Chicanos have
learned the maxim of American democratic politics that "the wheel that

squeaks the loudest gets the most grease." Some others have sought to redirect the focus of the 1960's to even more far-reaching efforts: "The Chicano movement . . . is in the process of transition from the ambiguous ideas and rhetoric of chauvinist cultural nationalism to the development of critical analysis of the structure of a capitalist society" (Munoz 1974:137). Finally, there are still a few who continue to attribute Chicano problems to Chicanos themselves.

Chicanozaje

The development of *Chicanozaje* (or Chicanismo, as it is sometimes called) is the most pervasive sign of the altered consciousness of Mexican-Americans. The term "Chicano" was seized upon by militants (especially youths) in the 1960's to express disdain for their "hyphenated" status as Mexican-Americans and to retain identity with their Mexican heritage. While many in the Mexican-American community rejected the term, associating it with the vulgarities of street life, its use spread until even establishment figures—white middle-class leaders included—had adopted it. In recent years more sophisticated objections to Chicanozaje have been raised: "The 'Chicano culture' of today is still characterized by negative aspects. The abstract defense of imaginary, entirely 'good' culture is nothing but the resurrection of the myth of the noble savage in a different disguise" (Fernandez 1977:152). This viewpoint, however, gives inadequate recognition to the all-encompassing scope of the word "Chicano," which covers the diversity of Mexican-American life-styles (Gomez-Quinones 1978:13).

Generally, Chicanozaje includes a historical awareness of the Chicanos' role as oppressed members of society. Chicanos stress the acts of being (how the past shaped them) and becoming (how they will shape the future). Equally important, they now realize that their past is a complex one of multiple heritages: "it is incredibly ancient on the one hand, and surprisingly new on the other. Indian, Spanish, Mexican, and Anglo elements have gone into its formation, and they continue to affect it" (Bacalski-Martinez 1979:19). Because of this background a whole range of cultural variation is possible. Some can favor the European side, others the Indian, or they can move in between seeking the cultural style that fits them (Sanchez 1976:85). Chicanozaje thus expands the boundaries of the age-old mestizaje tradition of Mexico. It is a fluid, dual cultural membership that gives a deeper meaning to the term "Chicano." Hence, "we are no longer Chicanos and yet . . . we are very much Chicanos . . . some of us are because we have found ourselves to be in a process of 'becoming': of adding, of multiplying, of subtracting, of dividing ourselves and others into moral categories—part of the process of constant creation" (Velez-I. 1979:46).

Fig. 9-7. Mestizaje heritage. (Drawing by Mary Nunez.)

Chicano arts

Both aspects of Chicanozaje—the past and the future—are apparent in the blossoming of Chicano arts since the 1960's. Contemplative artists incorporated a change of consciousness. Poets, writers, filmmakers, and muralists are known to create and maintain this state of mind (Cardenas De Dwyer 1975; Lowenfels 1973). East Los Angeles Chicano painters and muralists, and others as well, have interpreted the cultural-historical legacies of barrio dwellers. By creating a work of art they have brought a new awareness and focus to the people's experiences. "The murals show how the artist of the barrio sees his people. . . . They describe the anger in the barrio, the anger of being caught in a trap you cannot escape. The violence expressed is like that of a man who has his back against a wall and has nowhere to run" (Kahn 1975:119). The murals also drew on historical inspirations such as the Mexican Revolution and the Indian legacies, thus reminding viewers of the rich past and revolutionary potential of the Chicano people.

This type of consciousness-raising can be found in several areas of expression. For example, the *Teatro Campesino* (Rural Workers Theater) began as a medium to inform farm workers and others about the 1965-1970 grape boycott. Later it became a model for youth teatro groups throughout

Fig. 9-8. A and **B,** Murals in East Los Angeles.

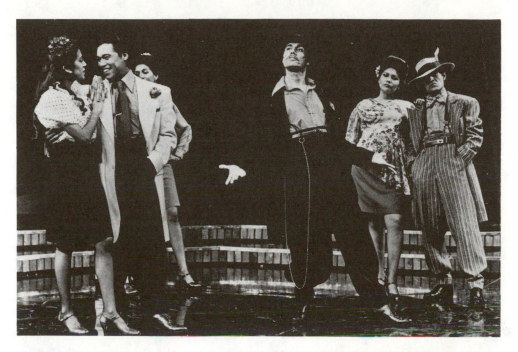

Fig. 9-9. A scene from *Zoot Suit* by Luis Valdez at the Center Theatre Group/Mark Taper Forum in Los Angeles.

the nation. These theater groups used dramatic interpretation to expose the conditions of the Chicano people. "When one considers the fact that the theater in the Southwest has always had a dual function, entertainment plus instruction, the appropriateness of the play for serving as the vehicle of cultural awareness and expansion becomes readily apparent" (Bacalski-Martinez 1979:33). Teatros have combined humor and satire to portray the multiple Chicano heritage. In this manner a consciousness is generated. People laugh, cry, or feel pain at the same moment, as if they were all of a similar mind. "All of the dramatic techniques used by the teatro were directed toward depicting the political situations and offering alternative solutions. The goal of the techniques was to produce immediate empathy in order to motivate action. They were symbolic of what 'ought' to have been done in reality" (Garcia 1978:40). The original Teatro Campesino, led by Luis Valdez, presented the successful play *Zoot-Suit*, which familiarized audiences with Chicano urban experiences.

Educational transformations

Similar changes are taking place in the Chicano educational experience. From Operation Head Start to the university, teachers and stu-

Fig. 9-10. Bilingual program classroom. (Courtesy Follow-Through Project, Cuca-monga, Calif.)

dents are comparing notes on the past and present (Samora and Simon 1977:218). In this exchange each learns from the other. Since most of the teachers are middle class, students regularly remind them of community needs. As a result, teachers find themselves responding to subtle pressures, even though they may have left the barrio years before. Student awareness is also altered as teachers present knowledge previously unavailable to them. Students have embraced a new social concern: "To that end, we pledge our efforts and take as our credo what Jose Vasconcelos once said at a time of crisis and hope: 'At this moment we do not come to work for the University, but to demand that the University work for our people'" (El Plan de Santa Barbara 1973:536) (Gomez-Quinones 1978:153-166).

One program offered by reformers was for bilingual education, an idea that has garnered increasing support from Anglo officials (Arvizu and Snyder 1977:1; Macias 1973:63). According to experts, Chicano educational liabilities have stemmed from a cultural, and specifically, a linguistic source. To correct this, schools were to give equal time and attention to English and Spanish. Thus, Chicanos and others would learn to appreciate their culture and language. Gradually, it was reasoned, the sense of Chicano inferiority engendered by traditional schooling would give way to a positive attitude toward themselves and education, and traditional Anglo ethnocentrism would begin its demise.

Government-supported experimental bilingual education programs began to tackle the "cultural" problem. It is no coincidence that most of these programs were started at the height of the movement (de la Garza 1979:106), although even reformist notions based on cultural criteria were considered too radical previously. After the programs were initiated, however, it was too late to rescind them. Both Anglo and Chicano educators found that the bilingual programs in large part improved student school performances (U.S. Commission on Civil Rights 1975:69). Also, parents and community leaders strongly supported bilingual education, for they had participated in its creation and implementation (Ballesteros 1979:161).

Revolution or reform?

While reforms made a contribution, some claim that leaders of these efforts exploited the Chicano movement (Munoz 1974:121). Rocco (1974:168) has argued that "this type of effort accepts and legitimizes, thus reinforcing, the institutions and processes through which demands are made." Thus, it is said, while such reforms (and others: the Southwest is now dotted with Chicano agencies and centers) have ameliorated suffering in Chicano communities and afforded the opportunity for more familiarity with dominant institutions, they have also allowed the same institutions to "co-opt" community leaders. Activist critics are quick to point out that in most instances reformers' pursestrings are not in the hands of Chicanos.

So far only the reform efforts within a cultural nationalist framework have been discussed. The intention here was not to downplay the importance of other factors but rather to reflect the tenor of the times. Chicanos were committed to improving their overall standard of living—schools, jobs, and so on—and they worked hard for these goals. However, leaders tended to emphasize cultural rights as a precondition leading to advances in other areas.

While cultural transformations were under way, some weak (even barely perceptible) class and color changes occurred. The spirit of the Mexican Revolution was instrumental in this slight stirring since cultural nationalists drew on the egalitarian revolutionary ideas of such leaders as Emiliano Zapata, Pancho Villa, and Ricardo Flores Magon (Fallows 1972:318-321). Unfortunately, "despite the political rhetoric of the last forty years, social values still continue to reflect the basic dehumanizing dimensions of the system, which hold possessions to be more important than people" (Rocco 1974:167). The movement gave hope for future generations, but the 1970's put brakes on those aspirations.

Fig. 9-11. A, Zapata and Villa meet near Mexico City. **B** and **C,** Villistas. (Courtesy Josefa V. Cordero.)

Social class and sexual equality

The median family income of the Spanish-surnamed population in 1969 was $7080 and that of the Anglos $10,750—a sizable gap (Briggs, Fosil, and Schmidt 1977:43). Ten years later, Chicano family income is still 70% of that for whites, or $11,742 as opposed to approximately $16,000 (Thurow 1979). Moreover, in 1979 almost 2.2 million Hispanic people were below the poverty level, and 1.4 million of these were of Mexican origin (Romero

1979:17). "While 9.3% of all families live below the official poverty line ($6,191 for an urban family of four in 1977) 21% of the general Hispanic Community and 19% of the Mexican American Community live below the poverty line" (Thurow 1979:3). Thus, despite an increase in the number of Chicanos in skilled and white-collar occupations, there was still a relative gap in income. Several observers (Romero 1979:19; Poston Alvirez, and Tienda 1977:40) have emphasized the persistence of discrimination as the primary barrier.

One national issue steadily gaining attention deals with equal opportunity for women, another class factor. *Chicanas* (Mexican-American women) are very much involved in that struggle, and in fact their role affects important cultural and socioeconomic dimensions (Melville 1980). Since historical conditions have relegated Chicanos to the lowest positions, Chicanas are even more disadvantaged than non-Chicano women (Gonzales 1979:81-99). In 1969 the salaries of working Chicanas averaged only a third of those of white female workers (Arroyo 1977:165).

The heroine of the classic labor film *Salt of the Earth* underscores the Chicana plight with these angry and insightful words (aimed not only at her husband but presumably at all minority men): "Do you feel better having someone lower than you? Whose neck shall I stand on to make me feel superior? And what will I get out of it? I don't want anything lower than I am. I'm low enough already. I want to rise. And push everything up with me as I go." Chicanas and other minority women are actively pursuing the end of their position as "twice a minority" (Melville 1980).

United States, Mexico, and undocumented immigrants

Chicano economic inequality is intertwined with the continuing saga of "as the United States goes, so goes Mexico." American interests have never relinquished some types of commercial investment in Mexico, and recent events illustrate the problems resulting from these investments. For example, in an effort to escape from United States labor unions many corporations (known as multinationals because they transcend national boundaries and move to whatever nation provides the cheapest workers) have built plants just across the Mexican border to tap the cheap source of labor (Fernandez 1977:131; Flores 1979). The growth of "sister" border cities along the United States-Mexican boundary has an economic basis: On the Mexican side, "about one-fifth to one-third of the wages earned by residents of these cities are earned in the United States" (Price 1973:9).

The 1970's witnessed the largest influx of undocumented Mexican workers yet, anywhere from 2 to 12 million (Cornelius 1978:10). (Previous periods of high immigration were the 1920's and 1950's-1960's.) These work-

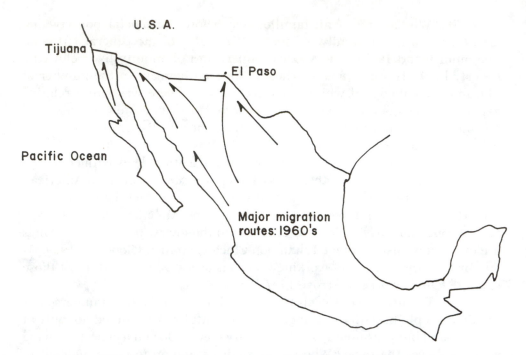

Fig. 9-12. Immigration routes in the 1960's. (Map by Jesus Medina.)

ers fill the low-paid, unskilled jobs no one else wants and, indeed, provide important services. They have nevertheless become a focus of concern for many people, including government officials, and some of the solutions to the "problem" have betrayed continuing ethnic discriminatory attitudes (Rios-Bustamante 1977). For example, Congressman Peter Rodino presented a bill that would allow employers to ask for place of birth identification from anyone "appearing" to be Mexican. Obviously, such a measure would infringe on the civil rights of millions of Mexican-Americans born in the United States. To resolve this difficulty, one naive apologist suggested that native Mexicans could wear badges.

Growing Chicano strength

Fortunately, Chicanos protested against discriminatory legislation and, with support from others, turned back efforts to control the flow of immigration in this manner. This is only one instance of the increased strength of the Chicano community in American politics and of the alliances sometimes formed with liberal whites and others. Another illustration is the successful outcome of the United Farm Workers' call for a boycott of California grapes and lettuce—farmers eventually recognized the union and California enacted progressive farm labor laws (Kushner 1975). La Raza Unida has at times influenced local elections (even winning several) and Chicano elected and appointed officials have increased in number at all levels of government. The Catholic Church has attempted to organize families into large neighborhood groups such as Communities Organized for Public Service (COPS) in San Antonio, The Organization of the Northwest (TON) in Chicago, and the United Neighborhood Organization (UNO) in Los Angeles.

These successes have by no means overcome all institutional discrimination against Chicano leadership, and factionalism among Chicano politicans has also retarded advances. Still, the few victories are sufficient to prove the merit of Rivera's (1974:219) observation: "Where Chicanos comprise a substantial proportion of the population, it should be possible to express Chicano consciousness through the . . . political system."

Indeed, there is ample reason to expect Chicano consciousness and political influence to continue to grow. The recent emergence of energy resources as a source of international prestige and power has been accompanied by the discovery of huge oil and natural gas reserves in Mexico. The new prestige that energy-consuming Americans will accord Mexico will in all probability influence the status of Chicanos in the United States. The Chicano population is also increasing rapidly—it now averages twelve percent in the Southwest overall and thirty-two percent in New Mexico (de la Garza 1979:117). Some observers (Scott 1979) are predicting that the Chicano population of Los Angeles will soon grow sufficiently to make California the first "Third World state" in the nation. The continuing massive immigration from Mexico will not only enlarge the Chicano population in the United States, but it will strengthen the links between the Chicano community and Mexico (Rocco 1974:175; Gomez-Quinones 1978:43). Moreover, it will add luster to Chicanozaje imagery (Ramirez 1978).

The legacy of the Chicano movement has not yet been worked out. Today's students and the professionals who emerged from among the students of the 1960's are fashioning new routes for change. One approach focuses on revolutionary concepts: "the student movement produced a very crucial element for the future, intellectuals with a class stand" (Gomez-Quinones 1978:46). Indian themes are also recurrent, echoing the militant resistance of ancient heroes such as Cuahtemoc or the profundity of contemporary mystics such as Don Juan Matus (Castaneda 1969). The process of change is weaving a newly distinct, yet diverse, pattern (Lux and Vigil 1979).

As might be expected, many hazards can accompany such a complex process. There still persists, for example, the problem of marginality; some people are unable to function adequately in any culture, much less

Fig. 9-13. Cholo montage. (Drawing by Mary Nunez.)

become creative cultural innovators. Obviously the barrio problem of gang warfare stems from many sources, but one cannot explain the cholo life-style without including cultural criteria. As previously noted, the cholo is marginal to the two main cultures. Some have patterned a life based on *la vida loca* (the crazy life). This is a subcultural model that over the years has become so institutionalized that "crazy" acts are accepted as normal. Considering the conditions that created this *vato loco* (crazy dude) tradition, it is no wonder that many who feel wronged by society believe it is the only way to survive in the United States. However, the majority of cholos follow a less destructive path, cruising with the cholas, getting high, and generally presenting an image of urban Chicano cool. Many simply behave like cholos because it is stylish and the "in thing" to do.

Chicanos: nativist acculturationists

The Chicano community on the whole has sought a more rewarding route. Those favoring the label "Chicano" have chosen their own name. It is a declaration of independence: "today this term refers to Mexican Americans who are no longer willing to be treated as second-class citizens. The Chicano takes pride in his cultural heritage and vigorously denies any suggestion that he is culturally deprived or in any way inferior" (de la Garza 1979:101). The term "Chicano" implies pride in a background of many and mixed heritages and the versatility to widen one's sociocultural persona. This pattern of nativist acculturation, in which the dominant cultural mode is learned and the native style kept, will lead American citizens away from ethnocentrism (Vigil and Long 1978). "Biculturalism is of tremendous advantage . . . for it carries with it . . . the ability to pick and choose constructively and eclectically from two different and useful cultures" (Arvizu 1974:125-126).

This pattern is based on cultural democracy: everyone's way of life is right and proper (Ramirez 1976:198). In such a setting, the future of the Chicano appears promising. "I would suggest that if we want to predict changes in the American continent, we should look at the Chicano; we must look at ourselves—for we reflect the western hemisphere in a state of cultural and social change" (Velez-I. 1979:48). As a socioculturally diverse population within the United States, Chicanos are in the forefront of this new age of "panhuman" awareness.

REFERENCES

Acosta, O. Z.: *The revolt of the cockroach people*, San Francisco, 1973, Straight Arrow Books.

Acuna, R.: *Occupied America*, San Francisco, 1972, Canfield Press.

Almaguer, T.: Historical notes on Chicano oppression: the dialectics of racial and class domination in North America, *Aztlan*, Spring and Fall, 1974.

Alvarez, R.: The psycho-historical and socio-economic development of the Mexican-American people. In Rosaldo, R., Calvert, R. A., and Seligmann, G. L., editors: *Chicano, the evolution of a people*, Minneapolis, 1973, Winston Press.

Alvarez, R.: The psycho-historical and socio-economic development of the Chicano society in the U.S. In Hernandez, C. A., Haug, M. J., and Wagner, N. N.: *Chicanos: social and psychological perspectives*, ed. 2, St. Louis, 1976, The C. V. Mosby Co.

Alvarez, S.: Mexican American community organizations. In Romano-V., O. I., editor: *El grito*, Berkeley, Calif., 1971, Quinto Sol Publications.

Alverez, J. H.: A demographic profile of the Mexican immigration to the United States, 1910-1950. In Rosaldo, R., Calvert, R. A., and Seligmann, G. L., editors: *Chicano: the evolution of a people*, Minneapolis, 1973, Winston Press.

Arens, W., and Montague, S. P.: *The American dimension: cultural myths and social reali-*

ties, Sherman Oaks, Calif., 1976, Alfred Publishing Co., Inc.

Arroyo, L. E.: Industrial and occupational distribution of Chicana workers. In Sanchez, R., and Cruz, R. M., editors: *Essays on la mujer*, Los Angeles, 1977, The University of California, Chicano Studies Center.

Arroyo, L. L.: Notes on past, present and future directions of Chicano labor studies, *Aztlan*, Summer, 1975.

Arvizu, S. F.: Education for constructive marginality. In Dillon, W., editor: *The cultural drama*, Washington, D.C., 1974, Smithsonian Institution Press.

Arvizu, S. F., and Snyder, W.: *Demystifying the concept of culture: theoretical and conceptual tools*, Sacramento, 1977, Cross Cultural Resource Center.

Bacalski-Martinez, R. R.: Aspects of Mexican American cultural heritage. In Trejo, A., editor: *The Chicanos: as we see ourselves*, Tucson, 1979, The University of Arizona Press.

Ballesteros, D.: Bilingual-bicultural education: a must for Chicanos. In Trejo, A., editor: *The Chicanos: as we see ourselves*, Tucson, 1979, The University of Arizona Press.

Barker, G. C.: *Social functions of language in a Mexican-American community*, Tucson, 1972, The University of Arizona Press.

Barrera, M.: *Race and class in the Southwest: a theory of racial inequality*, Notre Dame,

Ind., 1979, University of Notre Dame Press.

Barrera, M., Munoz, C., and Ornelas, C.: The barrio as an internal colony. In Garcia, F. C., editor: *La causa politica: a Chicano politics reader*, Notre Dame, Ind., 1974, University of Notre Dame Press.

Barrett, D. N.: Demographic characteristics. In Samora, J., editor: *La Raza: forgotten Americans*, Notre Dame, Ind., 1966, University of Notre Dame Press.

Bastide, R.: Color, racism, and Christianity. In Franklin, J. H., editor: *Color and race*, Boston, 1968, Houghton Mifflin Co.

Bayard, M.P.: Ethnic identity and stress: the significance of sociocultural context. In Casas, J., and Keefe, S., editors: *Family and mental health in the Mexican American community*, Los Angeles, 1978, U.C.L.A., Spanish Speaking Mental Health Research Center.

Bazant, J.: *A concise history of Mexico from Hidalgo to Cardenas, 1805-1940*, New York, 1977, Cambridge University Press.

Betten, N., and Mohl, R. A.: From discrimination to repatriation: Mexican life in Gary, Indiana during the Great Depression. In Hundley, N., editor: *The Chicano*, Santa Barbara, Calif., 1975, ABC-CLIO, Inc.

Blawis, P. B.: Tijerina and the land grants. In Duran, L. I., and Bernard, H. R., editors: *Introduction to Chicano studies*, New York, 1973, Macmillan, Inc.

Briggs, V. M., Jr.: *Chicanos and rural poverty*, Baltimore, 1973, The Johns Hopkins University Press.

Briggs, V. M., Jr., Fogel, W., and Schmidt, F. H.: *The Chicano worker*, Austin, 1977, University of Texas Press.

Bustamante, J.: Commodity migrants: structural analysis of Mexican immigration to the United States. In Ross, R. S., editor: *Views across the border: the United States and Mexico*, Albuquerque, 1978, University of New Mexico Press.

Camarillo, A.: Research note on Chicano community leaders: the G.I. generation, *Aztlan*, Fall, 1970.

Camarillo, A.: *Chicanos in a changing society: from Mexican pueblos to American barrios in Santa Barbara and southern California, 1848-1930*, Cambridge, Mass., 1979, Harvard University Press.

Camejo, A.: Lessons of the Los Angeles Chicano protest. In Duran, L. I., and Bernard, H. R., editors: *Introduction to Chicano studies*, New York, 1973, Macmillan, Inc.

Campa, A.: The Mexican-American in historical perspective. In Rosaldo, R., Calvert, R. A., and Seligmann, G. L., editors: *Chicano: the evolution of a people*, Minneapolis, 1973, Winston Press.

Cardenas, G.: Mexican labor: a view to conceptualizing the effects of migration, immigration and the Chicano population in the United States. In Teller, C., Estrada, L., Hernandez, J., and Alvirez, D., editors: *Cuantos somos: a demographic study of the Mexican American population*, Austin, 1977, University of Texas Press, Center for Mexican American Studies.

Cardenas De Dwyer, D.: *Chicano voices*, Boston, 1975, Houghton Mifflin Co.

Carter, T. P.: Mexican Americans: how the schools have failed them. In Duran, L. I., and Bernard, H. R., editors: *Introduction to Chicano studies*, New York, 1973, Macmillan, Inc.

Casso, H. J.: Higher education and the Mexican-American. In Tyler, G., editor: *Mexican-Americans tomorrow*, Albuquerque, 1975, University of New Mexico Press.

Casteneda, A.: Melting potters vs. cultural pluralists: implications for education. In Castaneda, A., et al., editors: *Mexican Americans and educational change*, New York: 1974, Arno Press, Inc.

Castaneda, C.: *The teachings of Don Juan: a Yaqui way of knowledge*, Berkeley, 1968, University of California Press.

Cline, H. F.: *Mexico: revolution to evolution 1940-1960*, New York, 1963, Oxford University Press.

Cockcroft, J. D.: *Intellectual precursors of the Mexican Revolution, 1900-1913*, Austin, 1968, University of Texas Press.

Cornelius, W. A.: *Mexican migration to the United States: causes, consequences, and U.S. responses*, Cambridge, Mass., 1978, Center for International Studies.

Cuellar, A.: Perspectives on politics. In Duran, L. I., and Bernard, H. R., editors: *Introduction to Chicano studies*, New York, 1973, Macmillan, Inc.

Cumberland, C. C.: *Mexico: the struggle for modernity*, Oxford, 1968, Oxford University Press.

de la Garza, R. O.: The politics of the Mexican Americans. In Trejo, A., editor: *The Chicanos: as we see ourselves*, Tucson, 1979, The University of Arizona Press.

de Leon, M.: The hamburger and the taco: a cultural reality. In Johnson, H. S., and Hernandez, W. J., editors: *Educating the Mexican American*, Valley Forge, Pa., 1970, Judson Press.

Diaz-Guerrero, R.: *Psychology of the Mexican*, Austin, 1975, University of Texas Press.

Diaz-Guerrero, R.: Mexicans and Americans: two worlds, one border . . . and one observer. In Ross, R. S., editor: *Views across the border: the United States and Mexico*, Albuquerque, 1978, University of New Mexico Press.

Dunne, J. G.: *Delano*, New York, 1967, Ambassador Books, Ltd.

Dworkin, A. G.: Stereotypes and self-images held by native-born and foreign-born Mexican-Americans. In Wagner, N. N., and Haug, M. J.: *Chicanos*, ed. 1, St. Louis, 1971, The C. V. Mosby Co.

Dworkin, A. G.: National origin and ghetto experience as variables in Mexican American stereotypy. In Hernandez, C. A., Haug, J. J., and Wagner, N. N.: *Chicanos: social and psychological perspectives*, ed. 2, St. Louis, 1976, The C. V. Mosby Co.

El Plan de Santa Barbara: the formation of Chicano studies programs. In Duran, L. I., and Bernard, H. R., editors: *Introduction to Chicano studies*, New York, 1973, Macmillan, Inc.

El Plan Espiritual de Aztlan. In Johnson, H. S., and Hernandez, W. J., editors: *Educating the Mexican American*, Valley Forge, Pa., 1970, Judson Press.

Emiliano, R.: Nathuatlan elements in Chicano speech. In Romano-V., O. I., editor: *Grito del sol*, Berkeley, Calif., 1976, Tonatiuh International, Inc.

Ericksen, C. A.: Uprising in the barrios. In Johnson, H. S., and Hernandez, W. J., editors: *Educating the Mexican American*, Valley Forge, Pa., 1970, Judson Press.

Fallows, M.: The Mexican American laborers: a different drummer. In Simmen, E., editor: *Pain and promise: the Chicano today*, New York, 1972, New American Library, Inc.

Fernandez, R. A.: *The United States-Mexico border*, Notre Dame, Ind., 1977, University of Notre Dame Press.

Flores, E. T.: Multinational Mexican workers: their struggles, the multidimensional attack on them and possible responses, *Zerowork* **3**, 1979.

Florez, J.: Chicanos and coalitions as a force for social change. In Mangold, M. M., editor: *La causa Chicana: the movement for justice*, New York, 1971, Family Service Association of America.

Foley, D. E., et al.: *From peones to politicos: ethnic relations in a south Texan town, 1900 to 1977*, Austin, 1977, University of Texas Press, Center for Mexican American Studies.

Forbes, J. D.: *Aztecas del norte: the Chicanos of Aztlan*, New York, 1973, Fawcett Books.

Frazier, E. F.: *Race and culture contacts in the modern world*, New York, 1957, Alfred A. Knopf, Inc.

Fuller, E.: The Mexican housing problem, Los Angeles (1920). In Cortez, C. E., editor: *Perspectives on Mexican-American life*, New York, 1974, Arno Press, Inc.

Galarza, E.: *Merchants of labor*, Santa Barbara, Calif., 1964, McNally & Loftin, Publishers.

Galarza, E.: *Barrio boy*, Notre Dame, Ind., 1971, University of Notre Dame Press.

Galarza, E., Gallegos, H., and Samora, J.: *Mexican-Americans in the Southwest*, Santa Barbara, Calif., 1969, McNally & Loftin, Publishers.

Gamio, M.: *Mexican immigration to the United States*, New York, 1969, Arno Press, Inc. (originally published in 1930).

Garcia, F. C., and de la Garza, R. O.: *The Chicano political experience*, North Scituate, Mass., 1977, Duxbury Press.

Garcia, J. C.: Teatro Chicano and the analysis of sacred symbols: towards a Chicano world-view in the social sciences. In Arvizu, S. F., editor: *Chicano perspectives on decolonizing anthropology*, Berkeley, Calif., 1978, Tonatiuh International, Inc.

Gardner, R.: *Grito: Reis Tijerina and the New Mexico land grant war of 1967*, New York, 1970, Harper & Row, Publishers.

Gecas, V.: Self-conceptions of migrants and settled Mexican Americans. In Hernandez, C. A., Haug, M. J., and Wagner, N. N.: *Chicanos: social and psychological perspectives*, St. Louis, ed. 2, 1976, The C. V. Mosby Co.

Gilbert, M. J.: Extended family integration among second-generation Mexican Americans. In Casas, J., and Keefe, S., editors: *Family and mental health in the Mexican American community*, Los Angeles, 1978, U.C.L.A., Spanish Speaking Mental Health Research Center.

Glick, L. B.: The right to equal opportunity. In Samora, J., editor: *La Raza: forgotten Americans*, Notre Dame, Ind., 1966, University of Notre Dame Press.

Goldschmidt, W.: *As you sow*, New York, 1947, The Free Press.

Gomez, D.: *Somos Chicanos: strangers in our own land*, Boston, 1973, Beacon Press.

Gomez-Quinones, J.: Plan de San Diego reviewed, *Aztlan*, Spring, 1970.

Gomez-Quinones, J.: The first steps: Chicano labor conflict and organizing 1900-1920, *Aztlan*, 1972.

Gomez-Quinones, J.: *The origin and development of the Mexican working class in the United States: laborers and artisans north of the Rio Bravo, 1600-1900*, Patscuaro, Mexico, 1977, Fifth International Congress of Mexican Studies.

Gomez-Quinones, J.: *Mexican students por La Raza: the Chicano student movement in southern California, 1967-1977*, Santa Barbara, Calif., 1978, Editorial La Causa.

Gonzales, N. L.: *The Spanish-Americans of New Mexico*, Albuquerque, 1967, University of New Mexico Press.

Gonzales, R.: Chicano nationalism: the key to unity for La Raza. In Rosaldo, R., Calvert, R. A., and Seligmann, G. L., editors: *Chicano: the evolution of a people*, Minneapolis, 1973, Winston Press.

Gonzales, R.: *I am Joaquin*, Denver, 1967, Crusade for Justice.

Gonzales, S. A.: The Chicana perspective: a design for self-awareness. In Trejo, A., editor: *The Chicanos: as we see ourselves*, Tucson, 1979, The University of Arizona Press.

Gonzalez, H. B.: Response to Chicano militancy. In Meir, M. S., and Rivera, F., editors: *Readings on La Raza: the twentieth century*, New York, 1974, Hill & Wang.

Gordon, M.: *Social class in American sociology*, New York, 1963, McGraw-Hill, Inc.

Grebler, L., Moore, J. W., and Guzman, R. C.: *The Mexican-American people*, New York, 1970, The Free Press.

Grebler, L., Moore, J. W., and Guzman, R. C.: The family: variations in time and space. In Duran, L. I., and Bernard, H. R., editors: *Introduction to Chicano studies*, New York, 1973, Macmillan, Inc.

Griffith, B.: *American me*, Boston, 1948, Houghton-Mifflin Co.

Guerra, M.: The Mexican-American child: problems or talents? In Johnson, H. S., and Hernandez, W. J., editors: *Educating the Mexican American*, Valley Forge, Pa., 1970, Judson Press.

Guzman, R.: The function on Anglo-American racism. In Meir, M. S., and Rivera, F., editors: *Readings on La Raza: the twentieth century*, New York, 1974, Hill & Wang.

Harrington, M.: *The other America*, New York, 1962, The Viking Press, Inc.

Heizer, R. F., and Almquist, A. J.: *The other Californians: prejudice and discrimination under Spain, Mexico, and the United States to 1920*, Berkeley, 1971, University of California Press.

Heller, C. S.: *New converts to the American dream*, New Haven, Conn., 1971, College & University Press.

Hernandez, D.: La Raza satellite system, *Aztlan*, Spring, 1970.

Hinojos, F. G.: Notes on the pachuco: stereotypes, history, and dialect, *Atisbos: Journal of Chicano Research*, Summer, 1975.

Hirsch, H.: Political scientists and other camaradas: academic myth making and racial stereotypes. In de la Garza, R., Kruszewski, A., and Arciniega, T., editors: *Chicanos and Native Americans*, Englewood Cliffs, N.J., 1973, Prentice-Hall, Inc.

Hoffman, A.: *Unwanted Mexican Americans in the Great Depression*, Tucson, 1974, The University of Arizona Press.

Hughes, E. C., and Hughes, H. M.: *Where peoples meet: racial and ethnic frontiers*, New York, 1952, The Free Press.

Inkeles, A., quoted in Toth, R.: Americans' traits: steady amid change, *Los Angeles Times*, Sept. 20, 1977.

Juarez, A.: The emergence of El Partido de la Raza Unida: California's new Chicano party. In Garcia, F. C., editor: *La causa politica: a Chicano politics reader*, Notre Dame, Ind., 1974, University of Notre Dame Press.

Kahn, D.: Chicano street murals: people's art in the East Los Angeles barrio, *Aztlan*, Spring, 1975.

Kahn, H.: *World economic development*, Boulder, Colo., 1979, Westview Press, Inc.

Kluckholm, F. R., and Strodtbeck, F. L.: *Variations in value orientations*, Evanston, Ill., 1961, Row, Peterson and Co.

Knowlton, C. S.: The neglected chapters in Mexican-American history. In Tyler, G., editor: *Mexican-Americans tomorrow*, Albuquerque, 1975, University of New Mexico Press.

Krueger, D. W.: The effect of urban-industrial values on the Indian life style. In de la Garza, R., Kruszewski, A., and Arciniega, T., editors: *Chicanos and Native Americans*, Englewood Cliffs, N.J., 1973, Prentice-Hall, Inc.

Kushner, S.: Long road to Delano, New York, 1975, International Publishers Co., Inc.

Kutsche, P.: The Anglo side of acculturation. In Helm, J., editor: *Spanish-speaking people in the United States*, Seattle, 1968, American Ethnological Society.

Lamb, B. P.: The early cinema views the Mexican-Americans. In Servin, M. P., editor: *Early southwestern minorities, Journal of the West* **XIV**:4, 1975.

Lewis, O.: *Five families: Mexican case studies in the culture of poverty*, New York, 1959, Harper & Row, Publishers.

Limon, J.: El Primer Congreso Mexicanista de 1911: a precursor to contemporary Chicanismo, *Aztlan*, Spring and Fall, 1974.

Linton, R.: One hundred per cent American. In Hayes, J. R., and Henslin, J. M., editors: *Introducing anthropology*, Boston, 1975, Holbrook Press, Inc.

Lopez, R.: The El Monte berry strike of 1933, *Aztlan*, Spring, 1970.

Lopez-McKnight, G.: Communication: the key to social change. In Mangold, M. M., editor: *La causa Chicana: the movement for justice*, New York, 1971.

Lopez y Rivas, G.: *The Chicanos: life and struggles of the Mexican minority in the United States*, New York, 1973, Monthly Review Press.

Lowenfels, W.: *From the belly of the shark*, New York, 1973, Random House, Inc.

Lux, M., and Vigil, M. E.: Return to Aztlan: the Chicano rediscovers his Indian past.

In Trejo, A.: *The Chicanos: as we see ourselves*, Tucson, 1979, The University of Arizona Press.

Macias, R.: Developing a bilingual, culturally relevant educational program for Chicanos, *Aztlan*, Spring, 1973.

Madsen, W.: *The Mexican Americans of south Texas*, New York, 1964, Holt, Rinehart & Winston.

Manuel, H.: *Spanish-speaking children of the Southwest*, Austin, 1965, University of Texas Press.

Marin, C.: Rodolfo "Corky" Gonzales: the Mexican-American movement spokesman, 1966-1972. In Servin, M. P., editor: *Early southwestern minorities, Journal of the West* **XIV**:4, 1975.

Martinez, C.: Community mental health and the Chicano movement. In Hernandez, C. A., Haug, M. J., and Wagner, N. N.: *Chicanos: social and psychological perspectives*, ed. 2, St. Louis, 1976, The C. V. Mosby Co.

Martinez, J. J.: Leadership and politics. In Samora, J., editor: *La Raza: forgotten Americans*, Notre Dame, Ind., 1966, Notre Dame University Press.

Martinez, T.: Advertising and racism: the case of the Mexican American. In Romano-V., O. I., editor: *Voices*, Berkeley, Calif., 1973, Quinto Sol Publications.

McWilliams, C.: *North from Mexico—the Spanish-speaking people of the United States*, Westport, Conn., 1968, Greenwood Press, Inc.

Meinig, D. W.: *Southwest: three peoples in geographical change, 1600-1970*, New York, 1971, Oxford University Press.

Meir, M. S., and Rivera, F., editors: *Readings on La Raza: the twentieth century*, New York, 1974, Hill & Wang.

Melville, M. B.: The Mexican-American and the celebration of the Fiestas Patrias: an ethnohistorical analysis. In Arvizu, S. F., editor: *Chicano perspectives on decolonizing anthropology*, Berkeley, Calif., 1978, Tonatiuh International, Inc.

Melville, M. B.: *Twice a minority: Mexican American women*, St. Louis, 1980, The C. V. Mosby Co.

Monsivais, C.: The culture of the frontier: the Mexican side. In Ross, R. S., editor: *Views across the border: the United States and*

Mexico, Albuquerque, 1978, University of New Mexico Press.

Monthly Labor Review: Industrial relations and labor conditions. In Rosaldo, R., Calvert, R. A., and Seligmann, G. L., editors: *Chicano: The evolution of a people*, 1973, Winston Press.

Monthly Labor Review: Conditions of Mexicans in California. In Meir, M. S., and Rivera, F., editors: *Readings on La Raza: the twentieth century*, New York, 1974, Hill & Wang.

Moore, J.: Colonialism: the case of the Mexican American. In Duran, L. S., and Bernard, H. R., editors: *Introduction to Chicano Studies*, New York, 1973, Macmillan, Inc.

Moore, J. W.: Social class, assimilation and acculturation. In Helm, J., editor: *Spanish-speaking people in the United States*, Seattle, 1968, American Ethnological Society.

Moore, J. W.: *Mexican Americans*, Englewood Cliffs, N.J., 1970, Prentice-Hall, Inc.

Moquin, W., and Van Doren, C., editors: *A documentary history of the Mexican Americans*, New York, 1971, Praeger Publishers.

Morales, A.: *Ando Sangrando*, La Puente, Calif., 1972, Perspectiva Publications.

Morin, R.: *Among the valiant*, Alhambra, Calif., 1966, Borden Publishing Co.

Munoz, C.: The politics of protest and Chicano liberation: a case study of repression and cooptation, *Aztlan*, Spring and Fall, 1974.

Murillo, N.: The Mexican American family. In Hernandez, C. A. Haug, M. J., and Wagner, N. N.: *Chicanos: social and psychological perspectives*, ed. 2, St. Louis, 1976, The C. V. Mosby Co.

Nabokov, P.: *Tijerina and the courthouse raid*, Albuquerque, 1969, University of New Mexico Press.

Negrete, L. A.: Culture clash: the utility of mass proteset as a political response. In Garcia, F. C., editor: *La causa politica: a Chicano politics reader*, Notre Dame, Ind., 1974, University of Notre Dame Press.

Nelson, E.: *Huelga*, Delano, Calif., 1966, Farm Workers Press, Inc.

Nelson-Cisneros, V. B.: La clase trabajadora en Tejas, 1920-1940, *Aztlan*, Summer, 1975.

Noel, D. L.: A theory of the origin of ethnic stratification. In Gelfland, D. E., and Lee,

R. K., editors: *Ethnic conflicts and power: a cross-national perspective*, New York, 1973, John Wiley & Sons, Inc.

Padilla, A. M.: Psychological research and the Mexican American. In Mangold, M. M., editor: *La causa Chicana: the movement for justice*, New York, 1971, Family Service Association of America.

Padilla, A., and Ruiz, R.: Prejudice and discrimination. In Hernanadez, C. A., Haug, M. J., and Wagner, N. N., editors: *Chicanos: social and psychological perspectives*, ed. 2, St. Louis, 1976, The C. V. Mosby Co.

Paredes, A.: The problem of identity in a changing culture: popular expressions of culture conflict along the lower Rio Grande border. In Ross, R. S., editor: *Views across the border: the United States and Mexico*, Albuquerque, 1978, University of New Mexico Press.

Paz, O.: *The labyrinth of solitude*, New York, 1961, Grove Press, Inc.

Penalosa, F.: The changing Mexican-American in Southern California. In Rosaldo, R., Calvert, R. A., and Seligmann, G. L., editors: *Chicano: the evolution of a people*, 1973a, Winston Press.

Penalosa, F.: Toward an operational definition of the Mexican-American. In Rosaldo, R., Calvert, R. A., and Seligmann, G. L., editors: *Chicano: the evolution of a people*, 1973b, Winston Press.

Pillisuk, M., and Pillisuk, P., editors: *Poor Americans: how the white poor live*, New Brunswick, N.J., 1971, Transaction Books.

Poston, D., Alvirez, D., and Tienda, M.: The high cost of being Chicano, *Human Behavior*, September, 1977.

Poston, L. P., and Alvirez, D.: On the cost of being a Mexican American worker. In Hernandez, C. A. Haug, M. J., and Wagner, N. N., editors: *Chicanos: social and psychological perspectives*, ed. 2, St. Louis, 1976, The C. V. Mosby Co.

Price, J. A.: *Tijuana: urbanization in a border culture*, Notre Dame, Ind., 1973, University of Notre Dame Press.

Ramirez III, M.: A mestizo world view and the psychodynamics of Mexican-American border populations. In Ross, R. S., editor: *Views across the border: the United States and Mexico*, Albuquerque, 1978, University of New Mexico Press.

Ramirez III, M.: Cognitive styles and cultural democracy in education. In Hernandez, C. A., Haug, M. J., and Wagner, N. N., editors: *Chicanos: social and psychological perspectives*, ed. 2, St. Louis, 1976, The C. V. Mosby Co.

Reisler, M.: *By the sweat of their brow*, Westport, Conn., 1976, Greenwood Press, Inc.

Rendon, A.: *Chicano manifesto*, New York, 1971, Macmillan, Inc.

Rios, S.: An approach to action anthropology: the community project, C.S.U.S. In Arvizu, S. F., editor: *Chicano perspectives on decolonizing anthropology*, Berkeley, Calif., 1978, Tonatiuh International, Inc.

Rios-Bustamante, A. J., editor: *Immigration and public policy: human rights for undocumented workers and their families*, Los Angeles, 1977, University of California, Chicano Studies Center.

Rippy, J. F.: *The United States and Mexico*, New York, 1926, Alfred A. Knopf, Inc.

Rivera, G., Jr.: Nosotros venceremos: Chicano consciousness and change strategies. In Garcia, F. C., editor: *La causa politica: a Chicano politics reader*, Notre Dame, Ind., 1974, University of Notre Dame Press.

Rocco, R. A.: The Chicano in the social sciences: traditional concepts, myths and images, *Aztlan*, Fall, 1970.

Rocco, R. A.: The role of power and authenticity in the Chicano movement: some reflections, *Aztlan*, Spring and Fall, 1974.

Rodriguez, O., editor: *The politics of Chicano liberation*, New York, 1977, Pathfinder Press, Inc.

Romano-V., O. I.: The anthropology and sociology of the Mexican Americans: the distortion of Mexican American history. In Romano-V., O. I., editor: *El grito*, Berkeley, Calif., 1968, Quinto Sol Publications.

Romano-V., O. I.: *Voices*, Berkeley, Calif., 1973, Quinto Sol Publications.

Romero, F.: *Chicano workers: their utilization and development*, Los Angeles, 1979, University of California, Chicano Studies Center.

Rosen, G.: The development of the Chicano movement in Los Angeles from 1967-1969, *Aztlan*, Spring, 1973.

Rubel, A.: *Across the tracks: Mexican Americans in a Texas city*, Austin, 1966, University of Texas Press.

Samora, J.: *Los mojados: the wetback story*, Notre Dame, Ind., 1971, University of Notre Dame Press.

Samora, J., and Simon, P. V.: *A history of the Mexican American people*, Notre Dame, Ind., 1977, University of Notre Dame Press.

Sanchez, D.: *Expedition through Aztlan*, La Puente, Calif., 1978, Perspectiva Publications.

Sanchez, F. A.: Raices Mexicanas. In Romano-V., O. I.: *Grito del sol*, Berkeley, Calif., 1976, Tonatiuh International, Inc.

Sanchez, G.: Educational change in historical perspective. In Castaneda, A., et al., editors: *Mexican Americans and historical change*, New York, 1974, Arno Press, Inc.

Sanchez, G. I.: History, culture, and education. In Samora, J., editor: *La Raza: forgotten Americans*, Notre Dame, Ind., 1966, University of Notre Dame Press.

Sanchez, G. I.: *Forgotten people: a study of New Mexicans*, Albuquerque, 1967, Calvin Horn Publishers (originally published in 1940).

Santana, R., and Esparza, M.: East Los Angeles blowouts. In *Parameters of institutional change: Chicano experiences in education*, Hayward, Calif., 1974, Southwest Network.

School and Society: School bias toward Mexican Americans. In Wagner, N. N., and Haug, M. J.: *Chicanos: social and psychological perspectives*, ed. 1, St. Louis, 1971, The C. V. Mosby Co.

Scott, A.: Anglos in city soon will reach minority status, *Los Angeles Times*, April 9, 1979.

Servin, M. P.: The Mexican-American awakes. In Servin, M. P., editor: *An awakened minority: the Mexican Americans*, Beverly Hills, Calif., 1970, Glencoe Press.

Servin, M. P.: The pre–World War II Mexican American. In Meir, M. S., and Rivera, F., editors: *Readings on La Raza: the twentieth century*, New York, 1974, Hill & Wang.

Shockley, J. S.: *Chicano revolt in a Texas town*, Notre Dame, Ind., 1974, University of Notre Dame Press.

Simmons, O. G.: *Anglo-Americans and change: Mexican Americans in South Texas: a study in dominant-subordinate group relations*, New York, 1974, Arno Press, Inc.

Simmons, O. G.: The mutual images and expectations of Anglo-Americans and Mexican Americans. In Duran, L. I., and Bernard, H. R., editors: *Introduction to Chicano studies*, New York, 1973, Macmillan, Inc.

Sowell, T.: *Race and economics*, New York, 1975, David McKay Co.

Spencer, M. H.: *Contemporary economics*, New York, 1977, Worth Publishers, Inc.

Starr, P. C.: *Economics: principles in action*, Belmont, Calif., 1978, Wadsworth Publishing Co.

Steiner, S.: *La Raza: the Mexican Americans*, New York, 1969, Harper & Row, Publishers.

Stowell, J. S.: The near side of the Mexican question (1921). In Cortez, C. E.: *Perspectives on Mexican-American life*, New York, 1974, Arno Press, Inc.

Swadesh, F. L.: The alianza movement: catalyst for social change in New Mexico. In Rosaldo, R., Calvert, R. A., and Seligmann, G. L., editors: *Chicano: the evolution of a people*, Minneapolis, 1973, Winston Press.

Tannenbaum, F.: *Peace by revolution: Mexico after 1910*, New York, 1933, Columbia University Press.

Taylor, P. S.: *An American Mexican frontier*, Chapel Hill, 1934, University of North Carolina Press.

Thurow, L. C.: Hispanics closing income gap, *Los Angeles Times*, May 5, 1979.

Tirado, M.: Mexican American community political organizations: The key to Chicano political power, *Aztlan*, Spring, 1970.

U.S. Commission on Civil Rights: *Mexican Americans and the administration of justice in the Southwest*, Washington, D.C., 1970, U.S. Government Printing Office.

U.S. Commission on Civil Rights: *Report 1: Ethnic isolation of Mexicans in the public schools of the Southwest*, Washington, D.C., 1971, U.S. Government Printing Office.

U.S. Commission on Civil Rights: *A better chance to learn: bilingual-bicultural education*, Washington, D.C., 1975, U.S. Government Printing Office.

Velez-I., C. G.: Ourselves through the eyes of an anthropologist. In Trejo, A., editor: *The Chicanos: as we see ourselves*, Tucson, 1979, The University of Arizona Press.

Vigil, D.: Marx and Chicano anthropology. In Arvizu, S. F., editor: *Chicano perspectives on decolonizing anthropology*, Berkeley, Calif., 1978, Tonatiuh international, Inc.

Vigil, D., and Long, J. M.: Unidirectional or nativist acculturation: A case for bilingual education. Unpublished paper, 1978.

Vigil, J. D.: *Adolescent Chicano acculturation and school performance: the role of social economic conditions and urban-suburban environmental differences*, Unpublished dissertation, 1976, University of California at Los Angeles.

Villarreal, J. A.: *Pocho*, New York, 1970, Doubleday & Co., Inc.

Villegas, D. C., et al.: *A compact history of Mexico*, Los Angeles, 1974, University of California, Latin American Center.

Wagley, C., and Harris, M.: *Minorities in the New World*, New York, 1958, Columbia University Press.

Webb, W. P.: *The Texas Rangers: a century of frontier defense*, Austin, 1935, University of Texas Press.

Weber, D. J.: *Foreigners in their native land*, Albuquerque, 1973, University of New Mexico Press.

Weber, M.: *The Protestant ethic and the spirit of capitalism*, New York, 1958, Charles Scribner's Sons.

Wright, D. E., Salinas, E., and Kuvlesky, W. P.: Opportunities for social mobility for Mexican-American youth. In de la Garza, R., Kruszewski, A., and Arciniega, T., editors: *Chicanos and Native Americans*, Englewood Cliffs, N.J., 1973, Prentice-Hall, Inc.

Zeleny, C.: *Relations between the Spanish-Americans and Anglo-Americans in New Mexico*, New York, 1974, Arno Press, Inc.

CONCLUSION

A LOOK TO THE FUTURE
1960's onward

IMPORTANCE OF HISTORY

To understand the Chicano people is to understand their history. It is to recognize that Chicanos have been shaped by a series of "social systems." The complex diversity that today characterizes Chicano life can be traced to the interaction of oppressed and oppressors, and the deprivations that mark most Chicano lives can in large part be traced to the same source. Even Chicano achievements, if they are to be fully assessed, must be measured against a history of sequentially imposed superordinate ruling classes.

More than four centuries of conditioned learning and relearning have inscribed certain patterns and traits into the Chicano character. It is a unique character, indeed, because of the variety of situations and changes. In some instances, no sooner were new customs learned than there was a new process of change. This history created a psychology of conquest, exploitation, and oppression, and the process was repeated for the Chicanos in the United States. In addition, many ways of thinking and acting were shaped by reactions to the several types of contact-conflict-change sequences. Successes were relatively few and, among these few, often Pyrrhic, save in one respect: The people and the culture changed, adapted, and survived. "History suggests that nations often learn from their defeats. What is important is that the lessons should be the correct ones" (Beloff 1978:18). As we have seen, there have been some positive results: (1) a strong tradition of work productivity, although others have benefited from it; (2) a syncretic culture that facilitates human interaction and understanding; (3) concern for family and friends in the face of adversity; and (4) almost habitual striving for equality and justice. The persistence of Chicanos, as demonstrated by their successes (however few), indicates that at least some correct answers have been learned. However, few would disagree that the Chicano community is also beset by a legacy of "wrong answers."

The Chicano community has now reached adulthood in the meta-phorical parallel of historical development and human growth. The meta-phor has served as a reminder that historical stages, like an individual's stages of development, are abstractions from a reality of continuous experi-ence, and the value of such abstractions is simply in their use for under-standing that experience. The metaphor also emphasizes the importance of past experience; just as the character of a man or woman is in large measure comprised of traits acquired in childhood, so are a people both a product of what their forebears have undergone and a contributor to what their descen-dants will become. Not least, the metaphor has provided a framework for understanding the ways in which distinctive social and cultural patterns arose, thus clarifying the relationship between contemporary habits and their historical basis and avoiding the tendency of social scientists to assess minorities within a zero-time framework. "For there must be some carry-over from the past, however attenuated" (Austin 1978:49).

LESSONS FROM EACH STAGE

Something new was learned in each maturational stage. The pre-Columbian period (embryonic and infancy years) supplied the foundation on which everything else was based. Foods that evolved during that period still comprise the staples of most Chicano households, and ancient motifs are prominent in the arts and folklore of the modern community.

The arrival of the Spaniards began the colonial period (child-hood). Under oppressive and exploitative conditions the Mexican people en-dured 300 years of underdevelopment—an inheritance that still affects many Chicanos' habits and beliefs. Overt racism and intraracial color preferences stemmed from this period, together with a landholder-peon social relation-ship that continues to hinder egalitarian movements. Technological im-provements were also introduced by the Spanish, as were the spiritual val-ues of the Catholic Church (which at times ameliorated oppression), but the major legacy of the Spanish period was a social structure based on racial and class inequality.

Eventually there was a movement by some Mexicans to break this stranglehold. During the period of Mexican independence and nationalism (adolescent stage), the people began to develop some authority for them-selves. This was a point of demarcation and separation from childhood. Chi-canos still celebrate that independence with annual *Cinco de Mayo* (Fifth of May) and *Dieciseis de Septiembre* (Sixteenth of September) parades, and the desire for control over their own destinies is reflected in the many commu-nity action and political groups. However, "childhood trainers" and elitists of the same type persisted as parental authorities, "keeping the natives in their places," while a growing number of disenfranchised workers fought for autonomy. While the Mexican people were in the throes of this awakening, the early adult stage was thrust on them. This period of time was doubly confusing; assimilation of adolescent strivings was made difficult by the imposition of a new (American) social order, with its own set of standards. Nevertheless, the early adulthood stage included experimentation and learning of new patterns; increasing awareness of the influence of the old patterns; and a broadening of perspective regarding the multidimensional world. In the beginning many were caught in the unusual dilemma of reconciling the unresolved problems of the childhood and adolescent stages and at the same time learning to integrate the new vistas of early adulthood. Despite this quandary, many experimented, learned from mistakes, and moved on in a never-ending cycle of resistance, protest, and organization. These processes were particularly important after the 1910 Mexican revolution, which brought new people and ideas into the United States. The end of this period saw a predominantly urban Chicano community, just beginning to flex its political and economic muscles, and its rural component engaged in a militant assertion of economic rights.

CONTEMPORARY STAGE—ADULTHOOD

As a result of events since the mid-1960's, Chicanos have reached a new plateau, adulthood, in which they can learn from previous stages and gain further maturity. However, they must not perceive each stage as a separate entity but rather must incorporate all the stages into one life story. The metaphor of history as an individual pattern of growth and development becomes awkward at this point: the declining strength of old age, followed by death, does not seem to be in the future for the Chicano people.

The Chicano population faces a hopeful, if rocky, future. While past events have taken their toll, Chicanos have nonetheless gradually advanced. Because of their high birth rate and the steady flow of Mexican immigration, by the end of the century they will become the nation's largest minority group. In addition, the growing importance of oil will markedly alter this country's past lukewarm attitude and behavior toward Mexico and by inference toward Mexicans in the United States. Both internal circumstances (population rise) and external events (the oil shortage) will shape the Chicano future. These facts loom larger when taken alongside the present movement to organize other Spanish-speaking groups (Puerto Ricans, Cubans, and other Latin Americans) into a Hispanic or "Latino" national network. Despite historical-cultural differences among Latinos, this is considered a politically expedient goal—especially in the light of growing movements toward self-determination in Latin America.

This "Latin American connection" will reaffirm the trend toward cultural democracy, perhaps expanding bilingual and multicultural learning programs nationally. Based on current demographic projections, Chicanos appear to be on the threshold of realizing their political power and thus strengthening their cultural rights. This is despite the fact that their educational performance still lags behind that of the majority population (Ogbu 1978:232-233).

The steady increase of Chicanos in the middle-income sectors since World War II adds immeasurably to their growing influence. Today there are a number of Chicano millionaires, something unheard of even twenty years ago (of course, a million dollars in this day of inflation is not what it used to be). Many Chicanos have moved up socioeconomically only after assimilation into the dominant culture. This pattern will undoubtedly continue for some, but many others have the new option of nativist acculturation. Some Chicano millionaires followed this strategy by establishing businesses among their own ethnic group.

Whatever cultural route is taken, however, this social mobility trend will undoubtedly grow. Even though movement activists caution against social aspirations, calling them a "sell-out," it is apparent that Chicanos have tired of a life of scarcity and want. Many Chicanos feel that their time for power and influence has come. Thus, affluence is a much-sought-after goal. Some people, of course, would use the acquired resources themselves. Others would use money to help the cause of Chicano self-determination. However, both goals, self- and other-centered, involve the question of "how to make a buck."

Racial barriers notwithstanding, it is clear that when a higher income level is reached, more doors open—or are broken down. In the past, racial discrimination was blatantly practiced, and it still is in many sections of the Southwest. However, especially in urban areas there is some relaxation of the barriers in the sense that they are now subtle and covert or apply mostly to poorer people. Chicanos are slowly destroying many racial and cultural myths that have hindered their participation in mainstream America. Although they still have a long way to go, they continue to struggle—some publicly, others privately—to attain a level of parity in all areas of society.

ECONOMICS AS A BASIS FOR CHANGE

A perspective of the adult stage of Chicano history must take into consideration the manner in which the economic sphere has dominated sociocultural features in each prior stage and has directed the shift from one stage to the next. Each historical period has had a particular class-culture-color conformation, and each stage has terminated in a contact-conflict-change sequence. While all aspects of the sociocultural configuration are important, careful reading of Chicano history indicates clearly the priority of economic issues. Many Third World peoples, as well as other ethnic minorities in the United States, have certain similarities with Chicanos because of the nature of the social class system in most parts of the world. They share with Chicanos a history of exploitation of natural resources and human labor and also the propensity to fight for justice and equality.

Several other patterns are traced by highlighting each historical stage. Biological needs were adversely affected throughout all the stages. Forced labor, loss of land, and inadequate incomes still cause malnutrition and other physical suffering. Moreover, economic exploitation resulted in a growing sense of emotional and status deprivation (Wolf 1969:276). Gross inequality on the basis of class and color was mitigated by the spread of Enlightenment philosophy in the late eighteenth century, but discrimination diminished only slightly. The struggle for independence continued into twentieth-century Mexico (Kimble 1963:150), but for most people the poorly conceived and implemented reforms have meant little. They remain locked in colonialism (Austin 1978:49). However, continued resistance and new economic resource potentials for Mexico offer prospects for improvement.

In the United States, exposure to a modern urban industrial system brought a host of new problems, many of which matched and even surpassed the worst features of the colonial period (Handlin 1951:68-75; Simpson and Yinger 1972:333). For the most part, "these elements of insecurity . . . were not confined to the conditions of the working day; they pervaded the total relationship of the worker to the economy" (Handlin 1951:74). Even the increased Chicano awareness resulting from independence could not fully comprehend or integrate all these transformations. Nevertheless, there arose a persistent and socially conscious method of resistance. Many adaptive strategies were used to ensure individual and group preservation. In a wide-ranging reaction to change, Chicanos fought, retreated, regrouped, organized, and demonstrated (Murguia 1975). They took various paths of national integration—assimilation, acculturation, cultural pluralism, and separatism, for example. Thus, "there is much evidence to support the new emphasis on ethnic change. The boundaries of ethnic groups—the definition of who is included and excluded as a member—can and do vary over time" (Horowitz 1977:7). The Chicano experience in the United States is underscored by participation in the fight for labor unions and the dual effects of the 1910 Mexican Revolution—immigration, thus ongoing cultural regeneration, and concomitant ideological influences for a more just society.

SEQUENCE OF SOCIOCULTURAL CHANGE

A summary of the maturational and historical development of the Chicano people leads to a discussion of the dynamics of sociocultural change. What similarities bind the stages together? What differences separate them? How does the trajectory of Chicano history compare with that of other peoples? The changes in each realm—socioeconomic (class), sociocultural (culture), and sociopsychological (color)—are rooted in "a world of those who have and those who have not" (Austin 1978:43). During the age of discovery and exploration, European states expanded onto the lands of Third World peoples. This was the beginning of colonial rule, "the domination imposed by a foreign minority, racially (or ethnically) and culturally different, acting in the name of a racial (or ethnic) and cultural superiority . . . and imposing itself on an indigenous population" (Balandier 1966:54) (Horowitz 1977:13). Colonialism and its modern variation, internal colonialism (Gonzalez-Casanova 1973:240-242), include "direct political control, indirect political control, and economic control . . . not just the 'old colonialism' of the European empires, but also the multitudinous forms of neocolonialism of the present period" (Caulfield 1974:189) (Barrera 1979:218).

The Chicano case is different from many others because it is sequential: One colonial structure was replaced by another, while a similar superordinate subordinate relationship was retained. Much of the ensuing ethnic conflict results from the disparity in wealth and resources. Whatever the general explanations for ethnic conflict—indeed, the condition can be traced from biblical times (Lipset 1978:125)—it is clear that economic motives apply in this instance. In almost every major stage colonization and native resistance to colonization were based on economic factors. Either simultaneous to the conqueror's victory or immediately afterward, the effort to explain or rationalize the takeover occurred. This generally meant the creation and refinement of prejudicial attitudes and discriminatory behavior. The culture and race of the victor were established as superior and those of the conquered as inferior. Thus, the conqueror's feelings of guilt were averted because the natives were thought of as subhuman, a lower form of cultural and racial life.

IDEOLOGY OF THE SOCIAL STRUCTURE

Economic imperialism was joined by cultural and racial imperialism (Schermerhorn 1970:117). Oppressed peoples have fashioned various types of responses to their condition (Edmonson 1960). Some fought to preserve their way of life by cloaking resistance in cultural themes (Horowitz 1977:14). Others avoided transformation by limiting contact with the new overseers (Migdal 1974:137). Whatever reaction strategies were used (and there were many local adaptations), one factor stands out: "dominant groups, sometimes minorities, discriminate against others in access to political power and economic and social advantages" (Lipset 1978:124). Thus, when writers discuss *social* problems (poverty, crime, housing, education, and so on), *cultural* problems (linguistic, value, and belief barriers), *racial* problems (inferior treatment, institutional racism, prejudice, and discrimination), and *psychological* problems (inferiority complex and marginality based on social-cultural-racial factors) of underclass ethnic minorities, they are generally talking about *economics*-related issues.

A historical perspective and knowledge of the currents described above are necessary requisites in understanding the social framework (Barrera 1974:17). Foley and co-workers (1977:48) write that "the notions of racial, cultural, and class superiority are so intertwined that they constitute one belief system." In many parts of the world an "ideology of the social structure" was created to preserve economic inequalities. This ideology encompasses local, national, and international networks. According to Hewitt (1977:151), many of the world's ethnic struggles have centered on these issues, causing over 10 million fatalities (in minor and major conflicts, from riots to extended wars) in the period from 1945 to 1970.

In the United States, as in many other countries, the ideology of oppression is in conflict with that of liberation. Yet, "the 'conflict of ideologies' is, of course, only a metaphor. Men or groups of men engage in conflict" (Beloff 1978:11). As noted previously, southern and eastern Europeans in the past underwent a type of "ideology of the social structure" oppression when they migrated to the United States. Their different "white" racial stock and cultural background barred them from wider opportunities. They also developed strategies similar to those used by Chicanos—cultural pluralism, assimilation, separatism, and militancy—to achieve social equality (Wagley and Harris 1958:285). The sociocultural life of many groups, both nationally and internationally, is affected by their powerless position. Thus, we must write "a history of the modern world in which we spell out the processes of power which created the present-day cultural systems and the linkages between them" (Wolf 1969:261).

In writing that history we might discover that social problems revolve around the issue of "haves vs. have-nots." This macrolevel analysis provides a clearer insight into a number of conditions affecting Chicanos, including the economic competition among the poor (a sort of national envidia) (Sassen-Koob 1973:114) and the cumulative effects of oppression in which intragroup frictions derive from the colonial period and intergroup conflicts from the present internal colonialism. However, "the study of culture change must take into account three orders of reality: the impact of the higher [dominant] culture; the substance of native life on which it is directed; and . . . change resulting from the reaction between the two cultures" (Malinowski 1945:26) (Spicer 1962:586; Migdal 1974:137). Integrally linked to this idea is the variability of contact-conflict-change sequences as dictated by the sociocultural traditions and environments of the native group and the colonizer. The student of change must heed Samual Ramos' warning (1962: 102) against over-romanticizing the native experience.

LEGACY OF PROBLEMS

Socioeconomic adaptations went hand in hand with other sociocultural changes in Chicano history. The family, education, religion, and other institutions have undergone a monumental upheaval in each stage. As noted previously, many surviving customs and traits were positive and beneficial. However, language and cultural values have been subjected to intense pressures. Individuals and groups either resisted accommodation to the dominant culture and fought for preservation of native traditions, or synthesized a compromise. These transformations have shaped a pattern that largely reflects a lower socioeconomic life-style. A closer examination of this pattern will be made only to dramatize the debilitating nature of underclass life, for many Chicanos have escaped poverty by using positive adaptation strategies.

Oscar Lewis has created the concept of "the culture of poverty," which in some ways explains the life of many Chicanos (Lewis 1959:16). Although critics have questioned the use of such an "omnibus" construct to explain the life of the poor (Leacock 1971; Valentine 1968), it is true that a cycle is created from one generation to the next among those in the lowest socioeconomic levels. Each successive generation inherits this world view, if only partially. However much they try to escape it—and some succeed—the overwhelming majority fail. Worse yet, many are unable to understand the roots of this cultural background; they live their lives as if they were the creators.

Envidia (envy) is another attitude resulting from economic deprivation. This is not an exclusively Chicano quality; it affects the poor generally. George Foster (1975:305) suggests in his theory of "limited good" that "if 'Good' exists in limited amounts which cannot be expanded, and if the system is closed, it follows that an individual or a family can improve a position only at the expense of others." Thus, there is the tendency to compete for limited resources by striving to keep others in the same group/class from obtaining them. While the opposite reaction, support for and cooperation with one another, also operates in a system of oppression, it appears that the process of underdevelopment has encouraged envidia in the Chicano people. During the 1960's movement, for example, there was great rivalry and dissension among leaders and groups, regardless if the idea or program being discussed was good or bad. Perhaps envidia beclouds the senses, making people call one another "Tio Taco," or traitor, without considering their worthiness or honesty.

The same economic rationale clarifies still another sociocultural practice—the high incidence of deviance and crime. Deviance is in large part the result of a lack of subsistence resources (Moore et al. 1978; Ianni 1977:66-78). If the social system were more just, there would be no need to resort to crime and deviance in order to survive. A recent study was made in East Los Angeles of lower-class and marginal groups who often are forced to follow deviant paths to success, such as the drug market (Moore et al. 1978). Many other former "second-class" citizens have become successful through deviant activities. In fact, only recently has the public turned their attention to "white-collar" crime.

The machismo syndrome is yet another example of cultural adaptation to poverty. Machismo has a positive aspect: males learn to protect family and home and become disciplined, responsible providers. Because oppressive conditions have been so bad, however, there is also a negative result. Many males seek an outlet by the indiscriminate sexual conquest of females, with the aim of lowering their status; escape from reality through alcohol and drug use; and fighting and even killing each other for relatively minor reasons. Both Spanish and Anglo-American colonialism contributed to this propensity. Indeed, it may be a way (however unfortunate) for the downtrodden to relieve anxieties and frustrations.

Finally, Chicanos have experienced a sense of inferiority and marginality. Racial and cultural imperialism supported the system of economic imperialism. Feelings of inferiority and marginality stem from the areas of race and culture in both the Spanish and Anglo-American systems. To understand this legacy, we must "take a backward look at the context in which similar phenomena have been appearing in the past" (Bettleheim and Janowitz 1950:108). Making people feel inferior because of how they look, speak, and/or act is clearly a mechanism to keep them socially immobile. An additional handicap is the establishment of social norms that keep those who are racially and culturally different marginal to most of society's groups and institutions: "individuals in this vanguard occupy marginal status, a position dangling between two social worlds" (Shibutani and Kwan 1965:352). Therefore, it is "the conflict of groups possessing different cultures which is the determining influence in creating the marginal person . . . and the typical traits are social-psychological" (Stonequist 1937:214). Several human dimensions are part of this experience (Gist and Dworkin 1972). Thus, "it is undeniable that cultural identity can persist despite multiple processes of change. . . . On the other hand, it is also clear that certain alterations and losses may seriously harm an identity" (Leon-Portilla 1974:3). Economic marginality is invariably at the root of this problem.

An analysis of the cultural transformations under the Spanish and, later, the Anglos offers an example of this and underscores the similarities between the colonial and internal colonial experiences. Spaniards (Anglos) neither accommodated nor appreciated Indian (Mexican) culture. "In almost all instances of inter-ethnic contact people of subordinate rank have sooner or later learned the ways of the dominant group" (Shibutani and Kwan 1965:470). As a result, cultural change was largely glorification of Spanish (Anglo) culture and destruction of Indian (Mexican) culture. Despite this pressure to assimilate dominant ways, however, many natives took the creative approach of amalgamating their culture with that of the dominant group. Thus, they innovated a new cultural style: Mexican (Chicano), a blend of Spanish (Anglo) and Indian (Mexican) elements without a precise delineation of the actual portion of each.

Some natives came to feel inferior because of this process. Other factors added to the burden: (1) they could not adjust to the Spanish (Anglo) mode; (2) the Spanish (Anglos) did not want them anyway; and (3) they were unable to fit into the new, syncretist Mexican (Chicano) culture. Lacking a definite strategy of adaptation, many became marginal to all three cultures—the dominant, subordinate, and syncretist versions. A sense of cultural inferiority and marginality resulted.

Racism compounded these problems (Van Den Berghe 1967). Eventually, race became a passport to social mobility, with Indian (Mexican) features effectively barring social advancement (Allport 1954). A further complicating factor was the rise of the hybrid, mestizo race. This phenomenon created an interesting situation, particularly since Indians were considered inferior to the Spanish. Many mestizos, especially those who looked Spanish, followed the racist colonial ideology. They attempted to change racial membership and thereby gain wider socioeconomic opportunities. Sometimes the goal included intermarriage with someone from the superior group.

In summary, "racism has affected life-style, value system, opportunities for education, work, housing, medical care and recreation of the victimized groups" (Kramer, Rosen, and Willis 1969:355-356). Racism and the other social patterns outlined above evolved through several stages of change and two major wars with other ethnic groups, an inheritance that compounds the problems of modern Chicanos.

RESIDUE OF CENTURIES OF HISTORY

If it is true that "differences in culture—tribal, peasant, civilizational—provide different modes whereby individual personalities acquire cultural identity" (King 1974:107), then it is equally correct that a cumulative effect pertains for a culture that has undergone a relatively rapid, 400-year transition. At present the Chicano intelligentsia are conducting a great debate, sometimes vociferously, more often quietly, about the sociocultural identity of the people. As they create ideologies based on one or another ethnic tradition of the past—Indian, Hispano, or mestizo—it might be well to remind them that all three traditions are important. The perspective one takes depends on several factors: the *people*, the *time*, and the *place*; or a dynamic, syncretic identity that combines sociocultural motifs from any of these factors. Thus, the study of a complex history requires a multiple perspective and, most significantly, complex and perhaps tentative answers to difficult questions.

The residue of their historical experience remains in the Chicano people. Many suffer mental conflict and anguish because of past and present conditions. It is hoped that the root causes of this dilemma have been explained. The purpose of this clarification is twofold: to understand the processes that have shaped Chicano behavior and, more importantly, to change the processes and reorder the behavior in some way. This introspective event can occur on an individual or group level, following any number of timetables.

There is also a positive side to the Chicano legacy: their ability to survive by fashioning syncretic adaptive strategies to many changing conditions. This is their core strength. The Chicanos' history has outfitted them with a variety of sociocultural perspectives in which to confront life. Indeed, this complex heritage makes it difficult to decide what path, or mixture of paths, to take. Nevertheless, in time, and perhaps in the near future, the right syncretic combination will be discovered to eliminate the worst features of the heritage of oppression.

REFERENCES

Allport, G.: *The nature of prejudice*, Cambridge, Mass., 1954, Addison-Wesley Publishing Co., Inc.

Austin, D.: Prospero's island. In Thompson, W. S., editor: *The Third World: premises of U.S. policy*, San Francisco, 1978, Institute for Contemporary Studies.

Balandier, G.: The colonial situation: a theoretical approach. In Wallerstein, I., editor: *Social change: the colonial situation*, New York, 1966, John Wiley & Sons, Inc.

Barrera, M.: The study of politics and the Chicano, *Aztlan*, 1974.

Barrera, M.: Race and class in the Southwest: a theory of racial inequality, Notre Dame, Ind., 1979, University of Notre Dame Press.

Beloff, M.: The Third World and the conflict of ideologies. In Thompson, W. S., editor: *The Third World: premises of U.S. policy*, San Francisco, 1978, Institute for Contemporary Studies.

Bettleheim, B., and Janowitz, M.: *Dynamics of prejudice*, New York, 1950, Harper & Row, Publishers.

Caulfield, M. D.: Culture and imperialism: proposing a new dialectic. In Hymes, D., editor: *Reinventing anthropology*, New York, 1974, Vintage Books.

Edmonson, M. S.: Nativism, syncretism, and anthropological science. In Edmonson, M. S., editor: *Nativism and syncretism*, New Orleans, 1960, Tulane University, Middle American Research Institute.

Foley, D. E., et al.: *From peones to politicos: ethnic relations in a South Texas town, 1900 to 1977*, Austin, 1977, University of Texas, Center for Mexican American Studies.

Foster, G.: Peasant society and the image of limited good. In Potter, J. M., Diaz, M. N., and Foster, G. M., editors: *Peasant society: a reader*, Boston, 1967, Little, Brown & Co.

Gist, N. P., and Dworkin, A. G., editors: *The blending of races: marginality and identity in world perspective*, New York, 1972, John Wiley & Sons, Inc.

Gonzalez-Casanova, P.: Society and internal colonialism. In Gelfland, D. E., and Lee, R. D., editors: *Ethnic conflicts and power: a cross-national perspective*, New York, 1973, John Wiley & Sons, Inc.

Handlin, O.: *The uprooted*, New York, 1951, Grossett & Dunlap, Inc.

Hewitt, C.: Majorities and minorities: a comparative survey of ethnic violence. In Heisler, M. O., editor: *The Annals of the American Academy of Political and Social Science*, vol. 433, 1977.

Horowitz, D. L.: Cultural movements and ethnic change. In Heisler, M. O., editor: *The Annals of the American Academy of Political and Social Science*, vol. 433, 1977.

Ianni, F. A. J.: New mafia: black, Hispanic, and Italian styles. In *Readings in anthropology 77/78*, Guilford, Conn., 1977, The Dushkin Publishing Group, Inc.

Kimble, G. H. T.: Colonialism: the good, the bad, the lessons. In Dean, V. M., and Harootunian, H. D., editors: *West and non-West: new perspectives*, New York, 1963, Holt, Rinehart & Winston.

King, A. R.: A stratification of labyrinths: the acquisition and retention of cultural identity in modern culture. In Fitzgerald, T. K., editor: *Social and cultural identity: problems of persistence and change*, Athens, Ga., 1974, Southern Anthropological Society, University of Georgia Press.

Kramer, M., Rosen, B. M., and Willis, E. M.: Definitions and distributions of mental disorders in a racist society. In Willie, C. V., Kramer, B. M., and Brown, B. S., editors: *Racism and mental health*, Pittsburgh, 1969, University of Pittsburgh Press.

Leacock, E. B., editor: *The culture of poverty: a critique*, New York, 1971, Simon & Schuster, Inc.

Leon-Portilla, M.: Anthropology and the endangered cultures. Delivered at the Seventy-Third American Anthropological Association Conference, Mexico City. Washington, D.C., 1974, American Anthropological Association.

Lewis, O.: *Five families: Mexican case studies in the culture of poverty*, New York, 1959, Basic Books, Inc., Publishers.

Lipset, S. M.: Racial and ethnic tensions in the Third World. In Thompson, S. S., editor: *The Third World: premises of U.S. policy*, San Francisco, 1978, Institute for Contemporary Studies.

Malinowski, B.: *The dynamics of culture change*, New Haven, Conn., 1945, Yale University Press.

Migdal, J. S.: *Peasants, politics, and revolution*, Princeton, N.J., 1974, Princeton University Press.

Moore, J. W., et al.: *Homeboys: gangs, drugs, and prisons in the barrios of Los Angeles*, Philadelphia, 1979, Temple University Press.

Murguia, E.: *Assimilation, colonialism and the Mexican American people*, Austin, 1975, University of Texas Press.

Ogbu, J. V.: *Minority education and caste: the American system in cross-cultural perspective*, New York, 1978, Academic Press, Inc.

Ramos, S.: *Profile of man and culture in Mexico*, Austin, 1962, University of Texas Press.

Sassen-Koob, S.: Non-dominant ethnic populations as parts of total society: Chicanos in the United States, *Aztlan*, 1973.

Schermerhorn, R. A.: *Comparative ethnic relations: a framework for theory and re-*

search New York, 1970, Random House, Inc.

Shibutani, T., and Kwan, K. M.: *Ethnic stratification: a comparative approach*, New York, 1965, Macmillan, Inc.

Simpson, G., and Yinger, M.: *Racial and cultural minorities: an analysis of prejudice and discrimination*, New York, 1972, Harper & Row, Publishers.

Spicer, E.: *Cycles of conquest*, Tucson, 1962, The University of Arizona Press.

Stonequist, E. V.: *The marginal man*, New York, 1937, Russell & Russell, Publishers.

Valentine, C. A.: *Culture and poverty*, Chicago, 1968, University of Chicago Press.

Van Den Berghe, P. L.: *Race and racism: a comparative perspective*, New York, 1967, John Wiley & Sons, Inc.

Wagley, C., and Harris, M.: *Minorities in the New World*, New York, 1958, Columbia University Press.

Wolf, E.: *Peasant wars of the twentieth-century*, New York, 1969, Harper & Row, Publishers.

Wolf, E.: American anthropologists and American society. In Hymes, D., editor: *Reinventing anthropology*, New York, 1974, Vintage Books.

BIBLIOGRAPHY

Gelfland, D. E.: Ethnic relations and social research: a reevaluation. In Gelfland, D. E., and Lee, R. D., editors: *Ethnic conflicts and power: a cross-national perspective*, New York, 1973, John Wiley & Sons, Inc.

Martinez, J. L., editor: *Chicano psychology*, New York, 1977, Academic Press, Inc.

Memmi, A.: *The colonizer and the colonized*, Boston, 1965, Beacon Press.

Rios-Bustamante, A. J.: *Mexicans in the United States and the national question*, Santa Barbara, Calif., 1978, Editorial La Causa.

Robinson, C.: *With the ears of strangers: the Mexican in American literature*, Tucson, 1963, The University of Arizona Press.

Spicer, E. H., and Thompson, R. H., editors: *Plural society in the Southwest*, Albuquerque, 1975, University of New Mexico Press.

U.S. Department of Commerce: *Persons of Spanish origin in the United States*, Washington, D.C., U.S. Bureau of the Census, 1977.

Vander Zanden, J. W.: *American minority relations*, Columbus, 1963, Ohio State University Press.

Weaver, T., editor: *To see ourselves*, Glenview, Ill., 1973, Scott, Foresman, & Co.

Wilkie, M. W.: Colonials, marginals and immigrants: contributions to a theory of ethnic stratification, *Comparative Studies in Society and History* **19**:67, 1977.

Index